Proceedings of the 2011 BALEAP Conference

EAP Within the Higher Education Garden: Cross-Pollination Between Disciplines, Departments and Research

Edited by
John Wrigglesworth

The global forum for
EAP professionals

Published by
Garnet Publishing Ltd.
8 Southern Court
South Street
Reading RG1 4QS, UK

Copyright © 2013 BALEAP.

Published 2013.

ISBN: 978 1 90861 471 1

British Cataloguing-in-Publication Data
A catalogue record for this book is available from
the British Library.

Production
Project manager: Kate Kemp
Editorial team: Sue Coll, Matthew George,
                     Kate Kemp, Jean McCutcheon,
                     Clare Roberts
Design and layout: Bob House

Printed and bound
in Lebanon by International Press: interpress@int-press.com

Contents

John Wrigglesworth

INTRODUCTION

Internationalisation, interdisciplinarity, combined honours, mixed method research, team-teaching, peer review – in simple terms, *bringing people and ideas together* to create something original and more suitable for a contemporary context – has increasing prominence in education. Cross-pollination was our guiding metaphor at the 2011 BALEAP biennial conference, to encourage practitioners of English for Academic Purposes (EAP) to showcase good practice in working and thinking together. EAP joins with specific disciplines to explore how language works to achieve the purposes of university courses; it works across institutions to ensure full participation from students from a variety of backgrounds; and it draws on many academic and research traditions to develop and improve its understanding of the teaching and learning needs of international students.

Few would dispute the importance of international students to the academic standing, vitality and financial soundness of universities worldwide. In his BALEAP conference plenary, Dominic Scott, Chief Executive of the United Kingdom Council for International Students (UKCISA), described the 'exponential growth in some of the key markets', traced back to the Prime Minister's Initiative (1999), which 'brought all parts of government together … around one table, saying we need a strategy to increase recruitment': an opening example of successful cross-pollination. He went on to argue that more than marketing is needed to ensure the quality of the international student experience, emphasising the need to work with academic staff to meet the needs of the contemporary student demographic and for financial advice and help with the transition between academic cultures. These themes were taken up and developed in another conference plenary. Janette Ryan, Director of the Teaching International Students Project at the Higher Education Academy, identified a compartmentalised approach within the Higher Education (HE) sector, with academics working alone and international students failing to make friends with their home-student peers. She called for a sharing of ideas both within and across universities, to help ensure increases in the quality of international student understanding and to maintain competitive advantage – examples where *more* cross-pollination is required.

Practitioners of EAP have a great deal to offer in developing the opportunities that international students bring. They can thus be a positive driver to enhance an individual student's experience, the international standing of a university (aka the league tables) and the economic sustainability of UK HE.

As EAP's professional body, BALEAP has the experience and membership to be a key player in ensuring the highest quality student experience. The BALEAP biennial conference is now an established feature of the academic calendar and the place where its membership comes together to debate and share good practice. The 2011 conference in Portsmouth was the 20th (including seven when known as SELMOUS); it offered over 80 presentations, and it was attended by 260 delegates.

BALEAP sees its role not only as a professional body and as a forum for discussion, but also as a catalyst for the pedagogical development of its members and of the research base of EAP theory. Along with the conference, Portsmouth also hosted the first in a series of Research Training Events (ResTES). Ian Bruce gave a masterclass on *Defining the research space: Literature reviews and research questions*, before going on to give his own plenary talk on the second day of the conference. There were six ResTES events in 2012, covering many of the research skills that underpin both a conference presentation and a research paper, and more are planned.

Another feature of the conference, which is relevant to these proceedings, was the relaunch of a much-expanded BALEAP website. The association has recently appointed a web officer, Martin Barge, to develop its online presence and the site contains details of all BALEAP activities, including conferences and Professional Issues Meetings (PIMs). Any interested EAP practitioner can now access videos of all the Portsmouth plenaries, and PowerPoint slides and handouts from over 20 sessions. Readers are encouraged to compare the affordances of the website with those of the printed proceedings and to speculate on the things that the composition and consumption of the written account brings to professional practice. Does cross-pollination from information technology lead to the extinction of a volume of papers?

EAP is regularly cross-pollinated with other disciplines, increasing its vigour, precision and scope. Regularly tapped gene pools include EFL theory and practice, discourse analysis, second language learning and assessment theory. Hybrids or sub-species that we were interested to see make a contribution at the conference were academic literacies, systemic functional linguistics, World Englishes and e-learning. In addition, we were keen to invite input from fields that perhaps seem tangential, but may have a contribution to make to certain aspects of EAP growth. We hoped the metaphor of cross-pollination would bring out the cross-disciplinary nature of our field, encourage an expansion in the number of voices driving its evolution, and offer participants a fun *leitmotiv* for their presentations.

Twenty-one presentations have been written up for these proceedings. There are papers from well-known authors: the established practitioners of the EAP garden.

There are also several papers by those who are new to writing up their research or to scholarly activity. Over the years, the proceedings' editors and team of reviewers have shown a commitment to supporting and offering formative feedback to colleagues joining the EAP conversation for the first time. We have tried to do the same while preparing the current volume.

The two plenary papers in Section I set the context for what follows. Janette Ryan opens the proceedings by arguing that the significant changes in the UK HE student demographic call for equally significant changes in institutional approach and pedagogy. By encouraging collaboration and deeper understanding of student needs, her research seeks to change the perception of international students by academics as a problem, so that they can participate with all students on an equal footing. She describes a Teaching International Students (TIS) project to maintain a web space for awareness-raising, debate and the sharing of ideas, and highlights the contribution that EAP practitioners make.

Ian Bruce's plenary paper looks at the challenges that students may experience as they start to enter their disciplinary discourse communities. Focusing on the process of negotiating written texts, he outlines a three-stage development approach to writing successfully for a particular academic audience. He concludes by suggesting that a genre approach to discourse best supports students through the process.

A feature of many of the papers at the conference, and reflected in the papers in these proceedings, is the difference in emphasis between those who teach to a mixed-discipline or general EAP student cohort and those who are able to deliver discipline-specific courses and test them accordingly.

Section II contains papers which develop ideas of discipline-specific pedagogy.

Joan Turner reports on a study into the different perspectives that academics take on proofreading. Using data from focus groups and semi-structured interviews, she shows how considerations about proofreading need to be developed along with those of the multiple socio-political dynamics of contemporary universities.

Maureen Finn considers the way that progression for PhD students turns on their ability to recognise and adopt the writing convention of their department. Basing her paper on an in-depth interview with an epidemiology professor, she discusses the challenges in communicating these conventions for both academics and students.

This challenge is taken up by Hilary Arnold and Simon Williams. They describe a process approach to PhD writing workshops, which is informed by Aristotelian concepts of the structure of knowledge. Supported with formative student feedback from a task-by-task self-reflection sheet and interviews, they offer practical suggestions for organising workshops and managing the expectations of the students who attend.

Nadya Yakovchuk and Julian Ingle describe two case studies using the Thinking Writing initiative at Queen Mary, University of London. They show how notions of good writing depend on perceptions of its purpose, content and discipline-specific characteristics within a student's immediate institutional context. They then go on to outline how co-teaching draws out dialogues within the pedagogic processes, issues of identity and power, and the ongoing nature of writing development for both students and professional academics.

Mary Davis and John Morley look at the difficult issue of establishing a boundary between the use of the words of others and the use of commonly used academic phrases. As part of the ongoing debate about plagiarism and the development of EAP materials to develop good practice with source use, they suggest criteria for the acceptable usage of academic phrases collected from 45 academics in an online survey.

Section III brings together research conducted in settings where the students are drawn from across an institution, and so works within general EAP principles and offers pedagogical strategies that students can use to develop their own learning.

Helen Armstrong and Suzanne Evans argue that generic, compulsory, in-sessional provision is good EAP practice. Drawing on their experiences at Teesside University, and academic results and feedback from students, they show how such an approach can help with integration, autonomy and core skills development.

Jackie Dannatt follows an action research approach to explore how reformulation and noticing techniques can be used to improve student writing. She provides data regarding the areas of language that students were able to notice and the progress they made.

A complementary strategy is provided by Francine Roussel, who describes the pedagogic pros and cons of MultiConcord, a parallel concordancer which offers users access to a corpus of well-translated texts and their originals. The corpus contains real language in use and allows for data-driven, independent learning.

Jianying Du presents an integrative model of student feedback designed to facilitate teacher-student interaction and thereby promote development in L2 writing and cognitive development. The paper reports on a case study which used qualitative and quantitative data to describe the application of the model in a Chinese university.

Gamze Oncul develops an approach to reading from William Grabe and applies it to EAP students. She explores strategies for designing reading courses within EAP for general academic purposes.

Rounding off Section III, Chitra Varaprasad evaluates an EAP programme in Singapore, which sought to combine general with specific EAP provision through the use of project work. The research analyses data from student perceptions of their progress and indicates that project work and the analysis of research articles from the student's own discipline does help to maintain a balance of provision.

Section IV brings together research that looks at assessment and academic argument. The papers here are predominantly discipline-specific in their focus.

Jenny Kemp and Glenn Fulcher argue that, where ESAP courses are provided, the validity of retaining general EAP marking criteria becomes questionable. Using travel agency discourse as an example, they show how performance decision trees can be created to provide a principled and valid measurement of a student's ability to perform authentic tasks and how this linguistic analysis and test construction might be applied to EAP.

Sarah Beaumont and Andy Gillett show how subject specialists and language teachers can work together to develop authentic materials and tasks to give students authentic preparation for a pre-MBA course. Using a statistical analysis of the marks given by the subject specialists and language teachers for an assessed discussion, backed up by interviews with the subject specialists, they argue that both sets are measuring the same thing and that language and content are inseparable.

John Slaght evaluates current thinking on reading assessments, with a particular emphasis on the authenticity of the tasks used for testing. He describes a state-of-the-art open-book EAP test developed at the University of Reading.

Fiona Dalziel and Carole Sedgwick look at the importance of argumentation in developing EAP practitioners' and their students' understanding of academic writing. Their comparison of teacher and student evaluations indicates that, to be well written, an assessment needs to be well argued.

Julia Molinari and Anne Kavanagh further develop this position by arguing that there is a need to define what we mean by critical thinking in order for it to be validly measured in integrated assessment (reading for writing). They offer some definitions by reviewing academic literature, textbook and exam board formulations, as well as presenting the results of a survey of student and tutor awareness of critical thinking.

Section V of the proceedings contains three papers that encourage good practice in learning, teaching and research.

Garry Dyck asks a critical question of his institution's pre-sessional course: what value does it add to students that is unavailable to those who fulfil the language entry requirements and are granted direct entry? Analysing data from a substantial number of students over several years, he finds that students who do the pre-sessional are significantly more likely to graduate.

Mick Kavanagh and Lisa Robinson report on a study in which 11 transcripts of post-observation discussion were analysed for recurrent themes. The results point to areas of professional development for EAP teachers and for those who observe them.

Rounding off the proceedings, Tijen Akşit offers a reflective paper on the use of action research by seven participants on an in-service professional development course. After reviewing the literature on action research, she gives a detailed report on the experience of one participant on the course, who conducted research to learn more about EAP students in Turkey and their reluctance to speak English in the classroom.

There is a wonderful mix of cross-pollination in the papers and great creativity in how new ideas have evolved in their various environments. Teaching and researching EAP looks certain to develop in energetic and inclusive ways, transforming how our students live and study in the future.

The 2013 BALEAP conference is in Nottingham under the theme *The Janus Moment in EAP; Revisiting the Past and Building the Future*. Given the vibrancy of BALEAP and the enthusiasm of its members, it promises to be a rewarding conference.

ACKNOWLEDGEMENTS

BALEAP conferences, in moving to different locations on each occasion, have different local teams working in conjunction with the BALEAP Executive. In Portsmouth, Nick Bertenshaw, Rose Clark, Claire Hutchinson, Linda Sterne and Lorraine Pickett-Rose worked with the main organisers, Richard Hitchcock and John Wrigglesworth. BALEAP thanks them for their hard work in putting together a smooth-running and enjoyable event. From the BALEAP Executive, tremendous energy and continuity have been provided over the last three conferences and 30 PIMS by Andy Seymour of Reading University; we thank him for all the advice and effort he has put in over the years and the support he gave the Portsmouth team. It's further evidence of cross-pollination.

Similarly, I'd like to thank the team of (originally anonymous) reviewers who gave advice and formative feedback on the papers in this volume: Olwyn Alexander, Mary-Anne Ansell, Edward de Chazal, Alex Ding, Nancy Gaffield, Andy Gillett, Julio Giménez, Richard Hitchcock, Steve King and Diane Schmitt.

And I'd like to give particular thanks to Jean McCutcheon for all her hard work on the proceedings. Jean co-ordinates the review process and copy-edits the final text. She is to be particularly thanked for making sure that things have run efficiently and on time.

SECTION I
Plenary papers

JANETTE RYAN

TRANSFORMATIVE INTERNATIONAL EDUCATION: COLLABORATIVE APPROACHES TO SUPPORTING INTERNATIONAL STUDENTS

This paper argues for a more collaborative approach to supporting teaching and learning for international students in UK higher education. It argues that universities can more effectively work to ensure the academic success of international students through a holistic and informed approach to meeting the learning needs of international students. In particular, it argues that, despite radical changes in the nature of the UK higher education student population, teaching and learning practices have changed relatively little, but that they need to change as students change, as do the contexts in which they are taught. This paper discusses how those who work with international students across universities can work together more effectively to provide better services for them, and discusses a national project that has been designed to achieve this. Interwoven through this discussion are reflections on the authors' own personal experiences as an international student and as a teacher of international students which demonstrate and illustrate how international education and intercultural learning experiences can be transformative, for not just international students, but also for their teachers and their UK student counterparts.

In this paper I draw on my own experiences of international education as an international student over the past 3 decades and my professional work in this area as a teacher and a researcher over the past 15 years. I have researched the teaching and learning experiences of international students in the UK and in Australia for many years, including a comparative doctoral study of approaches in Australia and the UK. My interest stems from my own personal background as an international student on four separate occasions. The first time was when I was in my early 20s, when I won an Australian Government scholarship to study Chinese language and modern Chinese literature in China in the early 1980s. This turned out to be the hardest thing I have ever done in my life, but, on reflection, the most enjoyable. The experience was both formative and transformative: it changed my life, changed the way I think, and made me the teacher and the researcher that I am today. In my current professional work as an Education academic and as Director of the UK Higher Education Academy's Teaching International Students Project, I try to convey this message to academics who are teaching international students and perhaps struggling with a sometimes heavy burden; they may not see the impact of what they are doing at the time, but they will change their international students' lives and transform their futures. It is this message that needs to be conveyed to all of those who work with international students in universities in countries such as the UK, from their teachers in the classroom to those who work with them in support services such as foundation and academic support programmes. The work that these staff do with international students is enormously important; it is challenging, but it is life changing for those involved.

My personal experiences also included two later periods as an international student in the UK, and I underestimated the challenges that this would bring. I speak the language so I anticipated few difficulties. I was therefore surprised to find that I experienced some of the same problems. To give one example of this – I was sitting in a postgraduate research methodology seminar and the lecturer began by talking about the Education Act of 1944 – I had no idea what that meant. It was clearly 'code' for a body of important information about the nature of the education system in the UK. I looked around and realised that the majority of the students in the class were international students (in fact, we had all introduced ourselves as such at the beginning of the class). If the lecturer had explained in a few sentences the significance of that act, she would have 'taken all of us with her' rather than leaving us somewhat baffled as to the meaning of the rest of the lecture. Although, after living in the UK for many years, I now know what that means, I didn't at the time and I was lost in that lecture, as were my international student colleagues. For me, this serves to illustrate one of the misconceptions about the learning needs of international students: that it is not just about language, and the way that students look may not be a good indicator of where they come from or what they know. It has to do with the fact that international students can bring with them a completely different range of experiences, expertise, ideas and perspectives, and teachers need to be aware of this and be prepared to learn from them as well as teach them.

To return to the main topic of this paper, I now focus on the changing nature of the student cohort in British higher education and what might constitute more effective approaches to teaching and supporting them. I discuss how those who work with international students can work together as a community to support them more effectively, and I suggest ways in which this might be achieved.

It is clear that the nature of the higher education student population in the UK is changing very rapidly. Along with changes as a result of widening participation measures, there has been a significant rise in the numbers of international students, with 16% or 1 in 6 students being an international student (UKCISA, 2011). The numbers in colleges and foundation programmes and on A-level programmes are also increasing as international students are starting to come a little earlier to improve their English and their chances of entering UK higher education. International students make up 12% of first-degree students but are enrolled predominantly within postgraduate programmes, comprising 68% of full-time taught postgraduate courses (UKCISA, 2011). On many postgraduate courses they are the majority. This means that international students are no longer a 'minority group' in the classroom; they are now 'everyone's business'. These changes underpin the reason for the establishment of the Teaching International Students (TIS)[1] project hosted by the UK Higher Education Academy.

The TIS project aims to work towards a more collaborative approach, so that those who work with international students in universities can share their ideas and expertise to provide better support for them. This requires a more holistic and sustainable approach. With these kinds of numbers of international students the dynamics in the classroom change, and the ways that academics work need to change, as well as the way that lecturers and tutors are supported. Overall, universities have been responding well to increases in international student numbers, and many universities across the UK have been investing in work on recruitment, marketing and in terms of the welcome – the 'soft landing' – that universities provide to students. But often the work stops there. Despite the radical changes in the student population, teaching and learning practices in universities have changed relatively little. Universities are often compartmentalised, with little contact occurring between different sections of the university. Academics by and large work on their own; they do have difficulties in teaching international students, but generally try to sort these out on their own and don't seek support or advice. This was the rationale for establishing the TIS project. We have subsequently discovered that there are often several academics within a university undertaking research on international students, but they are doing it on their own. They are unaware that there are other people within the university, sometimes within the same faculty, who are also working in this area. However, it can be very difficult for academics to make contact with other areas of expertise in the university, because they are very busy and have many other demands.

International students generally report that they do feel welcome in universities; they have often gone through an induction programme, or undertaken a foundation programme where they have felt very well supported, but then, when they move into the mainstream, they say that they can feel very unsupported, and everything can come to a 'crashing halt', and they can feel a sense of disappointment. Equally, lecturers sometimes expect that international students who have gone through foundation programmes will come into their classrooms with all of the skills and knowledge that

---

[1] http://www.heacademy.ac.uk/teaching-international-students

they need. They may be unaware of the limitations of IELTS and may erroneously believe that the problems that international students encounter will disappear if the required levels of IELTS at the university are raised. International students do sometimes need additional and continuing support, and one solution is to embed good practices of teaching and learning for international students within mainstream programmes and within the teaching and learning classroom. It is also often the case that language and learning support staff such as English for Academic Purposes practitioners can better understand the needs of international students than academics, but that expertise is not often shared. We appear to keep 'reinventing the wheel': identifying the same sorts of problems but not sharing solutions and ideas.

In my research in this area (Carroll & Ryan, 2005; Ryan, 2000; Ryan, 2002; Ryan, 2011; Ryan, 2012; Ryan & Slethaug, 2010) I have looked at the ways that universities respond to the teaching and learning needs of international students, and there are some unique features in the UK that make a strong argument for better support within universities. The international student profile is different in the UK from Australia, for example, where it is generally undergraduates who are international students. In the UK they are predominately postgraduates. This means that they are in the UK for a short period of time, and they may need to undertake research for a thesis and master the academic skills that they need in their new learning environment in a relatively short time. So their learning is much more intense. There is a very short period of time to work with students to assist them to be successful. The UK also has a different marking system from most other

countries, and international students can get quite a surprise when they first arrive and receive much lower marks than they are accustomed to. They may have previously been 'high flyers' and can get a shock when they think they have failed, or when they do fail, because it is such a steep learning curve for them. Lecturers often don't realise that they need to explain to them 'where they are', what they need to do and how well they are developing. The UK also has less continuous assessment than some other countries such as Australia and the US and involves more summative assessment and less feedback about how they are progressing. This means that lecturers need to build in earlier opportunities for feedback and support. International students also talk about how it is hard in the UK to make local friends, and some international students say that their greatest disappointment is that they have not made any local UK friends during their stay. I still have friends from 30 years ago when I was studying and working in China, and some of these have since become productive research collaborations. We are losing potential opportunities – not just for international students, but for home students as well – to mix with people from different backgrounds. If students are not getting this kind of support, this can also impact on their study; peer support is very important for success.

Another distinguishing feature of the UK system is a degree of complacency that I don't encounter in other countries. Lecturers often say to me, 'why should I change as a teacher, they come here for a British education – that is what they want'. Of course that is true – that *is* what they want – but they also want to be successful and they need to learn how to be successful within the British education system. Many other countries are entering the international student market – in Asia, in the Middle East, in Europe – offering courses in English to try and attract students away from Anglophone universities. The advantages that countries like the UK have had may not exist for that much longer, particularly when students are looking at fee structures and weighing the advantages and disadvantages. Academics have also told me, 'students often say to me what a wonderful system the UK is – you have taught me how to think' and I say, 'Yes, they say that in Australia and they say that in the US as well – students also say what a wonderful system there is in the US or Australia, I have learnt so much'. The point here is that we shouldn't be too complacent; we need to keep learning and listening to our international students.

I have been part of the research community in this area for the last 15 years and I have observed a change in how universities respond to international students over this period. There has been a major mind shift and this appears to be accelerating. In the early 1990s the focus was very much on how international students needed to change to fit into the UK system, and there was an emphasis on 'front loading' them or providing remediation programmes for particular academic skills. These are very important skills and international students need to learn them, but they are only part of the story. What was not considered were the knowledge and skills that international students bring to the learning environment and how their expertise and perspectives can be drawn upon to broaden the horizons of local students. Over the past decade there has also been a focus on what institutions need to do to in order to become more responsive to the needs of international students and to

internationalise the curriculum for all students. There has been an explosion of research in this area that examines not just how to 'fix up' international students, but how to cater for them and how to change teaching and learning practices so that they are more internationalised for all students. Currently, there is a focus on the future and sustainability of higher education across the world in a period of much change and uncertainty, but one of the things that has persisted in universities' academic agendas is internationalisation. Internationalisation can be found throughout universities' mission statements and permeates university policy and practice documents. This is an opportune time for communities like EAP to be bringing forth their expertise, because university managers and university policy makers are keen on globalising their operations and internationalising their curriculum. Initiatives such as internationalisation of the curriculum and 'internationalisation at home' (Crowther et al., 2000) are receiving much more attention and this provides opportunities for more collaborative working between research and practice communities; people are listening and are hungry for information.

However, there is still much work to be done, and I outline here some of the issues facing international students, drawing on my own research findings as well as those of others across several countries over the last decade or so. There are clear themes and issues that are coming through whether it is research on international students in Australia, New Zealand, China, the UK or Europe. In the UK international students are fairly satisfied with their learning experiences overall, but there are issues that they continue to report as being problematic. The most important one is unclear expectations – they don't know how to operate in their new learning environment. They may have been at school for perhaps 16 years or so in another system, and when they arrive in the UK they are not sure how, for example, they are meant to interact with the teacher, or how to write for a particular assignment. Learning how to write the perfect essay in another system takes time. Imagine how difficult it is for students coming from a very different kind of culture; it doesn't happen overnight. As mentioned above, I didn't have the required background knowledge that local students have, that body of information they have about the culture that acts as a 'shortcut'; there is a lot of cultural information behind the phrase 'the Education Act of 1944'.

International students also report difficulties with language, difficulties with assessment and difficulties participating in the classroom, the lab, the lecture theatre or seminar room. They also report that they sometimes encounter negative attitudes. Unfortunately, lecturers can make it clear that international students are more 'work' and are a challenge for them – and they *can* be more work. The TIS project aims to tease out these difficult issues and prompt discussion about how they can be addressed by working together to come up with 'smarter' solutions, including sharing expertise, so that it is not quite such hard work. International students do achieve as well as home students, but they need support in learning how to adjust and be successful, and there is much that lecturers can do to facilitate this.

It is clear, however, that there is a need for more work to be done. As part of the TIS project, we have analysed the last five years of the National Student Survey (NUS)

questions in relation to teaching and learning. As can be seen from Figure 1 for Q22 – 'Overall I am satisfied with the quality of the course' – international students are less satisfied than UK students. Over the five-year period, the difference between UK and international students' 'definitely agree' responses to the statement 'Overall I am satisfied with the quality of the course' is four percentage points (33.1% for UK students compared with 29.1% for international students). The difference seven years ago was quite dramatic and international students were far less satisfied, but this has slowly improved over time; this difference dropped from 8% in 2005 to 3% in 2009. This is perhaps because of more interest in international students, the PMI (Prime Minister's Initiative on International Education) projects, and the work that people are doing in universities. However, the statistics still show a four-to-five percentage point gap in all but one of the other questions to do with teaching and learning. As can be seen from the shaded areas highlighted in Table 1, international students' responses are clustered slightly further back into more ambivalent responses than local students. I personally think that is a real disappointment. International students make a big commitment and it is such a significant part of their lives and they should be even more positive than this.

It was with the aim of moving beyond the 'problematisation' of international students, often mentioned in the research literature, and towards examining effective and sustainable solutions to these issues and challenges that the TIS project was established. The United Kingdom Council for International Students (UKCISA) procured funding from the PMI scheme for a project on teaching and learning issues, as

Table I National Student Survey results 2005–2009 for UK and international students (EU and non-EU)

	Q22. Overall, I am satisfied with the quality of the course					
	Definitely disagree	Mostly disagree	Neither agree nor disagree	Mostly agree	Definitely agree	Total
UK (n=876,483)	2.9%	6.5%	9.0%	48.5%	33.1%	100.0%
International (n=81,966)	2.2%	5.8%	11.5%	51.3%	29.1%	100.0%
Total	2.8%	6.5%	9.2%	48.7%	32.8%	100.0%

this area had not previously been considered under the PMI programme. There has been more than 15 years' research on the 'problems' of international students, and the issues have been clearly identified. Much of the research, however, has been carried out when international students are newly arrived and still struggling. There has been little longitudinal research on students that can demonstrate their development and success. The aim of the TIS project is to share ideas, resources and expertise on how to better support teaching and learning for international students. Universities have a large pool of expertise among EAP practitioners and others who are working and researching in this area. There are individuals who are trying to change their practice and writing about their experiences and their successes, but there isn't as yet a strong and cohesive research community that can bring all of this together to assist those who are working with international students to change or enhance their practice.

Another aim of the project is to encourage a more holistic approach to the support of international students; there are so many different parts of the university that deal with students at different times but often there is no 'joining up of the dots'. This can be seen particularly when students are in some kind of distress where they are not doing well; they may be failing and nobody picks this up. Interestingly, it is often support staff, including people like librarians, who may notice that something is wrong, and when things go wrong for international students, they go terribly wrong. They may be a long way from home, there is a lot at stake and there is a lot of 'face' involved in how well they are doing (they may have family back at home who are investing in them). Sometimes we see international students in very tragic circumstances, where there may be something like an accusation of plagiarism, and then things can fall apart very rapidly for them. To prevent such situations occurring, there is a need to be proactive and preventative so that students don't get into these situations. I have been on academic plagiarism panels and I've seen the impact these can have on international students.

What the TIS project aims to do is to encourage understanding. What is it that leads up to an accusation of plagiarism? What is it that leads up to a withdrawal? What is it that leads up to a failure? How can we be doing better? The starting point is to understand what is going on. What are the difficulties for international students, what precisely is it that is difficult for them, what is it that might be unfamiliar? And how can we better support that? How can we address those issues in advance as part of our normative practice?

The first step is to try to understand the learning needs of international students. I always say to lecturers, 'You can't understand all of the cultural backgrounds for international students, particularly if there is a majority of them, but what you can do is develop a "meta-sensitivity"'. Lecturers need to have a good understanding of their own system and its requirements and be familiar with how it may be different from other systems. They need to know what it is that they require of international students that may be difficult or unfamiliar for them. The TIS project is trying to encourage a multi-disciplinary approach to this and is keen that the EAP community is involved to bring its specialist knowledge and expertise to bear and share with lecturers who may not have this knowledge and understanding. In order to do this, a major part of the TIS project has involved the establishment of a database as a 'one stop shop' for lecturers and others to locate current research and teaching and learning resources that can assist them to improve their practice. The intention is not to tell lecturers how to teach, and it is not a 'train the trainer' model. Its purpose is to raise awareness, prompt debate and share ideas and resources; it is up to individual lecturers to decide how they respond. The intention is to build a community of practice, so that those who work with international students understand that they are not the only ones who experience these difficulties. The hope is that they can work productively with others

to share ideas and try out new methods.

The International Student Lifecycle Resources bank[2] is designed for those who want to change or enhance their practice and includes teaching and learning resources and research articles. There are links to international databases, as there is a wealth of research that is constantly growing. As can be seen from Figure 1, the database is conceptualised around the international student 'lifecycle', from when students are starting to think about study and preparing to arrive, when they are learning in the 'classroom' and when they have their assessments, when they are in the community, and finally when they are preparing to move into employment. The topics in the database reflect the issues that are highlighted in the research as possible 'pressure points' for either staff or students. These may include issues such as: What is it in lectures that might be difficult for international students? What is it about reading that might be difficult for international students reading in a different language? It is important for staff to think not just about learning in the classroom, but also how universities can better prepare students before they come as well as after they leave. So, for example, there is a link from the database to the Prepare for Success project (http://www.prepareforsuccess.org.uk), as well as links to projects on employability.

All of the database resources are organised in terms of levels, so, for a novice in the area, there is a discussion of some of the issues that they may need to be thinking about, and, for more experienced staff, lists of further reading are provided for in-depth information and research evidence. Each area has an overview of common teaching topics and issues for the novice lecturer and selected resources showing how others have

---

[2] http://www.heacademy.ac.uk/international-student-lifecycle

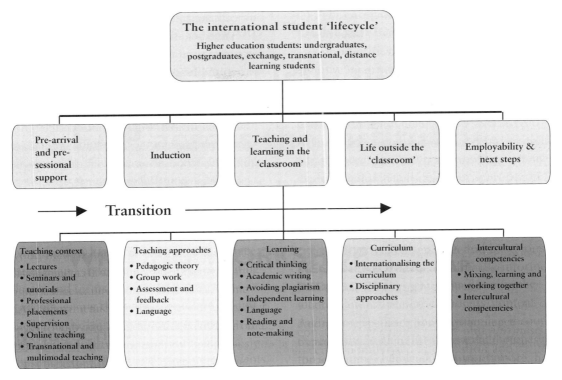

Figure I TIS International Student Lifecycle Resources Database

dealt with this issue and what success they have had. There are also links to other specialist sites and research databases for further evidence. One popular area of the site is the 'case stories' by teachers and by students – 'real life' stories that vividly illustrate the issues facing students and staff. These were obtained via a call through the Higher Education Academy Subject Centres, and there has been a good response with students saying, 'I need to tell lecturers about this'. Unsurprisingly, there are some areas of the website which are very popular – Critical Thinking, and Assessment and Feedback, are among the most visited areas. Lecturers want to know how they can work in a fairer way and in a way that is more embedded in their discipline and their work and is more sustainable for them.

Language, of course, is also an important area and one where many misconceptions arise. Many lecturers underestimate how difficult it is for an international student, particularly if they are operating in a different language. They may have no idea how much information international students will be taking in initially in a lecture. I had learnt Chinese for four years before I went to China and did a six-week intensive language course immediately before I went. I sat in lectures and I was absolutely lost and I missed most of what was going on for the first three months. If lecturers were able to understand that, then they may be able to understand why international students may be failing and then do something to address this. In the language section of the database there is a link to and explanation of IELTS (there are regular links to specialist sites). If lecturers don't understand IELTS and its limitations, then they will think that all of their or their students' problems will be solved by introducing a higher IELTS level, but it is not quite that simple. Even with high IELTS scores, students may still have difficulties. The project prompts lecturers to think in a more complex way about the needs of their students. Each section of the site provides suggestions for practice, 'top resources' for those who don't have much time and a reading list for further evidence. We have found this to be an effective way of engaging with academics. So, for example, in terms of the delivery of lectures, advice is provided about how to 'lighten the cognitive load' for students, how to present lectures in a way that doesn't overwhelm students, and lecturers are prompted to think about how they talk in a lecture, how they present information, how they can provide some sort of cognitive support for their students and how to use language that is intelligible for students.

As I have said, what seems to resonate most with lecturers (and this can be seen from analysis of the website hits data) are the personal stories of international students such as the one below. This excerpt from a case story by an international student about her language difficulties shows the compounding of problems for international students which is often not well understood by lecturers:

> *The biggest problem I have found is the listening skills. As an international student, one has to catch up with what the lecturers have stated in class. The teachers speak at a normal native speaker's pace. It is hard to follow the instructors in detail, which can be a barrier to grasp the key elements in handouts. Often, international students are ashamed to ask questions in class and even after class and let it be. Day after day, problems stick together and I do not know which to tackle first…*

(Excerpt from 'It takes us extra time', http://www.heacademy.ac.uk/resources/detail/internationalisation/case_story_language_xi_takes_extra_time)

These stories remind us of the importance of the work of those in universities who support international students. They also provide a strong rationale and motivation for continuing to support international students by working more collaboratively across universities to assist our international students to achieve success.

REFERENCES

Carroll, J., & Ryan, J. (2005). *Teaching international students: Improving learning for all.* London: Routledge.

Crowther, P., Joris, M., Otten, M., Nilsson, B., Teekens, H., & Wächter, B. (2000). *Internationalisation at home: A position paper.* Amsterdam: European Association for International Education (EAIE).

Ryan, J. (2000). *A guide to teaching international students.* Oxford: Oxford Centre for Staff Development and Learning, Oxford Brookes University.

Ryan, J. (2002). *University education for all? Teaching and learning practices for diverse groups of students.* Unpublished doctoral thesis, University of Ballarat.

Ryan, J. (2011). Teaching and learning for international students: Towards a transcultural approach. *Teachers and Teaching: Theory and Practice, 17*(6), 631–648.

Ryan, J. (2012). Internationalisation of doctoral education: Possibilities for the generation of new knowledge and understandings. *Australian Universities Review, 54*(1), 55–63.

Ryan, J., & Slethaug, G. (Eds.). (2010). *International education and the Chinese learner.* Hong Kong: Hong Kong University Press.

UKCISA (United Kingdom Council for International Student Affairs). (2010). *Higher Education Statistics.* Retrieved from http://www.ukcisa.org.uk/about/statistics_he.php#table2

Ian Bruce

The centrality of genre in EAP instruction

Introduction

This paper argues for a central role for genre in EAP courses, with particular reference to academic writing instruction. Three approaches to the teaching of writing are examined in relation to their capacity to develop EAP students' discourse competence, identity, voice and critical ability. The review concludes by arguing for genre-based instruction as the most suitable pedagogical vehicle for the teaching of academic writing in the EAP context.

When students enter university and begin to study in a particular subject area, they begin a process of mastering the literature, communicative practices and identities of their chosen discipline. Widdowson describes this adaptive process as 'bidding for membership' of a discourse community (1998, p. 10). As I see it, the main function of EAP courses is to assist students with their membership bid, in particular by helping them to develop as writers, so that they can join and participate in the discourse

community of their particular subject, an important part of which involves negotiating its written texts. As Prior states, '[i]n disciplinarity, much of the work on alignment is centring around texts, around the literate activities of reading and writing' (1998, p. 27). Therefore, the development of these skills, and in particular academic writing, is an important concern of EAP courses. In relation to this concern, I have previously proposed (Bruce, 2008; 2011) that the process of becoming accepted as a writer within an academic or professional discourse community involves three important developmental stages that are loosely sequential. They are:

- acquiring knowledge frameworks to be able to deconstruct and reconstruct the texts and related discourses of the discipline that the students aim to enter
- developing an authorial 'voice' and an 'identity' within the target discourse community

- exercising a critical competence to innovate, challenge, resist and reshape the discourses of the target academic community

These developmental stages outline the larger process of the successful launch of the academic or professional career of a writer. Typically, EAP courses, which tend to be brief and transitory, will probably only relate directly to the first and possibly the second developmental stages. However, an overall goal of EAP courses is to equip writers with the skills and knowledge that they need to analyse and master the texts and discourses of their chosen disciplines. Therefore, in this paper I consider three approaches to writing instruction, and specifically the potential of each approach to assist students in their development as disciplinary writers. These are the:

- process (and post-process) approaches
- critical literacy approach
- genre-based approach

The process (and post-process) approaches to writing instruction derive largely from the North American writing and rhetoric tradition (including *composition theory*). North American scholars of writing and rhetoric constitute an extremely large academic community with a long history, a large membership and its own organs of communication, such as the journals *College Composition and Communication* and *College English*. The second, the *critical literacy* approach to teaching writing, derives from theories of the relationship between the exercise of and response to power (such as proposed by Foucault, 1977, 1980) and Freire's notions of obstacles to learners posed by power structures in education (1979, 1994). The

critical literacy approach has questioned both the basis of pedagogy, including the assumptions and practices of teachers, as well as the object of pedagogy, such as the extent to which instructor-trained writers will perpetuate, rather than resist and reshape, the writing practices of their future disciplines. The genre-based approach to the teaching of writing, often used in mainstream schooling and second language teaching, has emerged from the fields of Systemic Functional Linguistics (SFL), educational studies and English for Specific Purposes (ESP). Genre-based pedagogy is concerned with the examination of examples of target-genre texts and their various constituent elements to enable student writers to construct their own examples of the same type of text. Within the scope of this paper, rather than review each of these approaches in detail, I discuss some of their key elements in relation to my suggested three stages of writer development.

STAGE 1: DEVELOPING KNOWLEDGE FRAMEWORKS ABOUT DISCIPLINARY TEXTS AND THEIR RELATED DISCOURSES

Theorists have proposed a number of models that aim to account for what is termed *communicative competence* in a language, referring to an individual's overall knowledge of and capacity to use a language. Most models of communicative competence propose an important sub-component, termed *discourse competence*, or in the case of one model, *textual competence*. Common to definitions of the concept of discourse competence is the idea that it relates to a language user's ability to arrange both content information and language appropriately, in order to create extended spoken or written texts from which coherent discourses may be derived. Discourse competence in writing involves the ability to bring together and integrate socially constructed knowledge, general rhetorical knowledge and linguistic knowledge. For EAP students to acquire this competence, Johns (1997, 2001) proposes that they need to be trained as discourse analysts, meaning that they need to develop knowledge frameworks and heuristic processes, in order to be able to deconstruct and reconstruct the texts of their particular disciplines. Therefore, the first criterion for the review of theories of writing instruction is their capacity to enable the novice writer to be able to analyse, deconstruct and reconstruct texts in their own subject area.

The 'process approach' to writing instruction (Flower & Hayes, 1981; Elbow, 1981; Emig, 1971; Murray, 1982) has tended not to focus on the uses of language in specific domains, such as on categories of text within academic discourse communities. Rather, it is centrally concerned with applying the knowledge of cognitive processes engaged in by writers in order to develop self-awareness and self-confidence in exercising the writing skill. Related to this concern about the personal aspects of writing processes, choice of writing topic also tends to involve issues of personal relevance and interest to the writer. As a consequence, language-related knowledge and skills are addressed on a 'need-to-know' basis in relation to the writer's own self-expression. This is usually done in an inductive way through conferencing, often at the stage of editing a draft text.

Post-process theorists moved from a focus on the writer's cognitive self to consideration of the social situation and construction of

writing and, in some cases, from the perspective of an external ideological positioning, such as, for example, a feminist position. The social situatedness of writing is reflected in classroom tasks and activities that reflect social constructivism (Lave & Wenger, 1991) and collaborative learning (Bruffee, 1995). Thus post-process theories, in moving from a focus simply on the writer, considered the *sociologics* of writing, including its interactive character. However, in post-process theories, the writer and the social activities that surround the writer do not tend to be linked in any systematic or principled way to the analysis of language in specific domains or contexts. In keeping with the post-process notion of the social situatedness of writing, North American genre theorists belonging to the group originally called *New Rhetoric*, and more recently rebranded as *Rhetorical Genre Studies*, consider genres (as categorisers of texts) by focusing principally on the social actions that surround texts (Devitt, 2004; Freedman & Medway, 1994; Miller, 1984). However, theorists in this school tend to avoid doing textual analysis, using the 'stabilised-for-now' argument of Schryer (1993, p. 208), claiming that genres are so rapidly changing that any synchronic textual analysis may misrepresent their rapidly evolving characteristics. Similarly, Freedman and Medway say that a text-analytical approach is seen as 'prescriptivism and [an] implicit[ly] static vision of genre' (1994, p. 9).

On the other hand, writing instructors, using the approaches to genre influenced by SFL and ESP, have attempted to link the construction of meaning in a social context to actual categories of text and their particular characteristics. In particular, the ESP approach has contributed a considerable body of research relating to the analysis and teaching of genres in academic settings. The core notion of a genre-based approach to writing instruction is that it provides opportunities for students to study and deconstruct prototypical examples of a target genre in order to develop their knowledge of its characteristics, and then use this knowledge as a basis for creating their own examples of the genre. Genre theory that provides that basis for such instruction is developing and ongoing. It is now considered that implementing a genre-based approach needs to include:

- a focus on ethnographic and textual knowledge, as well as propositional and meta-discoursal knowledge
- a principled pedagogy that includes cycles of synthesis and analysis

To summarise, the first stage of a writer's development involves developing the capacity to access the written texts and related discourses of their own subject area. Within the limited time frames of EAP courses, I propose that a well-theorised, genre-based approach may potentially provide access to this type of knowledge.

STAGE 2: DEVELOPMENT OF WRITER VOICE AND IDENTITY

A goal of those teaching academic writing in most contexts is that student writers develop their own *voice* in order to be able to communicate their own ideas in individual and innovative ways. The notion of voice is generally seen as an essential element of writer competence.

In the process approach to writing instruction, the idea of individual voice is a core element. Learner writers are

encouraged to harness cognitive principles of thinking, generating and organising ideas, and using recursive strategies for encoding their ideas into written texts. However, the process approach places little emphasis on the external factors of contextual knowledge and context-related communicative purposes and forms. It doesn't consider how these elements may influence the communicative interactions and the actual exercise of voice within specific contexts, such as, for example, in a particular academic discourse community. In the process approach, the focus on voice in writing is on a personal rather than a situated, disciplinary voice.

It is generally acknowledged that developing one's voice through writing (within the context of an academic community) is closely connected to reading and knowledge of the written texts of the same community. However, deriving appropriate discourses when reading an academic text, rather than involving personal interpretations of the text, requires access to the knowledge, communicative values and practices of the discourse community within which the text is located. Part of this may include what Widdowson (2004, p. 80) refers to as the *pretextual* values of specialist readers:

> Our understanding of a text, its realization as discourse, depends on the degree to which we can ratify the linguistic and contextual knowledge that its author presumes we share. This has to do with how far we can engage with the text at all. But there is a second condition that also comes into play: this has to do with what we are processing the text for, what we want to get out of it, the pretextual purpose which controls the nature of the engagement, and which regulates our focus of attention.

Thus, in an academic context, it is likely that the development of a writer's voice may not be merely an individualised voice, based on a heightened self-awareness of personal thinking and information-processing skills. Rather, it is an identity and a voice established and grounded within the texts of the particular discourse community, and effective communication involves drawing upon the identities, genres and communicative values that permeate the texts of that community. Thus, development of a disciplinary voice and identity in writing will be closely connected to reading; however, it will be reading that is orientated towards the academic practices and, specifically, the written genres of a particular subject discipline. As part of this orientation, voice will derive from understanding two closely related areas of subject practitioner knowledge – those of epistemological knowledge (Lea & Street, 1998) and *dialogism* (Bakhtin, 1986).

Epistemology refers to how a subject discipline views knowledge, its theory of knowledge, including how knowledge is validated or proven. This involves understanding of the subject's knowledge-creating processes, such as its research methods, and this understanding cannot be acquired solely in an EAP classroom. However, students can be encouraged to consider the connections between their subject's knowledge-creating processes and how they influence its knowledge-communicating forms, such as its research-reporting genres.

The second element that relates to voice is that of dialogism. The Russian formalist, Bakhtin, proposes that writing, like speaking, is *dialogic* – a dialogue between the writer and the reader – and, as a consequence, writing is constructed with the expectations and knowledge of the reader in mind. In developing Bakhtin's idea of dialogism, Hyland (2005, p. 39) identifies a set of language devices that are used to connect the writer with the reader, language devices which several theorists have termed *metadiscourse*. One example of the metadiscourse devices that he lists are *hedges*, which are expressions that withhold commitment and open dialogue, words such as 'might', 'perhaps' (different types of cautious language). Using Hyland's (ibid.) model, learner writers can be encouraged to examine the metadiscourse used in the written genres of their particular discipline in order to examine its particular ways of enacting voice.

STAGE 3: DEVELOPMENT OF A CRITICAL COMPETENCE

Across all sections of the academy, students' capacity for *critical thinking* (hereafter CT) is generally considered to be a core academic skill. However, operationalising CT and fostering its development through the tasks and activities of EAP writing courses can be problematic, since there is a multiplicity of approaches and views as to what it is and how it can be developed. Traditionally, critical thinking has been seen as a set of cognitive skills relating to informal logic and problem-solving, skills that are not specifically bound to a particular context. The assumption was that, if novice writers acquired this set of generalisable skills, they could then apply them in other disciplinary contexts. However, this view that CT is a set of generalisable, transferable skills has been challenged by a number of theorists and researchers reviewed by Ramanathan and Kaplan (1996, p. 242), who conclude that 'the transfer and general applicability of critical thinking/reasoning skills is at best a debatable one' and that the incorporation of CT into writing 'is situated and context/discipline-dependent'. The idea of critical thinking as a discipline-specific skill is also supported by the academic literacies movement.

Some also see a possible approach to the development of critical thinking by drawing on critical literacy theory and the related theory of *critical pedagogy*. Both of these theories have a socially transformative agenda. They reject the notion that learning should focus on a body of 'canonical' or standard knowledge. Texts are seen as social constructions, and CT involves their deconstruction to examine power relations that can be derived from different 'readings' or approaches to their interpretation. However, like Ramanathan and Kaplan, I suggest that EAP students need to focus on the development of how criticality is enacted within a particular disciplinary context, and that it involves, as Swales and Feak say, the ability of students to make evaluations 'within their [own] field's accepted standards of judgement' (2004, p. 180). I suggest that developing an understanding of the 'accepted standards of judgement' of a discipline requires familiarity with both its knowledge-creating processes and knowledge-reporting forms, such as its disciplinary genres.

Hyland (2003, p. 25) suggests that genres can provide a framework for focusing on critical thinking in relation to a specific context. He claims that 'learning about genres does not preclude a critical analysis but provides a necessary basis for critical engagement with cultural and textual practices'. Ultimately, exercising a critical competence within a particular discourse community involves a writer exercising their own authorial voice in creative ways that involve individualised and innovative use of the various aspects of discourse knowledge that are at their disposal. Or, as Canagarajah (2002, p. 599) puts it: '[t]o be really effective, I need to work from within the existing rules to transform the game'. This is the endpoint or goal for student academic writers. To reach this endpoint, however, requires a well-developed, analytical knowledge of the practices of the discipline and of the disciplinary genres that a student writer aims to control and eventually exploit.

CONCLUSION

To summarise, I argue that a genre-based approach to writing instruction potentially supports the three stages of writer development that I propose. First, it provides writers with a basis for deconstructing and reconstructing the texts and discourses of the discipline that they aim to enter. For most EAP practitioners, this type of top-down examination of a text in terms of its conventionalised features and discoursal interpretations will probably be the central activity of a genre-based approach to writing instruction. This type of activity scaffolds student efforts, then, to create their own examples of the same genre. Secondly, a genre-based approach can provide the basis for assisting novice writers to develop an authorial voice and an 'identity' within a target discourse community, especially in relation to communication through its written texts. This will involve examination of the generic features that relate to writer stance (see, for example, Bruce, 2011, pp. 93–96). Finally, a genre-based approach to writing instruction also provides the novice academic with the basis for developing a critical competence to innovate, challenge, resist and reshape the discourses of their chosen academic community. The third stage assumes mastery of the knowledge and skills of Stages 1 and 2, as well as a period of apprenticed engagement within a discourse community, in order to acquire the necessary disciplinary knowledge, including epistemology. However, in the EAP context it still may be possible to examine how critical thinking is expressed within disciplinary texts as an early step towards the development of this competence.

REFERENCES

Bakhtin, M. M. (1986). *Speech genres and other late essays* (M. A. Holquist & C. Emerson, Trans. 1st ed. Vol. 8). Austin: University of Texas Press.

Bruce, I. (2008). Theorising tertiary writing instruction: Accounting for the process, post-process, genre and critical literacies approaches. In *Proceedings of the TWN Biennial Colloquium: From here to there, December 2–3*, AUT University, Auckland, New Zealand.

Bruce, I. (2011). *Theory and Concepts of English for Academic Purposes*. Basingstoke: Palgrave Macmillan.

Bruffee, K. A. (1995). *Collaborative learning: Higher education, interdependence, and the authority of knowledge*. Baltimore: Johns Hopkins University Press.

Canagarajah, A. S. (2002). *Critical academic writing and multilingual students*. Ann Arbor: University of Michigan.

Devitt, A. J. (2004). *Writing genres*. Carbondale: Southern Illinois University Press.

Elbow, P. (1981). *Writing with power: Techniques for mastering the writing process*. New York: Oxford University Press.

Emig, J. A. (1971). *The composing processes of twelfth graders*. Urbana, Ill.: National Council of Teachers of English.

Flower, L., & Hayes, J. R. (1981). A cognitive process theory of writing. *College Composition and Communication, 32*(4), 365–387.

Foucault, M. (1977). *Discipline and punish: The birth of the prison* (A. Sheridan, Trans.). London: Penguin.

Foucault, M. (1980). Power and strategies. In C. Gordon (Ed.), *Power/knowledge: Selected interviews and other writings, 1972–1977*. New York: Pantheon Books.

Freedman, A., & Medway, P. (1994). *Learning and teaching genre*. Portsmouth, NH: Boynton/Cook Publishers.

Freire, P. (1979). *Reading and writing reality: Explorations into adult education*. New Delhi: Vishwa Yuvak Kendra.

Freire, P. (1994). *Pedagogy of hope: Reliving pedagogy of the oppressed* (A. M. A. Freire & P. Freire, Trans.). New York: Continuum.

Hyland, K. (2003). Genre-based pedagogies: A social response to process. *Journal of Second Language Writing, 12*(1), 17–29.

Hyland, K. (2005). *Metadiscourse: Exploring interaction in writing.* London: Continuum.

Johns, A. M. (1997). *Text, role, and context: Developing academic literacies.* Cambridge: Cambridge University Press.

Johns, A. M. (2001). The future is with us: Preparing diverse students for the challenges of university texts and cultures. In M. A. Hewings (Ed.), *Academic writing in context: Implications and applications. Papers in honour of Tony Dudley-Evans* (pp. 30–42). Birmingham: University of Birmingham Press.

Lea, M. R., & Street, B. V. (1998). Student writing in higher education: An academic literacies approach. *Studies in Higher Education, 23*(2), 157–172.

Lave, J., & Wenger, E. (1991). *Situated learning: Legitimate peripheral participation.* Cambridge: Cambridge University Press.

Miller, C. R. (1984). Genre as social action. *Quarterly Journal of Speech, 70*(2), 151–167.

Murray, D. M. (1982). *Learning by teaching: Selected articles on writing and teaching.* Montclair, NJ: Boynton/Cook.

Ramanathan, V., & Kaplan, R. B. (1996). Some problematic "channels" in the teaching of critical thinking in current L1 composition textbooks: Implications for L2 student-writers. *Issues in Applied Linguistics, 7*(2), 225–249.

Swales, J. M., & Feak, C. B. (2004). *Academic writing for graduate students: Essential tasks and skills* (2nd ed.). Ann Arbor: University of Michigan Press.

Schryer, C. F. (1993). Records as Genre. *Written Communication, 10*(2), 200–234.

Widdowson, H. G. (1998). Communication and community: The pragmatics of ESP. *English for Specific Purposes, 17*(1), 3–14.

Widdowson, H. G. (2004). *Text, context, pretext: Critical issues in discourse analysis.* Malden, MA: Blackwell.

SECTION II

EAP and the disciplines

JOAN TURNER

NON-POLLINATING PERSPECTIVES ON THE WRITTEN: THE CASE OF 'PROOFREADING'

INTRODUCTION

Following on from an earlier BALEAP paper (Turner, 2010), in which student demands on the EAP practitioner were discussed alongside expectations of language proficiency and the often underestimated rigours of how that might be achieved, a systematic research project was undertaken to look at the differing perspectives on 'proofreading' that prevail in the academy. The word 'proofreading' sits in scare quotes because the practice and assumptions around it have taken on symbolic significance such that it does not mean 'proofreading' in the usual pedagogic or pre-publication sense.

The paper also draws on audience participation and comment during the BALEAP conference presentation itself, especially their responses to the possible interventions, if any, desirable on a piece of student text. It further situates the issues within the wider contemporary context of English as an International Language (EIL).

THE RESEARCH PROCESS

The aim of the research was to solicit the views of EAP practitioners, students and discipline-based academic staff in relation to proofreading. To this end, I held one focus group with EAP practitioners, and drew on a wide-ranging discussion on the BALEAP mailbase (Autumn 2007), in which practitioners discussed the pros and cons of setting up a proofreading service, as had been requested at one institution. Student perspectives were gathered through nine small focus groups and four semi-structured interviews. A small grant from the British Academy helped to recruit two focus group organizers and moderators, who were themselves research students and had experience of the methodology. The third range of data, from academics in the humanities, social sciences and visual arts, was gathered through seven semi-structured interviews with the author, specifically relating to the topic of proofreading, while a further three interviews on expectations of academic writing, conducted at an earlier time, were also drawn on. The use of focus groups and semi-structured interviews is well documented in the research methodology literature relating to qualitative research, see for example Denzin and Lincoln (2000), Gobo, Gubrium, Seale and Silverman (2004), Silverman (2004) and Berg (2009).

All the data was recorded and transcribed and a thematic analysis conducted on the results. It emerged that the discourses from the three different groups were very different in themselves. These discourses can be characterized as:

a) *pedagogic*, that is, concerned with student learning and the educational value of practitioner teaching (EAP practitioners)
b) *affective*, showing a wide range of worries and anxieties, but also desire, and an energetic search for solutions in their terms, which often meant engaging proofreaders (the students)
c) *conventional*, revealing expectations of 'correct', well-written academic prose.

Proofreading, even if done by others, was not seen as problematic (the academics).

While some cross-over topics emerged within these discourses, some of which will be discussed and illustrated below, in the main, the tenor of the discussions was tripartite, as characterized.

PROOFREADING, ETHICS, ROLES AND RESPONSIBILITIES

Relating to proofreading as a specific practice, whether paid or voluntary, Harwood, Austin and Macaulay (2010, p. 54) define it as 'third-party interventions (that entail some level of written alteration) on assessed work in

progress'. The notion of 'some level of written alteration' signals the wider concern of their paper, which deals with ethics and integrity in proofreading. Indeed, ethics and integrity is closely related to the practice of proofreading, as also emerged in the data I drew on, especially in relation to student and EAP practitioner perspectives. The following quote from a focus group student expresses the sense of unfairness:

> … but if you get a higher mark just because someone made your sentences better, then I think this is not fair.

Discussing student expectations of proofreading in relation to drop-in sessions with an EAP advisor, the following quote from a participant in my EAP practitioner focus group sums up professional feeling on the issue:

> We should be working with students to highlight weak areas that need to be improved and giving them examples of how to improve it but we certainly shouldn't be going through crossing every 't' and dotting every 'i'. I absolutely don't think that is our job. (Excerpt from EAP practitioners' focus group).

From a different angle, but similarly related to roles and responsibilities, the following post from the BALEAP mailbase discussion succinctly juxtaposes a widely recognizable institutional context with the ethical issues:

> A lot of supervisors here have sent students to see the learning advisors/EAP tutors here and without explicitly saying so, create an expectation that we are going to proofread these dissertations. This allows them to give the ethical issues a body swerve and pass the problem on to someone else. (Excerpt 1 from BALEAP mailbase discussion.)

It is my contention that such supervisors don't actually see it as an ethical issue, but rather see it as part of the EAP practitioner's role in providing language support. Our role tends to be under-analysed at an institutional level. Assumptions about language, and specifically related to the widespread terminology of 'language support', tend to be on a par with the process of proofreading; that is, not very demanding, at least much less so than the rigours of getting to grips with the subject of study. Our rejection, of course, of a proofreading or proofreading-like role for our work, then fits into a process of perennial displacement. If we don't do the work that supervisors want us to do, who does? Some EAP departments then farm the work out, as it were, to individual proofreaders, whether on a formal or informal basis, but this is obviously not satisfactory (see also, Harwood et al., 2009). In fact the whole process masks deeper underlying issues, which do not get addressed.

The perspective on proofreading from my semi-structured interviews with discipline-based academics did not include any immediate association with ethics or integrity. They were concerned rather with their own professional practice as academics, of being able to read student work without hindrance. As one put it:

I think that the problem with text, which is full of those kind of proofreading errors, they are so distracting that it makes it very difficult to read the larger argument. (Semi-structured interviews, excerpt 1)

The importance to the reader of smooth-flowing text is reinforced by the following comment from another academic interviewee:

And I also think that the presentation of the written work in terms of the language used, the succinctness of presentation of ideas, the syntax, the spelling and so on, is crucial to creating a positive impression in the reader's mind, and particularly in the examiner's mind. (Semi-structured interviews, excerpt 2)

By negative association, then, the way in which errors get in the way of a smooth read indicates the importance of the written in itself, what I have elsewhere called 'writtenness' (Turner, 2011). This means that error-free writing could be seen as an important part of addressing the academic audience.

RECONFIGURING EAP PEDAGOGY?

Addressing the finer points of audience expectation, which often gets talked of as 'proofreading' but is actually much more, has implications for EAP pedagogy. It blurs the distinction often made between overall structure and 'surface' level issues. For example, in the discussion on the BALEAP mailbase, one post describes how a 'checking' service was set up, with attendant constraints:

The [checking] service was set up with quite strict guidelines for use: tutors would be restricted in what they did, concentrating on 'surface' grammatical features in order to make texts more readable, and students would only be able to use the service once supervisors were happy with the content. (Excerpt from BALEAP mailbase discussion, 2).

This all sounds professionally appropriate, but its idealism is countermanded by another excerpt:

Also, as we all know, the limits (stick to grammatical tweaking) are not practical. (Excerpt from BALEAP mailbase discussion, 3).

Commensurate with the focus on discourse and genre, and insights into the overall structuring of texts from discourse analysis, EAP writing pedagogy has developed a discourse of 'surface' features of texts and the implication that they are less important. Does the contemporary demand for proofreading perhaps suggest the need for a re-evaluation here? In other words, is 'surface' very much not surface, but crucial to meaning making and interpretation, as well as being important in the higher education context to addressing the academic audience? To illustrate the exigencies and inconsistencies of dealing with what might be seen as 'surface' features, responses of the BALEAP audience at the Portsmouth, 2011 conference to an excerpt of text will be discussed. The excerpt of text was as follows:

> *This acknowledgement towards the diversity of Englishes should raise the attitudes of the participants of the international communication to try to understand each other.*

The audience was asked whether they would leave the text as it was, or if they made changes, what they would change. The first, and most common mention of change related to the word 'towards'. Another frequently mentioned desirable change was to the second 'of the', which people wanted to change to 'in'. A few people suggested leaving the excerpt as it was, as the general import was clear. Some would simply have put a question mark alongside the text, while others would have written 'do you mean awareness?' in the margin. One person also made the point that words that we didn't respond to, such as 'diversity', might not have been the best choice for the student to have made. Would 'diversification' for example have expressed

the argument more clearly? This is a good point. Often we know with certainty when the word choice is wrong, but this example points to the limitless possibilities of intervention, as well as omission.

The only actual change that was made by an academic reader was to substitute the second 'of the' for 'in'. One wonders whether perhaps it was the repetition of 'of the' in quick succession that jarred stylistically with the reader or whether it was the collocation 'participation in' that needed to be redressed. There are, however, occasions where 'participation' could be followed by 'of the'. So does this textual annotation represent a learning opportunity for the student? It struck me that it was actually much more important semantically, collocationally and logically, to change the expression 'raise the attitudes'. However, it's not simply a question of substituting 'awareness' for 'attitudes', as the whole sentence reads awkwardly in standard 'inner circle' (Kachru, 1988) English. The problem is that to reword the sentence would take time and space, which is not compatible with the process of reading an extensive amount of text. Nor does this fit with the assumption that, if one made proofreading changes, they would be perfunctory. The issue of speed and time constraints occurs even in routine EAP marking. It can be easier just to alight on something that can be simply changed, rather than suggest the detailed re-working of a whole paragraph. This point was made by a member of the audience at the BALEAP session. So, ultimately, we would have to admit that there are times when our reading mode is indeed that of proofreading.

What is overwhelmingly apparent from the above task, as well as numerous examples from observational experience, are the multiple inconsistencies of intervention in student texts, and the uncertainty of learning outcomes for the student of those interventions. Proofreading is in effect never-ending. A supervisor often further proofreads an already 'proofread' text. In one case that I know of, an external examiner suggested 264 changes to a thesis which the student had already had proofread. Two readers will often make different proofreading changes.

WORKING WITH ENGLISH AS AN INTERNATIONAL LANGUAGE

The textual excerpt was chosen also for the irony that it dealt with the topic of international English. Should we be more open to EIL and the internationally inflected (also in writing) voice of the student? Should we be open about the fact that many intellectually highly capable students will possibly never achieve the optimum level of written language proficiency in English to best convey their ideas and arguments? There is also an alternative question which arises: what does it mean, in terms of English language, to gain a degree, especially a research degree, at an 'inner circle' institution? Should written proficiency in English as the academic language of 'inner circle' institutions be more rigorously pursued, and importantly, be recognized as an achievement in its own right? The experience of the following focus group student, who paid for the services of a proofreader because, as she said: 'I was thinking they might make my text... into

fluent and nice English', exemplifies a lot of the problems here. She was disappointed because, 'in the end they only corrected my spelling mistakes and the very main grammar mistakes'. The student wants her text to sound 'English', as opposed to betraying her own (European) linguistic background. She assumes this can be done through a proofreader. Shouldn't she rather be encouraged, not only by EAP staff but also her own academic department, to achieve a higher degree of proficiency in English? Uptake of those suggestions would, of course, require a change in institutional culture, whereby the development of high-level English language proficiency ran parallel to the study of the subject. Such an aspiration also adds high-level language proficiency to the purposes of EAP, and does not restrict its practice to a supporting role. A further desirable practice might be to include the EAP practitioner, or 'literacy broker' as Lillis and Curry (2006, 2010) call it, in relation to helping multilingual academics publish in English, as a recognized and established part of the process of getting a research degree, where arguably, the written is as important as the research.

The socio-political dynamics of what circulates under the term 'proofreading' make it less an either/or issue for EAP centres (we do it or we don't), and more one of critical engagement with its myriad issues. Such issues are at the heart of the reception of written work in the contemporary academy, and EAP practitioners should be at the heart of policy making and practice around it.

ACKNOWLEDGEMENT

I'd like to acknowledge the support of a small grant from the British Academy, received in a joint bid with Mary Scott, of the Institute of Education, London. What is reported relates only to my half of the funding.

REFERENCES

Berg, B. L. (2009). *Qualitative research methods for the social sciences*. Boston: Allyn & Bacon.

Denzin, N. K., & Lincoln, Y. S. (Eds.) (2000). *Handbook of qualitative research* (2nd ed.). Thousand Oaks, CA: Sage.

Gobo, G., Gubrium, J., Seale, C., & Silverman, D. (Eds.). (2004). *Qualitative research practice*. London: Sage.

Harwood, N., Austin, L., & Macaulay, R. (2009). Proofreading in a UK university: proofreaders' beliefs, practices, and experiences. *Journal of Second Language Writing, 18*, 166–190.

Harwood, N., Austin, L., & Macaulay, R. (2010). Ethics and integrity in proofreading: findings from an interview-based study. *English for Specific Purposes, 29*, 54–67.

Kachru, B. B. (1988). ESP and non-native varieties of English: Toward a shift in paradigm. In D. A. Baumgarten & R. Chamberlain (Eds.), *ESP in the classroom: Practice and evaluation* (pp. 9–28). Hong Kong: Modern English Publications, in association with The British Council.

Lillis, T., & Curry, M. J. (2006). Professional academic writing by multilingual scholars. Interactions with literacy brokers in the production of English-medium texts. *Written communication, 23*(1), 3–35.

Lillis, T., & Curry, M. J. (2010). *Academic writing in global context*. London: Routledge.

Silverman, D. (Ed.). (2004). *Qualitative research. Theory, method and practice*. London: Sage.

Turner, J. (2010). Supporting academic literacy: Issues of proofreading and language proficiency. In G. Blue (Ed.), *Developing academic literacy* (pp. 39–51). Oxford: Peter Lang.

Turner, J. (2011). Re-writing writing in higher education: the contested spaces of proofreading. *Studies in Higher Education, 36*(4), 427–440.

MAUREEN FINN

WRITER TURNED GATEKEEPER

INTRODUCTION

There is a need for both PhD students and EAP tutors to develop an understanding of their relevant discourse communities because of the situated nature of thesis writing. Students' knowledge is constructed within their social community. As writers they need to see themselves, and be seen, in a context which is as clearly defined as possible, in order to judge the effect of purpose, setting and audience on rhetorical strategies (Hyland, 2000). From a teaching perspective, the concept of discourse community has provided a useful organising principle in EAP. It has set a research agenda relating to genres and communicative conventions, and has led to the subsequent use in teaching of the knowledge gained from this research, in order to help students take their place in their academic communities (Hyland & Hamp-Lyons, 2002).

This study sets out to ascertain whether, or how far, it is possible to build up an understanding of the academic context of a PhD student in a single interview with a senior academic and if this knowledge can be applied to deliver effective in-sessional academic writing classes for a group of international PhD students in the Faculty of Medical and Human Sciences in a UK university. To this end, it looked for practices and norms within the Department of Epidemiology, using Swales' (1990) framework of six defining characteristics of a discourse community, in order, firstly, to understand the practices of the academic context within which these students operate, and, secondly, to be aware of the restraints and demands of the types of writing they are expected to produce within this context.

THEORETICAL BACKGROUND

THESIS WRITING

Good writing is not simply a question of learning formulae in order to produce language-like behaviour (Widdowson, 1983,

p. 102). Students, when writing at PhD level, face a series of complex problems that need to be resolved if they are to be successful academically. Firstly, they need to build the frameworks necessary to understand texts in their discipline, in order to see how knowledge is constructed and developed (Bruce, 2011; Woodward-Kron, 2002). For example, they need to recognise the rhetorical/pragmatic intent of the author of the sources they are using and to know how to attribute content to these sources when it is incorporated into their own work (Swales, 1990; Hyland, 2000). They need to demonstrate a clear understanding of the specific order in which information is presented in a thesis and show the ability to produce an academic style that is both explicit and concise (Swales, 1990; Paltridge, 2002; Bitchener & Basturkman, 2006; Biber & Gray, 2010). Secondly, students need to develop their own voice within their target community (Bruce, 2011). This involves being able to convey what they see as important, choosing material, deciding how to present it and indicating how they feel about their subject matter (Hyland, 2010). Thirdly, it is necessary for PhD students to demonstrate a critical competence that will allow them to contest and reshape disciplinary knowledge (Bruce, 2011; Woodward-Kron, 2002). In order to produce writing that is analytical rather than simply descriptive, they need to critique established knowledge; they should have their own clear line of argument in their writing, and be able to position the material they take from their sources in order to support the points they make; and they need to be able to evaluate phenomena using appropriate criteria (Woodward-Kron, 2002). Students, therefore, need to manage different types of high-level information, or

meta-knowledge, if they are to communicate clearly to their supervisors and examiners, through their written work, an understanding of the knowledge and practices of their discipline.

DISCOURSE COMMUNITIES

Widdowson (2003) describes communication as being possible only where there is a degree of convergence between the worlds inhabited by the participants. Writer and reader have to cooperate in making meaning. Problems arise when there is a difference in linguistic knowledge, as might occur when PhD students are writing in their L2, but the difficulties in thesis writing described above are faced by both native and non-native speakers. Widdowson's second point, therefore, is particularly relevant in the EAP context; difficulties are not only linguistic, but arise when 'the participant is not a member of the culture for whom the text was designed' (ibid., p. 68). This academic culture is described by Swales (1990, pp. 24–27) as a 'discourse community' – that is, a group of individuals who are not limited by locality, but who are connected by specific interests. They join up in order to further shared goals, which, in turn, influence the way communication is carried out in the group.

Swales proposed a framework of six defining characteristics in order to identify such a community:

- common public goals
- mechanisms of communication which permit individuals to participate in the group
- shared information and feedback within the group
- the use of genres that belong to the community and are used to further its purpose
- highly technical texts

- a number of members with an appropriate level of expertise, but also a balance between experts and novices, to allow for the continued existence of the community

The definition of 'discourse community', however, is contested. Hyland (2000) notes the wide range of participants, varying degrees of identification with goals and the variety of uses to which the same texts and genres can be put by members. These comments are echoed by Hyland and Hamp-Lyons (2002, p .7), who warn against interpreting a discourse community as 'determinate, static, autonomous' or considering it to have 'predictable arenas of shared and agreed-upon values and conventions'. Woodward-Kron (2004) points out that discursive practices can be influenced by a variety of participants. All of these elements combine to create a lack of certainty and cause problems for students, particularly those who come from different cultural backgrounds, as they attempt to work out which voices to listen to and which influences to accept while writing up their research.

Borg (2003) charts a shift of emphasis from discourse community to communities of practice (Wenger, 2000; Wenger, McDermott & Snyder, 2002) as a possible response to the difficulties of definition, suggesting that Wenger's definition of communities of practice as the 'social' containers that make up the building blocks of a social learning system is not subject to the 'more diffuse' understandings that are attached to discourse community. In addition, Lave and Wenger's social learning theory (Wenger, 1998, p. 100–101) provides a useful model of how newcomers might become part of a community of practice.

Access to and acceptance as a member requires an awareness of the beliefs, values and conventions of the community, and this sort of knowledge is not usually acquired formally (Flowerdew, 2000). Legitimate peripheral participation, as Lave and Wenger (Wenger, 1998, p. 100–101) describe the process whereby newcomers engage mutually with other members and become included in the community, might provide the means by which this necessary information is attained.

For PhD students and EAP tutors, then, key issues emerge from this discussion. There is a clear emphasis on the importance of the discourse community and on the recognition of its demands and practices, as a context for student theses. For the purposes of this study, despite its contested nature, Swales' framework, described above, was chosen in order to analyse the interview for evidence of a discourse community and how it might be communicated to students. It was used because it is, as Swales points out, 'sufficiently narrow' (1990, p. 22) to exclude marginal possibilities and so produce an operational definition.

GENRE

Swales (1990, p. 58) defined genre as 'a class of communicative events, with a shared communicative purpose, i.e., genre used to accomplish an action' (Miller, 1984, p. 151 in Askehave & Swales, 2001). These purposes are recognized by the discourse community and provide a rationale for the genre. The rationale impacts on both the structure of the discourse and choice of content and style. But if the definition of 'discourse community' is contested, that of 'genre' is a battleground. Responses to Swale's definition included argument about communicative purpose and public goals, and the addition of a psychological, or cognitive, level of genre construction, to account for tactical aspects of genre, thus emphasising its nature as a dynamic social process (Bhatia, 1993, p. 16). There was also discussion about the difficulty of identifying genres as distinctive entities, because of change brought about by the requirements of particular communities (Widdowson, 2003). Swales (2004, p. 61) commented that accepting an easy definition of 'genre' might well get in the way of accurate analysis of new genres.

Reaching agreement on an operational definition continues to be a central problem (Bruce, 2011). Bruce describes two broad tendencies in classification, which correspond to the two major divisions described by Swales in 2001. The first, 'social genre', is concerned with the socially recognised functions of texts, which are seen to be influenced by context, participants and communicative purposes. The second, cognitive genre, is rhetorically motivated and is concerned with the study of organisation and linguistics, dealing with general categories of text, such as argument, explanation and reporting. He considers these categories to be complimentary rather than mutually exclusive, and suggests that together they permit the examination of both discoursal and textual elements of a genre (Bruce, 2010). Key issues here for PhD students and EAP tutors lie in Bruce's argument for a critical approach to genre based on local learner need and recognition that it may include socially constructed knowledge, rhetorical or text-type knowledge and linguistic knowledge (Bruce, 2011).

The focus of in-sessional writing classes is to support students' development as academic writers, and an awareness of the genres in use in their (potential) discourse community can usefully inform in-sessional course structure and classroom discussion. In order to reach some understanding of these genres, as presented by the interviewee, Swales' description (1990, p. 26) of discoursal expectation has been used. This suggests a focus on appropriacy of topics, form, function and position of discoursal elements and the roles texts play within the discourse community. Despite the contested nature of the definition of genre, this list is a practical starting point and so has been used to frame the discussion of requirements for students' PhD theses in the Department of Epidemiology.

THE STUDY

The study sought to obtain information required to develop and improve in-sessional writing classes for PhD students. It aimed to look for evidence of a discourse community and the genres it uses in a specific department in the Faculty of Medical and Human Sciences (FMHS), based on a single interview with a Professor of Epidemiology at a UK university.

The specific objectives were to:
- look for characteristics that would identify a group of individuals as a discourse community
- explore departmental expectations that students will recognise the restraints and demands of the genres in use in the department
- explore departmental expectations that student writing will conform to these demands

METHODOLOGY

The interview was set up through interdepartmental contacts at the university. It was semi-scripted and the questions (Appendix I) presented a week before the interview was scheduled. It deals with the interviewee's opinions on the qualities of good and bad writing, and the process of writing a PhD for the Department of Epidemiology is systematically described. The session was filmed by university technical staff: ethical concerns were covered by obtaining informed consent to the interview, and release forms were signed to allow the material to be used for teaching purposes. Once recorded, the interview was transcribed. In order to analyse the voluminous data which resulted from the transcription, framework analysis was used. This qualitative research method was originally developed for applied policy research, as a comprehensive method of working through raw data systematically, towards concepts that explain social behaviour (Richie, Spencer & O'Connor, 2003).

STAGE ONE

The first stage of data analysis involved immersion in the data, in order to become familiar with it and to develop an overview of the main ideas. While reading, notes were made and recurring ideas collated into groups of similar themes, so that they could be organised into a conceptual framework (Richie et al., 2003). A draft framework of broad headings was produced and then applied back to the transcript of raw data to explore the fit, and the data were indexed (ibid.). With larger amounts of data this process might lead to revision of the draft framework. In this case, with a transcript of 5,000 words, minor adjustments were made. After indexing according to the theoretical framework, the data were then reorganised to summarise them into thematic charts, and these summaries or blocks of data matched to the relevant theme in the framework, under the heading of 'descriptors'. All data, even if apparently unrelated to the objectives of the study, had to be included. The final stage consisted of mapping and interpretation in order to synthesise data (ibid.). At this point, some themes and sub-themes merged and the theoretical framework was revised. This final stage (major themes and descriptors) forms part of Table 1 overleaf.

STAGE TWO

At this point, the emergent themes and major descriptors were searched for evidence of both a discourse community, and the use of genres within this community. In order to do this, they were compared to Swales' framework (1990, pp. 24–27) of six defining characteristics of a discourse community. The characteristics are listed overleaf in Table 1, which presents the results of stage two.

Table 1 Major themes to emerge from the interviews

Major themes	Descriptors	Swales' framework
Roles	Reviewer PhD supervisor PhD examiner	6. A threshold level of members with a suitable degree of relevant content and discoursal expertise 3. Uses participatory mechanisms primarily to provide information and feedback
Expert writer	Text type knowledge Linguistic knowledge Difficulties in writing Solutions to problems Writing techniques	
The role of scientific texts	Text as product Text as transaction Text as story Text as a scientific exercise	1. A broadly agreed set of common goals 2. Mechanisms of intercommunication among its members 4. Utilises and therefore possesses one or more genres in the communicative furtherance of aims
Content and organisation of a PhD in the Department of Epidemiology	Structure of the whole Predictability Academic writing Academic discourse	5. In addition to owning genres, a discourse community has acquired some specific lexis

RESULTS AND DISCUSSION

This section will look briefly at characteristics of a discourse community according to Swales' definition, analyse texts produced in the department and look for evidence that students are expected to be able to recognise and comply with rules governing the production of these texts.

EVIDENCE OF A DISCOURSE COMMUNITY

There are a number of indications of the status of the speaker within his academic community. The majority of these are references to his role as supervisor in the Department of Epidemiology, explaining the control he exercises over students' work, highlighting the pitfalls they face and encouraging them to be critical of their own work. He mentions his role as a PhD examiner, which adds to his authority, and he indicates his seniority in the department by commenting that he reviews the work of his colleagues, and is at ease with doing so. Evidence from the recording shows him an expert in his field; this allows him to give a large amount of relevant information during the interview and validates the content of what he says.

Extract 1

When I am reviewing, say, drafts from students or even more senior people, as well as when I edit chapters from textbooks and papers, I am aware that the biggest problem is people not following a logical sequence of events.

There is an indication here that in the department there are recognised mechanisms for sharing information and for participating in the life of the community. The speaker is at ease giving feedback and he manages a variety of genres (dissertation drafts, chapters in textbooks, papers), all of which validate and develop the purposes of the department both internally (student drafts) and externally (work published commercially and in academic journals). There is also the implicit suggestion that the community maintains a level of membership by allowing entry to those who show evidence of sufficient expertise: students will be awarded PhDs, if their drafts are reviewed and corrected in the required manner and may, with time and editing, become published authors.

GENRES WITHIN THE DEPARTMENT

There are also expectations about the role or purpose a text will have within the

community, and in Extract 4 the speaker makes clear the role of a PhD thesis within the academic community.

Extract 4

Now, let's be honest, for most people doing a PhD, you are often set the question by your supervisor and you are often writing the background when you are into the meat of doing it. And, to be truthful, you are sometimes having to justify asking those questions, even though it wasn't you who asked them. But it's not dishonest. As a scientific exercise, it's quite reasonable to do that, even retrospectively.

He is aware that students might respond negatively to the task they are asked to carry out and argues in favour of the processes by which they are included in the community (Wenger, 1998, p. 100–101). There is also a comment about PhD students 'playing the game', a possible indication of shared public goals, achieved by agreed practices within a community.

Within the discussion on the use of genre to further a community's aims, Swales (1990, p. 26) refers to discoursal expectations. These include the appropriacy of the form in which content is presented. In the extract below, the speaker explains the consequences of not following the requirements for the presentation of numerical information.

Extract 2

Where you fill your text, your prose with lots of figures, it's almost impossible to understand. I don't think any of us has the capacity to read a paragraph where 30 or 40% comprises numbers or brackets or formulae. If you've got that sort of material, put it in a table, put it in a figure, put it in a diagram, and your text can illuminate that.

A second expectation is the text will have a specific function and the elements of the text will appear in an agreed sequence or position. This point is stressed constantly by the speaker throughout the recording and is backed up by numerous concrete examples from his field of practice; organisation is both a support to the writer and an essential part of producing an acceptable text for supervisor, examiners and the editors of scientific journals. In Extract 3, the speaker clearly states that anyone writing for him needs to be aware of the set order in which information is presented, within the genres they are expected to be proficient in.

Extract 3

So the way I look at it is, there are no surprises. So I'm writing an article, I'm reading an article and the article will say, 'These are the following sections', then you give the sections and then you summarise the sections, because the main problem is that sometimes you are struggling to work out where one piece fits in with the other.

Swales refers to the use of highly technical texts as an indication of belonging to a specific group and notes that shared terminology often takes the form of abbreviations and acronyms. In Extract 5 below, the speaker recognises this, and reveals both how students attempt to gain entry to the discourse community by manifesting what they believe is appropriate linguistic behaviour, i.e., (real) academic writing, and how standards are reasserted by the expert.

Extract 5

And one of the things that bedevils a lot of scientific writing is the desire to use abbreviations. And my recommendation, where possible, unless they're standard ones like DNA for example, (is that) to make up

abbreviations just for the purposes of your own piece often can make for a very, very difficult piece of writing to understand.

DEPARTMENTAL EXPECTATIONS

The extracts from the speaker indicate a hierarchy within the community (students as opposed to 'more senior people', the authoritative tone of the speaker himself) and the possibility of changes of status within the group.

In this context, Wenger's (2000, p. 233) description of the boundaries in communities of practice is useful in analysing the positions of both post-graduate student and supervisor within discourse communities. He states:

At the boundaries, competence and experience tend to diverge: a boundary interaction is usually an experience of being exposed to a foreign competence.

The problem is complex. Supervisors have to maintain standards, which mean that they 'perform gatekeeping roles' (Borg 2003, p. 400). At the same time, they also have to manage a process by which newcomers can become part of the community (Wenger, 1998, pp. 100–1).

Part of this process, the construction of texts, is of concern to the EAP tutor. The interviewee placed emphasis on text-type knowledge, linguistic knowledge and writing techniques, all of which form part of standard in-sessional courses. However, there is also evidence of the need for focus on different types of academic discourse, such as being explicit and concise, and being critical and analytical, and this content is less easy to deliver. There is evidence in the recording of the support offered to students, but also of assumptions of expertise and skills that may be beyond students' current linguistic and organisational abilities. The speaker discusses below his expectations that students will be concise. It is also interesting to note the speaker's response to the phrases commonly taught in academic writing classes, in Extract 6 below, which indicate, in this case at least, that standard EAP practice may not be aligned with the requirements of academics in the departments.

Extract 6

The other thing that I think is really important, when you go back, is, have I been concise? What's so easy is to write is the same thing in two or three different ways, or to use expressions like, 'It has been shown that…'. Meaningless expression. You know, 'One more important aspect is…'. These things don't add, they're padding, and I think there is a need to write concisely.

Students are also expected to produce critical analysis rather than description, a complex process of interpretation, argumentation, evaluating and persuasion. The ability to carry out these tasks successfully, with reference to key texts, is seen to result from shared knowledge within a discipline and might present considerable problems for less proficient writers (Woodward-Kron, 2002).

Extract 7

I think that one of the problems I see in the background is that students in my experience are very good at saying, 'Smith et al. 1994 did this, Jones et al. in 1998 did that, Brown et al. in 2002 did that'. Fine. But how do I then take all this and interpret what has been learned in the field? And a really good background is one that is just more than being descriptive but is analytical.

CONCLUSION

The limitations of this piece of research are clear; there is only one interviewee, from a single university and he is representative only of his own department. The findings from this study, therefore, can only be tentative. The available data is confirmatory, giving evidence of a defined and recognisable discourse community, with shared goals, though these remained implicit during the interview. There was communication between members, and journal articles and chapters in books were indicated as means of sharing information. There was participation at different levels within the community; the roles of reviewer, supervisor and examiner were highlighted and the central role of feedback to PhD students discussed in detail. The interview shed light on the use of genres in the community. These were described as (relatively) stable texts, with very clear, and indeed rigid, discoursal expectations; specialist language was used carefully and the interviewer controlled this within student-produced texts. The data showed ways in which the discourse community is communicated to new members; the interviewer conveyed a deep understanding of his role in developing and supporting students as they attempt to gain membership of his specific discourse community.

FURTHER RESEARCH

Students frequently have problems in carrying out the kind of writing they have to produce at PhD level. In particular, students who come from different cultures and different academic backgrounds have considerable trouble in understanding departmental requirements. Given that the information on expectations about what a thesis will contain and how it must be organised was clear and detailed, and given that it is context-dependant, it might be valuable to do further research into these expectations in different departments.

REFERENCES

Askehave, I., & Swales, J. M. (2001). Genre identification and communicative purpose: A problem and a possible solution. *Applied Linguistics, 22*(2), 195–212.

Bhatia, V. K. (1993). *Analysing genre: Language use in professional settings.* Harlow: Longman Group UK Limited.

Biber, D., & Gray, B. (2010). Challenging stereotypes about academic writing: Complexity, elaboration, explicitness. *Journal of English for Academic Purposes, 9*(1), 2–20.

Bitchener, J., & Basturkman, H. (2006). Perceptions of the difficulties of postgraduate L2 thesis students writing the discussion section. *Journal of English for Academic Purposes, 5*(1), 4–18.

Borg, E. (2003). Discourse community. *English Language Teaching Journal, 57*(4), 398–400.

Bruce, I. (2010). Textual and discoursal resources used in the essay genre in sociology and English. *Journal of English for Academic Purposes, 9*(3), 153–166.

Bruce, A. (2011). *The centrality of genre in EAP instruction and research: Addressing issues of theoretical diversity and construct validity.* [Video]. Retrieved April 02, 2012 from http://www.baleap.org.uk/baleap/conference-events/conference/conference-2011

Flowerdew, J. (2000). Discourse community, legitimate peripheral participation, and the nonnative-English-speaking scholar. *TESOL Quarterly, 34*(1), 127–150.

Hyland, K. (2000). *Disciplinary discourses: Social interactions in academic writing.* Harlow: Pearson Education Limited.

Hyland, K. (2010). Constructing proximity: Relating to readers in popular and professional science. *Journal of English for Academic Purposes, 9*(2), 116–127.

Hyland, K., & Hamp-Lyons, L. (2002). EAP: issues and directions. *Journal of English for Academic Purposes, 1*(1), 1–12.

Paltridge, B. (2002). Thesis and dissertation writing: An examination of public advice and actual practice. *English for Specific Purposes, 24*(2), 125–143.

Richie, J., Spencer, L., & O'Connor, W. (2003). Carrying out qualitative analysis. In J. Richie, & J. Lewis (Eds.), *Qualitative research practice. A guide for social science students and researchers* (pp. 219–262). London: Sage Publications.

Swales, J. M. (1990). *Genre analysis: English in academic and research settings.* Cambridge: Cambridge University Press.

Swales, J. M. (2004). *Research genres explorations and applications.* Cambridge: Cambridge University Press.

Wenger, E. (1998). *Communities of practice: Learning, meaning and identity.* New York: Cambridge University Press.

Wenger, E. (2000). Communities of practice and social learning systems. *Organisation, 7*(2), 225–246.

Wenger, E., McDermott, R., & Snyder, W.M. (2002). *Cultivating communities of practice.* Boston: Harvard Business School Publications.

Widdowson, H. G. (1983). *Learning purpose and language Use.* Oxford: Oxford University Press.

Widdowson, H. G. (2003). *Defining issues in English language teaching.* Oxford: Oxford University Press.

Woodward-Kron, R. (2002). Critical analysis versus description? Examining the relationship in successful student writing. *Journal of English for Academic Purposes 1*, 121–143.

Woodward-Kron, R. (2004). 'Discourse communities' and 'writing apprenticeship': An investigation of these concepts in undergraduate Education students' writing. *Journal of English for Academic Purposes, 3*(2), 139–161.

APPENDIX 1

SCRIPT
About writing

Could you say a few words about how you recognise good writing?

what problems do students usually have?

problems with medical terminology?

how do you know writing is bad?

why are papers commonly rejected for publication?

Could you describe how you set about producing a piece of writing?

do you have a particular place to write?

how much revision do you do?

any words of advice on revision?

Can you tell us briefly what you would expect to find in the different sections of a PhD?

how do you approach note taking?

the aims and objectives chapter?

introduction?

a good literature review?

the methodology chapter?

results chapter?

conclusions chapter?

suggestions for future research?

HILARY ARNOLD AND SIMON WILLIAMS

ARBITRATING BELIEFS ABOUT LEARNING TO WRITE IN THE PhD WRITING WORKSHOP

INTRODUCTION

Research training for postgraduate students has an increasingly high profile and high take-up rate. This is particularly the case with workshops on academic writing, which are often oversubscribed. In the course of the writing workshops we have provided for research students at the University of Surrey over the last four years, a challenge we have faced is that participants have mutually conflicting expectations of the workshop process and content. Since students may only attend one workshop on a particular theme, it is clearly important that content should match their expectations. At first, we sought to prescribe what we taught by defining the ideal workshop task and creating a template to satisfy everyone, but our desire proved to be misguided. Instead, adapting our modes of evaluation and learning in order to understand participants' needs and wants in terms of their writing stage proved more useful. Specifically, Aristotle's structure of knowledge and his

concepts of *episteme*, *techne* and *phronesis*, recently popularised in education and technical writing (e.g., Eisner, 2002), helped us to interpret the range of student feedback we regularly received, to map it against stages of learning and to include in each workshop a range of tasks to fit these stages; it also helped us to reflect on the nature of the opportunities for feedback we provided. Our rationale is that socialisation through iterative forms of evaluation enables students to express their needs more clearly and to attempt tasks of higher complexity in the writing workshops. This paper describes the evolution of our feedback mechanisms and our interpretation of participants' responses within the institutional constraints of our remit as writing tutors, and how we learned from both.

THEORETICAL BACKGROUND

Aristotle's conceptualisation of forms of knowledge continues to inform subsequent models of teaching and learning, for example Bloom's taxonomy of learning (1956), Lea and Street's (1998) approaches to teaching EAP writing and Richards' (2002) theories of teaching. Table 1 summarises the relationships between these conceptualisations of knowledge or their application, with the most concrete, external and objective interpretations across the top row. For example, a skills approach to writing might use explicit knowledge of form to teach sentence-level linguistic features such as grammar, spelling and punctuation; it is *epistemic* because the conventions being taught are systematic and widespread, and there is little need for personal judgements from writer or teacher. Richards (2002) sees much science research as necessarily proceeding at this descriptive level, e.g., accounts of empirical projects.

The second row of the table illustrates a genre approach to writing, applying the functions of texts produced by a discourse community to teach rhetorical patterns, which are often at paragraph level, e.g., identifying the gap in the subject literature in an introduction; it is *technical* because the conventions being taught are systematic and confined to a group of language users, and there is some scope for personal judgements from writer or teacher, e.g., in choosing the so-called block, chain or thematic organisation of paragraphs to compare and contrast subject material. In a similar way, Richards (2002) suggests that philosophy proceeds by manipulating models and theories.

The third row of the table illustrates an academic literacies approach to writing, which requires familiarity with power relations within a culture to evaluate a text; it is *phronetic* because the conventions being taught are a combination of the subjective and the social; it demands judgements from writer or teacher on how and whether to apply or adapt conventions. Richards (2002) considers arts and crafts subjects are taught in this way; actually, they cannot be taught explicitly because their production relies on

Table 1 Analogies between forms of knowledge, writing stages and workshop tasks

Aristotle: forms of knowledge	Bloom's taxonomy (1956)	Lea & Street (1998): approaches to teaching EAP writing	Richards (2002): theories of teaching	Language focus	Writing workshop tasks
episteme	knowledge	skills	science research	form	sentence-level information giving
techne	application	genre	theory–philosophy	function	paragraph-level patterned writing
phronesis	evaluation	academic literacies	art–craft	discourse	whole-text writing with reflection

the breaking of conventions, and so the texts produced are unpredictable. Aristotle's conceptualisations of knowledge forms are chosen to contextualise the work reported in this paper because they are the most general and have the advantage of making fewer associations with particular writing movements.

SITUATION

In October 2007, the Department of Languages and Translation Studies at the University of Surrey introduced an ongoing scheme of writing workshops and one-to-one consultations for PhD students. This project is financed through Roberts' funding and focuses on a process approach to developing research students' writing skills across disciplines. The scheme runs across the University and is designed to appeal to all research students irrespective of their background, stage of research or level of skills. The workshops and consultations aim to increase students' awareness of the demands of writing tasks encountered in a programme of research. Samples of the students' own writing are used as a basis for study, analysis and development.

Since our programme of writing workshops began, approximately 500 students have chosen from a repertory of 15 themes and 3 to 5 workshops per term. Each workshop lasts 3 hours and is led by 2 facilitators and attended by up to 20 research students from mixed disciplines. The largest student attendance by faculty is represented by Engineering and Science, reflecting its relative size in the university. The teaching style is interactive and collaborative, involving individual and group activities, and combining tutor-

selected materials and students' own work. The content is process-oriented and the sessions are specifically advertised as 'writing' rather than study skills workshops.

As researchers, the participants have been trained to be critical; they are time conscious, and have high expectations and a clear notion of what they want. They identify themselves as a separate constituency within the University, preferring to attend their own dedicated courses, which have been funded separately. EAP writing tutors, too, see the workshop participants as atypical, not least because of their mix of first languages, including English.

ISSUES

During the course of the writing workshops, several issues have become apparent from participant reaction within them and from post-workshop evaluations. The research students who attend them often have a mindset where writing is very considered and as a result they can be paralysed by the notion of academic writing as anything less than polished production. In contrast, we as workshop facilitators expect instant and superficial writing output, e.g., in response to a free writing exercise.

Initially, simple three-part student evaluations ('Why did you attend the workshop?', 'What did you learn?' and 'What change would you recommend?') seemed useful in helping us understand participants' needs, but there were a number of complicating factors in our interpretation and response: because workshops were attended as 'one-offs' rather than as a series, it was difficult to measure any long-term development in participants' writing, and their contrasting expectations were typified by the following comments given in response to the same workshop:

> *I want to know about writing, not actually do it in the workshop.*

> *Excellent to be obliged to write something in the workshop. Even if it is just a draft, something was done.*

In circumstances where a participant might come to only one workshop, managing expectations at the start of the session became an important way of responding to earlier evaluations. Participants were asked to sit in faculty groups, and a novel procedure was introduced whereby they were given coloured Post-it notes to record their expectations individually. They then worked in their groups to sort them into categories. The colour of the Post-it note showed the student's year, e.g., 1st, 2nd, 3rd or the equivalent for part-time students. The first time the procedure was tried, the participants collectively grouped the notes into three categories approximating style, format and content, confirming earlier feedback that most students wanted to learn about writing structure and organisation (comparatively fewer wanted grammar) and how to improve their own writing within the discipline. This was reflected in the popularity of the various workshop tasks, which could notionally be divided into three types: e.g., aspects of style, rhetorical moves and critical feedback on writing (see samples of tasks below).

<u>Use noun-based phrases instead of *wh~* clauses</u>.

1(a) A road atlas can help in estimating **when we arrive** at our destination.

1(b) A road atlas can help in estimating **the time of arrival** at our destination.

<u>Rewrite</u>

2(a) A glance at a geological atlas will reveal **where these limestones occur**.

2(b) ....

Figure 1 Aspects of style

Write the number of the appropriate sentence in the table below:

1. A number of studies have suggested that high intake of low glycaemic index foods and non-starch polysaccharides (NSPs) may benefit diabetics (Green et al., 2000, Ketab et al., 2004; Wang, 2007).

2. Kim (2007) found that blood glucose and lipid levels improved after consuming a low glycaemic index (GI) diet.

3. Dietary carbohydrates (CHOs) are known to have a strong impact on blood glucose levels (Jones, 2001).

4. However, the health benefits of a low GI diet remain to be fully analysed.

Focus	Citation	Tense	Sentence
General statement	INFORMATION PROMINENT	present tense *is / are*	*Example 3*
Medium focus	WEAK AUTHOR PROMINENT	present perfect *has / have ~ed*	
Narrow focus	AUTHOR PROMINENT CITATIONS	simple past *~ed*	
Identifying the gap	-	present tense *is / are*	

Figure 2 Rhetorical moves
(Adapted from Weissberg, R., & Buker, S. (1990), *Writing Up Research*. London: Prentice Hall. Authors named in Figure 2 are fictional.)

- With another participant, team up with two others (i.e., 4 people, 2 x 2).
- Exchange proposals you have written.
- Take turns in vetting the proposals and applying editing filters, using the feedback sheets provided.

Figure 3 Critical feedback on writing a conference proposal

The style and format tasks were most popular, and the critical feedback task elicited the polar evaluations.

The comments of workshop participants could be seen in terms of the types of knowledge described by Aristotle, namely *episteme*, *techne* and *phronesis*, glossed as 'theoretical', 'productive' and 'socio-ethical' (Saugstad, 2002), and as 'certain knowledge', '"savvy" knowledge' and 'ethical reflection' (Schryer, Lingard & Spafford, 2005) respectively (for related discussions, see Bridgeford & Moore, 2002; Beckett, Agashae & Oliver 2002; Birmingham, 2004; Hawk, 2004). These models make it possible to see the three task types as building on one another in terms of cognitive complexity. Further, because Aristotle saw these knowledge stages as progressive, it would be natural that the participants should be encouraged to move from a stage of *episteme*, or skills-based learning to write, expressed by the desire for 'knowledge about', to *techne*, a more practice-based form. The participant's final aim should be the *phronetic* stage, as in academic literacies, the ability to self-consciously choose a style and approach to suit the situation. Thus, whilst information about writing is necessary for novice writers, it cannot be sufficient for them to produce texts suitable for the communities of practice they aspire to engage in (Lave & Wenger, 1991). For that, more specific examples and guidance are needed, as practised by representatives in the field. To become an independent writer capable of making original contributions requires an independence of approach developed only by a combination of critical self-reflection and an exchange of ideas with others in the field.

COLLECTING FEEDBACK

As workshop facilitators, we have used four different means of collecting feedback from participants: hard copy, online questionnaires, interviews and focus groups. Conventional means of collecting feedback in hard copy at the end of each workshop was discontinued by the programme administrators in favour of online evaluations. However, these were less timely, completed by fewer participants and did not always get passed to the tutor concerned. In response, the workshop facilitators introduced a self-reflection sheet, on which participants recorded their response task-by-task. It was these self-reflection sheets that produced the contrasting comments.

We also conducted a small number of semi-structured interviews with former participants to get a better idea of their experience. After identifying students who were available for interview, our criteria for selection were whether the student had attended a writing workshop and had followed up with regular writing tutorials over a period of time (six months to two years). We felt such participants would have a better understanding of the rationale behind the approach we offered and therefore be in a better position to evaluate it. Three interviews were conducted, using questions suggested by the questionnaire responses (see Figure 4).

The findings suggested that interviewees had a heightened awareness of their writing needs and how they wanted to progress, and were not necessarily expecting EAP tutors to solve their writing problems for them.

> What writing workshops have you attended? Why that one / those?
>
> What did you expect from the writing workshop(s)
>
> Do you think they've made any difference (to your writing)? How?
>
> What did you think of the format of the workshop?
>
> How would you run a writing workshop?
>
> Is there anything else you do / have done to develop your writing? What?
>
> What kind of writing do you think you'll do in the future?

Figure 4 Semi-structured interview questions

Following the procedure adopted by Flint, Oxley, Helm and Bradley (2009) and Oxley and Flint (2008), comments extracted from the interviews then provided some of the prompts for a 'dialogue sheet' that became the stimulus for a focus group meeting. Other prompts came from the student evaluations. A dialogue sheet is a tool developed at the Royal Institute of Technology (RIT), Stockholm, to encourage student reflection (Blomqvist, Handberg & Naeve, 2003). At RIT, dialogue sheets were used to socialise freshers with their peers and get them talking positively about learning. A dialogue sheet is simply an A0 sheet of paper, on which are printed a number of questions and tasks. (See Appendix, Figure 5, for an example.) The questions and tasks are stimuli for the six to eight people who sit around the paper, each in front of a particular question or task. Each person is responsible for reading theirs out and then commenting on it, to initiate a round of discussion. The same person is also responsible for noting the outcomes for that stage on their part of the sheet. The procedure means that everyone takes the lead at some point and everyone has the chance to contribute to each point; this reduces the possibility of the event being dominated by one or two people. The aim is to stimulate the sort of discussion that encourages participants to reflect on the prompts.

The focus group at Surrey lasted for 90 minutes. Seven participants were invited to attend on the basis of their workshop attendance and availability and rewarded with book tokens. They represented a range of nationalities and first languages: Polish, Indonesian, British English (two), American English, American English/Japanese and Brazilian Portuguese[1]. The quotations were transferred to three A0 sheets, each sheet containing quotations judged to represent a particular knowledge stage. Representative quotations were:

- *The course had many practical tips and suggestions* (episteme sheet).
- *I learned a lot from evaluating a text* (techne sheet).
- *I always find it very valuable to meet and hear the views of other students* (phronesis sheet).

With hindsight, it was probably unnecessary to produce separate sheets because, firstly, participants made similar points regardless of the quotation and sheet they were working on, and secondly, there was insufficient time for the focus group to work its way through all three sheets.

The method for conducting the focus group meeting was based on World Café: Café to Go! procedure (www.theworldcafe.com), with one variation: to allow for differences in

---

[1] One participant was also an interviewee, but had not participated in a face-to-face interview.

self-confidence, a particular consideration in groups of speakers of various first languages, participants were given two minutes to reflect on the comment in front of them – e.g., 'It's good to be in a workshop group from the same faculty or department to make discussion easier' – before introducing it and giving their response. In the event, other people around the table then gave their response to the original comment and to others' reactions to it – in what became a discussion – before the second quotation was read out, and so on. It was not the case that each person around the table gave their reaction in turn before a general discussion occurred. Participants were also encouraged to write their comments on the dialogue sheet. The focus-group discussion was audio-recorded on two MP3 players placed on the table. The size of the group suggested that it might be difficult to hear all participants on the recording if only one machine was used. The recordings were afterwards listened to by both authors and transcribed.

Time only allowed for discussion of the *episteme* and *techne* sheets, but, as noted above, participants' contributions tended to follow set themes, e.g., the Indonesian student considered compulsory subject-specific writing workshops were needed at the start of a PhD programme; the Polish student thought writing was best learned through practice; and the North American student thought anything was worth trying once. Their comments were summarised from the transcription and classified into Aristotle's knowledge types as follows:

- *Subject specific workshops are needed at the start of a PhD (techne).*
- *At home, it's assumed I've already learned what I need (episteme).*
- *Could we set up a student writing group? (phronesis).*

A contribution from the Polish student, viz.

I agree that attending a session at the beginning might be a good idea, but it may be too [unfamiliar] for you to participate unless it's a very general course. It raises questions of field-specific issues as well.

revealed the inherent contradictions within the group's thinking, which could be summarised as:

Timing: compulsory workshops for new students

versus

Content: subject-specific.

As the Polish student pointed out, subject-specific content is difficult for newly-arrived research students to relate to as they have not yet acquired sufficient background knowledge. Faced with such diverse opinions and the dilemmas they produced, the participants agreed to disagree: 'OK, if you say so', was a blunt rejoinder at one stage.

The data collection reported in this study was an iterative process that can be summarised as:

1. Students' evaluations of workshops via individual hard copy collected at the end of workshops, online evaluations and self-reflection sheets recording a student's response task-by-task.
2. Students' expectations via groups and, later, individually classified as
   - style
   - format
   - critical feedback on writing.
3. Semi-structured interviews using questions based on expectations and comments in evaluations (see Figure 4).

4. Focus-group prompts from student comments in interviews and evaluations organised and analysed in categories similar to those in Table 1.

OUTCOMES

What we learned from the focus group was that we too have to accept contradictions in the needs of writing workshop participants. There will never be a silver bullet (a favourite metaphor used in the focus-group meeting) to devise the perfect task or the perfect workshop. Workshop participants will inevitably be at various points in the Aristotelian stages of knowledge, irrespective of their language, culture, subject and career stage. What facilitators can do is offer within each workshop a varied set of activities as luminous stepping stones, enabling participants who are ready to proceed from one stage of knowledge to another. Facilitators can also seek to offer a varied set of evaluation modes, so that participants, rather than being constrained by *techne*-like forms that are convenient to administer, are encouraged to express themselves in *phronetic* dialogue. This allows their voices to be heard. As a result of the suggestion by one of the students in the focus group, we set up a structured monthly writing group, run by the research students but with a tutor present. The aim of these group meetings is to peer review each other's writing. One of the participants expressed her surprise that having first come to a workshop with a sample of her writing for study, analysis and development twelve months ago, she was now being invited to read this paper and do the same for us. We began the programme of workshops seeing ourselves more as information givers; now,

we see ourselves as collaborators involved in a cyclical process with the students.

CONCLUSION

We set out to establish a process approach to developing research students' writing and we as facilitators have also gone through a process of learning and development. The collection of formative evaluations highlighted the differences in participant expectations and prompted us to create different workshop tasks, to manage the sessions differently and to change our methods of collecting feedback.

It seems that the workshop expectations of the PhD students need to be managed in three ways: (1) providing information about each task before and after, so satisfying students' needs for *episteme*; (2) providing a mix of tasks focusing on writing form, function and discourse in every workshop, so satisfying students' general and specific needs for *techne*; (3) providing group feedback and eliciting student discussion of each other's work wherever possible, so satisfying students' needs for *phronesis*. Meanwhile, the structured monthly writing group run by the research students focuses more on peer editing and review, so providing an additional forum for *phronetic* learning for a minority.

We propose to arrange further student interviews and focus groups to access views not expressed in other forms of evaluation. Personal interviews and focus groups have provided the qualitative feedback that has led to critical analysis of what we as EAP tutors do and what we seek to continue to do: to try and engage with writers on several levels – as students, subject experts, participants and informants.

REFERENCES

Beckett, D., Agashae, Z., & Oliver, V. (2002). Forum: Just-in-time training: techne meets phronesis. *Journal of Workplace Learning, 14*(8), 332–339.

Birmingham, C. (2004). Phronesis: A model for pedagogical reflection. *Journal of Teacher Education, 55*(4), 313–324.

Blomqvist, U., Handberg, L., & Naeve, A. (2003). New Methods for focusing on Students' Learning Process and Reflection in Higher Education. Proceedings of the 28th IUT Conference. Växjö, Sweden. Retrieved October 10 2011 from http://cid.nada.kth.se/pdf/CID-238.pdf

Bloom, B. S. (1956). *Taxonomy of Educational Objectives, Handbook I: The Cognitive Domain.* New York: David McKay.

Bridgeford, T., & Moore, M. (2002). Guest editors' column. *Technical Communication Quarterly, 11*(2), 125–128.

Eisner, E. W. (2002). From episteme to phronesis to artistry in the study and improvement of teaching. *Teaching and Teacher Education, 18*(4), 375–385.

Flint, A., Oxley, A., Helm, P., & Bradley, S. (2009). Preparing for success: One institution's aspirational and student focused response to the National Student Survey. *Teaching in Higher Education, 14*(6), 607–618.

Hawk, B. (2004). Toward a Post-Techne—Or, Inventing Pedagogies for Professional Writing. *Technical Communication Quarterly, 13*(4), 371–339.

Lave, J., & Wenger, E. (1991). *Situated Learning: Legitimate Peripheral Participation.* Cambridge: Cambridge University Press.

Lea, M., & Street, B. (1998). Student Writing in Higher Education: An academic literacies approach. *Studies in Higher Education, 23*(2), 157–172.

Oxley, A., & Flint, A. (2008). Placing student voices at the heart of institutional dialogue. *Educational Development, 9*(3), 14–16.

Richards, J. C. (2002). Theories of teaching in language teaching. In J. C. Richards & W. A. Renandya (Eds.), *Methodology in TESOL: An anthology of current practice* (pp. 19–25). New York: Cambridge University Press.

Saugstad, T. (2002). Educational theory and practice in an Aristotelian perspective. *Scandinavian Journal of Educational Research, 46*(4), 373–390.

Schryer, C. F., Lingard, L., & Spafford, M. M. (2005). Techne or artful science and the genre of case presentations in healthcare settings. *Communication Monographs, 72*(2), 234–260.

Weissberg, R., & Baker, S. (1990). *Writing Up Research.* London: Prentice Hall.

APPENDIX

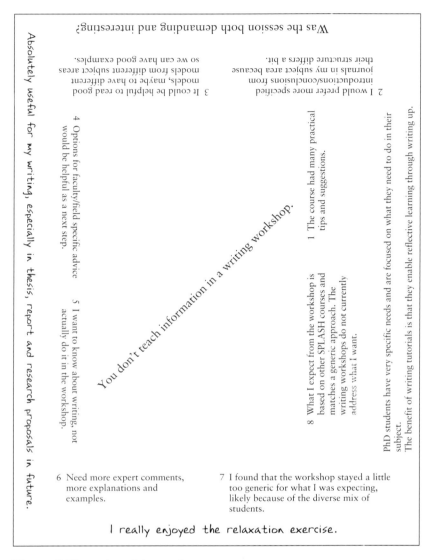

Was the session both demanding and interesting?

Absolutely useful for my writing, especially in thesis, report and research proposals in future.

3 It could be helpful to read good models, maybe to have different models from different subject areas so we can have good examples.

2 I would prefer more specified introductions/conclusions from journals in my subject area because their structure differs a bit.

4 Options for faculty/field specific advice would be helpful as a next step.

1 The course had many practical tips and suggestions.

You don't teach information in a writing workshop.

8 What I expect from the workshop is based on other SPLASH courses and matches a generic approach. The writing workshops do not currently address what I want.

5 I want to know about writing, not actually do it in the workshop.

PhD students have very specific needs and are focused on what they need to do in their subject.
The benefit of writing tutorials is that they enable reflective learning through writing up.

6 Need more expert comments, more explanations and examples.

7 I found that the workshop stayed a little too generic for what I was expecting, likely because of the diverse mix of students.

I really enjoyed the relaxation exercise.

Figure 5 The *techne* dialogue sheet

Nadya Yakovchuk and Julian Ingle

Working with Departments to Develop Students' Writing: Two Examples of Collaborations on Medical Degrees at Queen Mary, University of London

Introduction

Within the theory and practice of writing development in UK tertiary education, there has been a move in the last decade towards working more closely within departments and individual disciplines to address students' writing needs. Although the 'generic/discipline-specific' debate is perennial to EAP (and writing development work in general) and both approaches have their purposes and value (Hyland, 2006; Alexander, Argent & Spencer, 2008), as Hyland and Hamp-Lyons (2002, p. 6) state, 'it is important for EAP to … establish practices that challenge the widely-held assumption that academic conventions are universal and independent of particular disciplines as this … leads learners to believe that they simply need to master a set of

transferable skills'. This resonates with Lea and Street's (1998) position against the conceptualization of writing as a 'set of atomised skills' that, once acquired, can be transferred to other contexts; they emphasize the importance of considering writing (critically) in the context of specific disciplinary discourse communities and their norms.

This paper aims to contribute to the debate by sharing our experience of embedding writing development within disciplinary contexts. The two projects discussed are recent collaborations in which the authors have participated. The first addresses ways of improving the quality of second-year medical students' written responses to short-answer questions (SAQs) in exams, one of the main forms of assessment on the Bachelor of Medicine, Bachelor of Surgery (MBBS) degree.

The second, a more established collaboration, involves a series of writing workshops developed and co-taught with the Centre for Sports and Exercise Medicine (CSEM), which prepare fourth-year medical students on an intercalated degree for writing their research project for assessment and possible publication in the *British Journal of Sports Medicine (BJSM)*. We discuss these case studies in light of some of the current theoretical debates in the area of writing development and offer some practical suggestions on how to initiate and sustain collaborations with departments, establish co-teaching and develop highly contextualized writing materials suitable for both L1 and L2 students.

PUTTING THEORY INTO PRACTICE

John Bean (2011) extended Beaufort's (2007) conceptual model of writing expertise to outline a range of knowledge and skills needed to be able to produce 'expert insider prose' within a discipline (i.e., to be able to write as a historian, a sociologist, a biologist, etc.). These capabilities include subject matter knowledge, genre knowledge, disciplinary discourse knowledge, rhetorical knowledge, writing process knowledge and information literacy. The need to possess such a wide range of competencies highlights the complex nature of academic writing and the importance of including, where possible, subject specialists in writing development work. According to Monroe (2003, p. 5), 'all meaningful acts of writing are unavoidably complex negotiations with particular contexts, purposes and audiences. In higher education, these negotiations take place within particular disciplines'.

Since its inception, the Thinking Writing (TW) initiative at Queen Mary, University of London, has been working to improve the quality of students' writing by establishing close collaborations with subject specialists and, through these collaborations, exploring the potential of writing for acquiring disciplinary knowledge and for developing students' thinking in the discipline – both 'writing to learn' and 'learning to write' (Britton, 1982). TW's work has drawn on insights from a range of fields, including Writing Across the Curriculum (WAC) and Writing in the Disciplines (WiD) (Monroe, 2003, 2007; Russell, 2002), genre analysis (Swales, 1990; Bhatia, 1993; Martin & Rose, 2003), argument theory (Willard, 1989; Andrews & Mitchell, 2001), Systemic Functional Linguistics (SFL) (Martin & Rose, 2003; Halliday & Matthiessen, 2004) and Academic Literacies (Lea & Street, 1998; Lillis & Scott, 2007).

Our way of working with departments has similarities to other modes of discipline-specific writing development which have been emerging in the sector (e.g., Sloan & Porter, 2009; Wrigglesworth & McKeever, 2010). This approach, however, often goes beyond an assessment focus and explores the potential of writing for learning, reflection and professional practice, and, in some cases, challenges disciplinary conventions around writing. The background work we do often involves analyzing how learning outcomes for a course or programme are reflected in the written assignments, discussing whether the assignments set by the tutor reflect some of the epistemological underpinnings or ways of thinking in the discipline and the demands of the wider professional field, as well as trying to understand academics' beliefs about learning and assessment. This work also entails close analysis of subject-specific text types and students' written assignments, which often leads to materials or course development and co-teaching with staff from the discipline. A number of accounts of different aspects of TW's work have been presented elsewhere (e.g., Mitchell & Evison, 2006; Mitchell, 2010; Horne & Peake, 2011; McConlogue, Mitchell & Peake, 2011).

The two case studies below illustrate how this works in practice. The first demonstrates a more instrumental and target-oriented approach to writing, driven primarily by students' need to develop content knowledge and to be able to demonstrate this in exams. The second involves a more developmental approach and focuses on facilitating students' 'acculturation' to their discipline and developing their research writing. Both collaborations have involved extensive dialogues with disciplinary tutors about what constitutes good writing in their contexts, what functions such writing is expected to fulfil and how this can be co-taught.

CASE STUDY 1: SHORT-ANSWER QUESTIONS

A) CONTEXT

Initiated by the head of the second-year MBBS in the School of Medicine and Dentistry (SMD), Dr. C., the project addresses concerns about the quality of students' writing on the degree. (Among students accepted each year onto the degree, fewer than 10% are international, although there are significant numbers of home students from ethnic minority backgrounds who are either bilingual or have English as an additional language). We chose to work on short-answer questions (SAQs[1]), a task medical students do repeatedly throughout their degree. According to Dr. C., one of the problems common to students' SAQ answers was that they would write statements of fact that were scientifically correct but did not provide explanations as to why they were relevant to the questions.

B) PROCESS OF COLLABORATION

Our starting point was to read through batches of students' SAQ scripts from a range of medical specialisms.[2] Having gained a feel for the content, we analyzed the types of writing required by the questions, and looked at the high scoring responses for any patterns or similarities. Broadly speaking, the questions required three different types of writing: descriptive (e.g., defining terms or listing facts), explanatory and cause-effect relations (this would often take the form of 'explain the significance of x with regard to …'), and more applied questions, in which a specific problem or set of symptoms are analyzed (these would often involve a specific scenario, e.g., 'given x scenario, why does y happen?').

---

[1] An SAQ section of an exam is usually allocated 20 minutes and is worth 20 marks. A range of very short written responses is required, from a sentence to a paragraph, on topics within medical specialisms, such as Locomotor, Histology or Metabolism. Questions are sometimes framed by a short case history or a contextualizing statement, which would often have been covered earlier in problem-based learning sessions (see Appendix 1 for a typical SAQ).

[2] The authors would like to acknowledge the role of our colleague Kelly Peake for her contribution at this important initial stage, and subsequently in the development of the online resource.

Premised on the integration of disciplinary and specialist knowledge with our linguistic analysis of SAQs and transcripts, the design of the learning resource encompassed awareness-raising activities on the features of writing good quality SAQs, practice at identifying question types, peer evaluation of five students' answers to a question from Biochemical Metabolism (see Appendix 2) and a short activity on nominalization.

C) Feedback and ways forward

We trialled the activities in two different settings: a lecture and a small seminar, and both sessions were co-taught with Dr. C. and a member of staff from TW. From the short feedback questionnaires completed by students, they found the peer marking of a range of previous students' answers particularly useful. They valued the opportunity to follow up with the subject specialist why certain marks were awarded or not, and discover more about the marking process itself. In the feedback from the first time the session ran, about a third said that they would prefer not to do the language-based activities and wanted more examples of student answers to a range of SAQs. From discussions with Dr. C., his thoughts were that some medical students are quite instrumental in their approach and would therefore only be interested in the SAQ examples themselves, as this content focus is what improves their grades. Nevertheless, we all felt that some analysis of linguistic functions was important and should remain in the activities. After the material had been refined (tightening up the language activities and adding a longer SAQ worth five points), the majority said they enjoyed the language activities but still wanted more examples from a range of subject areas to peer review.

More SAQ topics will gradually be incorporated into the existing material with the aim of developing and piloting an on-line self-access resource (or reusable learning object – RLO) for second-years, with a new version adapted for first-years.

Case study 2: research writing workshops

A) Context

Third- and fourth-year MBBS students can choose to study for a BSc on an intercalated degree programme (iBSc). Although there is homogeneity in their academic performance, given that they are selected on their academic ability, there is considerable diversity of educational and ethnic background of the cohort. The vast majority, however, have English as L1. Assessment for the Centre for Sports and Exercise Medicine's (CSEM) iBSc includes a research project, which is given considerable importance, reflected in its weighting (50% of the total mark for the BSc). Of equal significance is the department's desire to ensure as many research projects as possible reach a publishable standard. A perceived disparity between the students' ability to articulate their research in vivas and presentations versus written projects was one of the prompts that initiated this collaboration.

B) Process of collaboration

TW and CSEM co-designed a series of writing sessions to improve the quality of students' writing, which, with further direction from CSEM supervisors, would ideally bring it to a publishable standard. The four 2.5-hour workshops co-taught by the subject tutor and a member of TW run in the second semester. To identify students' experiences of, and beliefs about, reading and writing in the medical sciences, activities asking them to reflect on their own practices of reading and writing have been included. A number of free-writing exercises and discussions have been designed to explore some of the 'taken for granted conventions' (Lillis & Scott, 2007, p. 11) and the 'impact of power relations on student writing' (ibid., p. 12). For example, the 2011 cohort were keen to discuss the significance of author order in co-authored journal articles, questioning the status of each author and what their position in the list might mean. The subject co-tutor explained the significance of first and last author, in particular the anchoring role of the last author, who may well have come up with the original idea, but who may not have contributed much to the writing itself. The academic status of the last author was discussed in relation to the possibility of getting published and how this could be an important factor. As 'novice' researchers they could, it was argued, be on a journey towards the status of last author. There were concerns about their role as student researchers being abused; for example, that they could be used as a source of work in research projects but would not receive the recognition. The subject co-tutor commented that they had to 'earn their spurs' or 'serve their time' in the research community. Also, systematic literature reviews and research articles from the *BJSM* have been analyzed in terms of their linguistic and organizational features. The value of co-teaching when, for example, looking at the coherence of sections of a literature review, is that both the linguistic moves and the methodological quality of the paper can be discussed simultaneously.

C) FEEDBACK AND WAYS FORWARD

The process of collaborative teaching opens up opportunities for insight into each other's disciplines and the ways in which knowledge is constructed and communicated. In this case, the approach to co-teaching is premised on an evolving dialogue between the tutors themselves and between the tutors and the students. In written feedback, students commented that they appreciated having the perspectives of someone from a different disciplinary background, in this case the humanities. Inevitably, as a reflection of their diverse needs and interests, some students were more interested in the language-based activities, whereas others preferred those with more of a content bias, such as analyzing methodological quality of research studies for literature reviews in terms of, for example, sample size, experimental design and baseline matching. However, there was consensus about the value of peer reviewing each other's and previous students' writing. Common to a significant majority of this feedback is that students say they feel more confident as writers.

There have been two developments in the co-teaching with CSEM this year. Students who had just completed the CSEM iBSc and whose research projects were approaching a publishable standard took part in a semi-structured, three-day writing retreat facilitated by the same co-teachers. Secondly, the option of fully incorporating the writing workshops into the assessed framework of the iBSc has been proposed by the course lead.

DISCUSSION

These case studies demonstrate how the same general approach can be adapted to, and shaped by, two different teaching and learning contexts. We think that these examples highlight the need for, and value of, situating writing development work within its disciplinary context. Although the case studies draw on the same discipline and level, the distinctive nature of the immediate contexts – modules, tasks and purposes of writing (exams vs. writing for research and publication) – means that the collaborative modes we adopt, the materials we produce, and the co-teaching sessions we undertake vary significantly.

CO-TEACHING AS A DEVELOPMENTAL PROCESS

Grounded in the belief that learning about writing is best done within the social and intellectual context of the discipline, the co-teaching on the iBSc opened up possibilities for an exchange of ideas not only between the co-teachers and the students, but between the co-teachers themselves. Coming from different backgrounds – humanities and medical sciences respectively – each had to negotiate their own conceptions about writing in the sciences and humanities, and students were integral to these debates. What emerged was a dialogue, or rather, multiple dialogues on different levels: co-teachers/students, writing specialist/subject specialist, student/student, students/the discipline, students' research/their target audience (their module assessors and potentially the *BJSM* readers), and so on.

What these dialogues helped to reinforce, firstly, was the idea that writing and language are not that distinct from the knowledge that students develop. In contrast to a more traditional view of the relation between knowledge and language in which the latter is understood as a transparent – and neutral – system of signs used to represent knowledge (the view that, as Turner (2011) argues, is deeply embedded in the western intellectual tradition), the writing workshops on an intercalated degree opened up opportunities for dialogue between the tutors and the students in which the distinctions between content and language became somewhat blurred.

Secondly, this multi-dialogic encounter provided a space in which it was possible to explore, albeit in a limited way, notions of writer identity and power relations existing in that particular context, something that the recently emerged field of Academic Literacies is particularly concerned with[3] (Lea & Street, 1998; Lillis & Scott, 2007).

Thirdly, this on-going interchange was developmental for the co-teachers themselves in that they were able to gain insight into each other's worlds. According to Turner (2011, p. 434), academics often have a tacit understanding of the discipline and the way knowledge is articulated within it, but they 'do not always know that they have this rhetorical knowledge and cannot readily explain it to others'. Indeed, this is something that the TW team regularly come across when working in the disciplines – although the subject specialists may be experienced and published writers themselves, they are not always aware that they are doing what they do and therefore rarely question why they do it. In this case, the disciplinary co-teacher's 'learning trajectory' mainly related to being able to

---

[3] This aspect of our work is explored in detail in another publication – Ingle and Yakovchuk (Forthcoming).

articulate the specific writing conventions in his discipline and relate them to how the discipline works epistemologically and ontologically. For the writing specialist, the collaboration was equally enriching and opened up a deeper and much more nuanced understanding of a specific sub-discipline's scientific writing and how it operates within HE and beyond.

Finally, what we hoped this work would substantiate is the notion that we should start and end with a view that the ability to write in all its manifestations should be seen as something that requires continual development, and should not be viewed as an ability or skill a student lacks for a variety of reasons. This is in line with what has started happening across the EAP sector: a shift away from a 'deficit' model to what could be called a more developmental approach to student writing. Indeed, as some research suggests, even established academics with many years of writing experience still do not see themselves as 'finished products' in terms of their personal writing development (Murray & Newton, 2009).

CONCLUSION

We believe that Thinking Writing's approach is a possible way forward for those wanting to explore disciplinary writing, and that it can be used effectively in an EAP context. Over the last decade, we have developed collaborations with many departments in the college (see Mitchell, 2010; Horne & Peake, 2011; McConlogue, Mitchell & Peake, 2011). Inevitably, the stories of our collaborations differ: some colleagues are more receptive to our ideas

than others. All our collaborations are localized in that they start with the concerns of a particular teacher in the context of a particular module. The crucial factor in developing successful partnerships is to find disciplinary staff who are open to some of our ideas and are committed to investing time and effort into thinking about their approaches to teaching and learning.

Another key factor in working collaboratively in a particular discipline is to have the time not only to build relationships with subject specialists, but to get a thorough understanding of the materials and concerns that staff and students want to address. It takes time to grasp unfamiliar content, assignments and writing practices. It also takes time to find ways of working effectively with disciplinary colleagues on both a professional and a personal level, and develop strategies and materials that will respond to the specific needs of their students and their disciplinary contexts. When co-teaching works, the exchange of insight between the co-tutors in front of and with the students enriches our and their understanding of the disciplinary and educational contexts in which we are learning and writing.

The examples presented in this paper are by no means finished 'products' – they are evolving collaborations which are refined year on year. We are learning from what works and what does not as much as, we hope, our disciplinary colleagues are. We also hope that, as writing developers, we are really *learning* about writing in particular disciplines – something that only a close engagement with the issues of epistemology, ways of arguing and specific disciplinary writing conventions, can achieve.

REFERENCES

Alexander, O., Argent, S., & Spencer, J. (2008). *EAP essentials: A teacher's guide to principles and practice*. Reading: Garnet Publishing Ltd.

Andrews, R., & Mitchell, S. (2001). *Essays in Argument*. London: Middlesex University Press.

Bean, J. C. (2011). *Teaching rhetorical reading of primary scientific literature to first-year undergraduates: A two-stage writing assignment*. Paper presented at the 2011 EATAW Conference at the University of Limerick, Ireland.

Beaufort, A. (2007). *College writing and beyond: A new framework for university writing instruction*. Logan, UT: Utah University Press.

Bhatia, V. K. (1993). *Analysing genre: Language use in professional settings*. Harlow, Essex: Pearson Education Limited.

Britton, J. (1982). Writing to learn and learning to write. In G. Pradl (Ed.), *Prospect and Retrospect: Selected Essays of James Britton* (pp. 94–111). Portsmouth, NH: Boynton/Cook.

Halliday M. A. K., & Matthiessen, C. (2004). *An Introduction to Functional Grammar* (3rd ed.). Oxford: Oxford University Press.

Horne, D., & Peake, K. (2011). Writing Hazards. In M. Deane & P. O'Neill (Eds.), *Writing in the Disciplines* (pp. 103–121). Basingstoke, Hampshire: Palgrave Macmillan.

Hyland, K. (2006). *English for Academic Purposes: An advanced resource book*. Abingdon: Routledge.

Hyland, K., & Hamp-Lyons, L. (2002). EAP: issues and directions. *Journal of English for Academic Purposes*, 1(1), 1–12.

Ingle, J., & Yakovchuk, N. (Forthcoming). Writing development, co-teaching and Academic Literacies: Exploring the connections. In T. Lillis, K. Harrington, M. Lea & S. Mitchell (Eds.), *Working with Academic Literacies: Research, Theory, Design*. Anderson, S.C: Anderson, S. C.: Parlor Press.

Lea, M. R., & Street, B. V. (1998). Student writing in higher education: An academic literacies approach. *Studies in Higher Education*, 23(2), 157–170.

Lillis, T., & Scott, M. (2007). Defining academic literacies research: Issues of epistemology, ideology and strategy. *Journal of Applied Linguistics*, 4(1), 5–32.

Martin, J. R., & Rose, D. (2003). *Working with discourse: Meaning beyond the clause*. London: Continuum.

McConlogue, T., Mitchell, S., & Peake, K. (2011). Thinking Writing at Queen Mary, University of London. In C. Thaiss, G. Bräuer, P. Carlino & L. Ganobcsik-Williams (Eds.), *Writing programs worldwide: Profiles of academic writing in many places*. Parlor Press/WAC Clearinghouse.

Mitchell, S. (2010). Now you don't see it; now you do: Writing made visible in the university. *Arts and humanities in higher education*, 9(2), 133–148.

Mitchell, S., & Evison, A. (2006). Exploiting the potential of writing for educational change at Queen Mary, University of London. In L. Ganobcsik-Williams (Ed.), *Teaching academic writing in UK higher education* (pp. 68–84). Hampshire: Palgrave Macmillan.

Monroe, J. (2003). Writing and the Disciplines. *Peer Review*, 6(1), 4–7.

Monroe, J. (2007). Writing, assessment, and the authority of the disciplines. *Educational Studies in Language and Literature*, 8(2), 59–88.

Murray, R., & Newton, M. (2009). Writing retreat as structured intervention: margin or mainstream? *Higher Education Research and Development*, 28(5), 541–553.

Russell, D. R. (2002). *Writing in the academic disciplines: A curricular history* (2nd ed.). IL: Southern Illinois University Press.

Sloan, D., & Porter, E. (2010). Changing international student and business staff perceptions of in-sessional EAP: using the CEM model. *Journal of English for Academic Purposes*, 9(3), 198–210.

Swales, J. M. (1990). *Genre analysis: English in academic and research settings*. Cambridge: Cambridge University Press.

Turner, J. (2011). Rewriting writing in higher education: the contested spaces of proofreading. *Studies in Higher Education*, 36(4), 427–440.

Willard, C. A. (1989). *A Theory of Argumentation*. Tiscaloosa, Alabama: The University of Alabama Press.

Wrigglesworth, J., & McKeever, M. (2010). Writing history: A genre-based, interdisciplinary approach linking disciplines, language and academic skills. *Arts and Humanities in Higher Education*, 9(1), 107–126.

APPENDIX 1

Below is a typical question from the SAQ exam on Biochemical Metabolism, worth three marks. In this case, the context is provided by the initial two sentences and the question is then broken down into three parts, each worth one mark.

Q. The enzyme pyruvate dehydrogenase (PDH) catalyses the conversion of pyruvate to acetyl CoA in the mitochondria. Some children have a deficiency of this enzyme activity.
(3 marks)

Explain why:
a) some of these children can be helped by a dietary supplementation with B group vitamins.
b) these children accumulate lactate and alanine in their blood.
c) these children have impaired neurological function.

APPENDIX 2

Below is a slide with an evaluation task and a slide of one student's answers with the tutor's original script comments:

Awareness of Strong and Weak Answers

Look at the six answers to the question below and mark them as if you were the tutor – what mark would each of them receive? What strengths/weaknesses does each one have?

Question:
Explain the significance of lactic acid with respect to energy metabolism during exercise. (2 marks).

Figure 1 Evaluation task and sample question

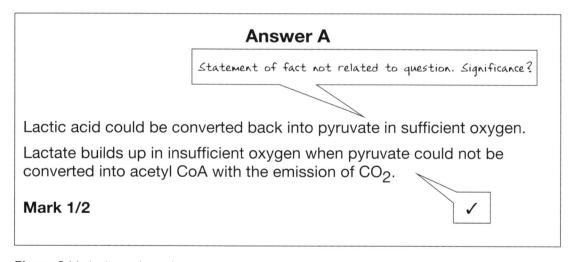

Figure 2 Marked sample student answer

MARY DAVIS AND JOHN MORLEY

'USE YOUR OWN WORDS': EXPLORING THE BOUNDARIES OF PLAGIARISM

INTRODUCTION

The guidelines given to students about plagiarism often refer to the use of other people's 'words':

> Plagiarism is presenting the ideas, work or words of other people without proper, clear and unambiguous acknowledgement.

(Manchester University: Guidance to students on plagiarism, 2010)

> Plagiarism is presenting or submitting someone else's work (words or ideas), intentionally or unintentionally, as your own.

(Oxford Brookes University, Library guide – Plagiarism avoidance, 2011)

Furthermore, studies of plagiarism have established that most attention is paid to it at the word level (Angelíl-Carter, 2000). The text-matching tool, Turnitin, which has been almost universally adopted in UK higher education for plagiarism detection, operates purely by identifying words in student text that are the same as the source text (Davis,

2007). This seems to have created a tendency for academics to concentrate very heavily on the words students use, particularly if they can be traced to sources. It is very common for academics to give the task instruction 'use your own words', but this may be confusing and difficult for non-native students (McGowan, 2005), especially if they do not feel they own words in English (Handa & Power, 2005) or feel that the words of others are better than their own (Thompson, 2005). Researchers have questioned ownership of words for some time, many influenced by Bakhtin (1981), who saw that words come from others before they are used by an individual.

There is an ongoing debate about owning words: some consider using certain words from others as acceptable practice, others connect it with plagiarism (Flowerdew & Li, 2007). Indeed, at the word or phrase level, the guidelines above are unclear about where the boundaries of plagiarism lie, for all of the words and phrases we employ in speech and writing belong to the speech community of which we are a part. Related to this is the fact that much of the language that we produce has been shown to be phraseological or formulaic in nature (Pawley & Syder, 1983; Sinclair, 1991; Wray, 2002) and this is a recognised feature of academic writing in particular (Nattinger & DeCarrico, 1992; Hyland, 2008). Indeed, a writer's display of a range of commonly used word combinations, together with subject-specific terminology, is a way of illustrating a degree of mastery within their discipline. Their use may also be a way for a writer to establish common ground with other members of their discourse community.

Importantly, research has shown that there is a much greater incidence of non-standard phraseology in non-native speaker writing, reflecting a general lack of awareness of preferred phraseological structures (Howarth, 1998; Paquot, 2010). Even if they have a well-developed knowledge of English grammar and vocabulary, non-native users of English often still tend to have a restricted repertoire of phraseological constructions. This fact has been recognised within the field of EAP, and many practitioners acknowledge that helping learners notice useful common phrases in academic texts adds a valuable dimension to EAP pedagogy. One well-known EAP textbook, for example, gives the following advice:

> Borrowing the words and phrases of others can be a useful language learning strategy. Certainly, you would not be plagiarizing if you borrowed items that are commonly or frequently used in academic English. (Swales & Feak, 2004, p. 172).

The assumption here is that such phrases are common property and that, once identified, they can be 'borrowed' and reused by other writers, in this case non-native speaker students. The particular example given to students in the textbook referred to above is: '*The results from this experiment seem to suggest that…*'. This type of phrasal construction has been termed a 'sentence builder' by Nattinger and DeCarrico (1992, p. 165) since it provides a framework for a complete sentence, and it also allows for the possibility of variation.

However, the kind of advice given by Swales and Feak appears to be at odds with university guidelines on plagiarism. The aim of this paper was to try to understand more about the boundaries of where plagiarism begins and ends, in relation to the use of phrases and words. In particular, we wanted to explore the views of academics on this question. For this purpose, we designed a short questionnaire, which we sent to academics representing a range of disciplines at two British universities.

Just over 60 academics were invited to participate via a personalised email which contained a link to an electronic survey tool. Around half of those surveyed were known to the researchers. In the end, 45 completed the online questionnaires from the following disciplinary areas: social science and education (9), maths and physical sciences (3), life science (3), health (7), arts and humanities (11) and business (9). As we were conscious of the heavy workloads of our colleagues, the electronic questionnaire was designed to be completed in less than ten minutes. It presented a combination of closed and open item types so that both quantitative and qualitative data could be gathered.

One of the aims of the questionnaire was to elicit academics' views about the approach of encouraging students to identify and reuse commonly used phrases. Question 3 asked respondents to indicate whether they agreed or disagreed with the advice presented in Swales and Feak's textbook (see above); Question 4 then asked whether they thought this advice might also be helpful for native speakers; and Question 5 asked respondents to comment openly on this advice.

The questionnaire also sought to obtain the respondents' views on what kind of phrases they felt could be reused, so that we could try to ascertain what features these shared. Question 6, therefore, presented a series of 32 phrases (see Appendix), ranging from commonly used phrases containing just 2 words to phrases containing over 21 words. Within this range were phrases containing just one 'generic content word' to phrases containing over nine 'generic content words'. In this study, 'generic content words' were understood to be lexical words (as opposed to function or grammatical words) which were not bound to particular disciplinary domains. These phrases were taken from the *Academic Phrasebank*, an open online resource of commonly used academic phrases, organised according to the typical communicative moves found in research writing. In addition, for contrastive purposes, a number of phrases contained content words which were associated with specific disciplines, and some consisted of quite original constructions. Finally, Question 7 invited respondents to comment on the considerations that had led them to decide whether a phrase might be reused or not.

RESULTS AND ANALYSIS

In this section, the results from the questionnaire will be presented and analysed in the form of respondents' comments and a table to analyse opinions about phrases. Firstly, in response to Question 3, the majority of respondents (77%) indicated that the advice given by Swales and Feak would be useful to students whose first language is not English. A slightly higher proportion of respondents (84%) felt that this advice might also be useful for native speaker students. For this question no 'Not sure' response was available, so a small number of responses may have been 'forced'; nevertheless, we were surprised by the number who thought it was useful for native speaker students to follow this advice.

The majority of respondents then gave reasons, from their perspectives as academics, as to why they thought the advice given by Swales and Feak would be helpful for both non-native and native speakers. A representative view was: 'Most academic disciplines have their own vocabulary and even style of expression, and students need to be able to use these facets of specialist language appropriately'. Some participants highlighted the need to understand why this was useful as a learning strategy and even suggested that some academics do not understand this: 'the advice is obviously useful to students but perhaps needs to be more widely considered by academics who may not understand such learning strategies'. Drawing attention to this may be an important way that EAP can contribute to teaching in the academic disciplines. The comments indicate that greater awareness of this area could be very useful for both academics and their students.

Some respondents gave the insightful view that the borrowing had to be done from other sources to ones being used for ideas: 'Plagiarism does not arise from "using the same words" but from using the same words to say the same thing' and 'If you "borrow" a common phrase such as "have a profound impact on" from a writer whose sentence you are paraphrasing at the time, then you are plagiarising, because your sentence will resemble the writer's too closely'. Thus, it is useful to recommend using reading to make lists of common phrases, but not to use reading for common phrases when that same reading source is simultaneously being used to cite an idea.

Furthermore, some respondents had concerns about non-native speakers' ability to understand phrases, reuse them appropriately and to understand which are frequently used: 'The simple borrowing of words can lead to a situation where a speaker/writer is being misled into communicating something subtly different from the intended meaning' and 'I think that students who have poor command of English will not have the sophistication to understand the difference between commonly or frequently used terms (and others)'. The concerns here from content tutors are that second-language writers would struggle to use these phrases on their own.

Moreover, respondents said that a key issue was knowing when a phrase is common or frequently used. One view was that this could be an issue for native speakers as well as non-native speakers, (perhaps where the native speaker was unfamiliar with the field or had weak academic skills): 'The danger is that students, perhaps both NNS and NS, don't have a clear sense of what items are "commonly or frequently used in academic English" and as a result borrow "items" that are less common as well'. This once again

highlights the importance of integrating teaching about phrasal use into academic study, as well as encouraging students to read widely in their discipline, so that this 'sense' could be developed.

For Question 6, the phrases in the survey (full list in appendix) were categorised into one of four patterns of response. These are presented with sample phrases in Table 1.

Group 1 comprised phrases which more than 95% of respondents felt could be reused in another piece of writing without constituting plagiarism. The mean length in total number of words is 4.8, and the average number of 'generic content words' per phrase is 2.4. In addition to the low number of content words, it is worth noting that many of these phrases can be used to establish the general context of a study and to begin sentences or sections.

Group 2 consisted of phrases which between 80% and 94% of respondents felt could be reused by students in their own writing without constituting plagiarism. For this group, the mean length in total number of words is 8.4, and the average number of generic content words per phrase is 4.1. Despite the longer lengths of these phrases (around twice that of Group 1), their reuse in writing was still deemed to be acceptable by the majority of respondents. This suggests that the length of the phrase is not in fact a major determinant of whether a phrase can be reused, at least with phrases containing up to nine words. Another characteristic of the phrases in Group 2 is that some of them exhibit an evaluative quality: they express a value or position in 'main weakness' or 'most striking'. Nevertheless, whilst they may not be value neutral, their generic nature is such that most respondents felt that they could be reused.

Table I Phrases and opinions about reuse

Groups and opinions about reuse	Total words/ content words
Group 1: more than 95% felt could be reused	
– within the field	3/1
– to account for this	4/1
– it has been demonstrated that	5/1
– in this paper I argue that	6/2
– recent evidence suggests that	4/3
Group 2: between 80% and 94% felt could be reused	
– the findings of the current study are consistent with	9/4
– the main weakness of this study was the lack of	10/4
– an issue that was not addressed in this study was whether	11/4
– a significant difference between the two conditions	7/4
– the single most striking observation	5/4
Group 3: between 50% and 80% felt could be reused	
– much of the research up to now has been descriptive in nature	12/5
– the research to date has tended to focus on X rather than Y	13/5
– a set of stable energy levels	6/4
– however, there are limits to how far the idea of X can be taken	13/5
– the relationship between a diet high in fats and poor health has been widely investigated	15/8
Group 4: more than 75% felt could NOT be reused	
– deliberately and incisively debunks such myths	6/4
– it has become a catchword used to label and delegitimize political movements	12/7
– in their insularity and absolutism, both groups scare each other into existence and are reflections of the enemies they create	20/12
– Dawkins is deaf to theology	5/2

Group 3 contained phrases that, depending on which phrase, between 50% and 80% of respondents felt could be reused in student assignments without constituting plagiarism. For this group, the mean length in total number of words is 13.5, and the average number of generic content words per phrase is six. Two aspects of these phrases probably had a bearing on the decision of up to half of respondents to indicate that it would not be appropriate to recycle some of these phrases. First of all,

they are all comparatively long phrases. The number of content words per phrase is also comparatively high. Secondly, some of the content words were not generic but rather seemed to be bound to particular domains, such as 'energy levels', 'diet high in fats', 'poor health'. The slotted elements in some of the phrases, X and Y, might also have been interpreted by some respondents as representing subject-related content (although this was not the intention in the research design).

Finally, Group 4 consisted of phrases that more than 75% of respondents felt could not be recycled without plagiarism being committed. For the last three of these, there was almost unanimous agreement that they should not be reused (94% of respondents). Although, on average, these are not as long as phrases in Group 3, these phrases all seem to contain content words associated with particular academic domains. In addition, all contain fairly or very original phrasal constructions: at least three seem to express a strong evaluative stance on the topic, and the last one employs metaphor.

When respondents were asked why they had identified phrases in the previous section as plagiarism or not, some very enlightening views were given. Their comments can be placed into four categories: originality, specificity, evaluative nature and length of the phrase. Some boundaries are suggested from their comments.

Respondents drew attention to the originality of the phrase, in that phrases which were idiosyncratic, metaphoric, elaborate, unusual and rarely found would not be acceptable for students to reuse. An example of this from the given phrases was 'Dawkins is deaf to theology' (which has alliteration and the metaphor of deafness). One respondent defined these highly original phrases as: 'Unnecessary words or over-elaborate words (that) state more than the basic meaning of the phrase' and another called them 'a way of expressing something that has some individuality'. Thus we can establish a boundary here that rarely used phrases can be seen as belonging to authors and cannot be borrowed.

Similarly, respondents distinguished between the generic and specific nature of the phrase. Where it was considered generic, it was deemed acceptable, while specific

claims, specific topics and specialised content words would not be acceptable for reuse. The specific nature of the phrase is also related to the degree of stance contained in it, what one respondent called 'clearly interpretive strings'. Another respondent explained that 'the cases I feel are dodgy are those in which an opinion is strongly expressed'. Thus we establish what appears to be another boundary, in that phrases containing an author's particular point of view cannot be reused.

Interestingly, the respondents did not include the length of a phrase as an important criterion for determining whether the reuse of a phrase constituted plagiarism. One respondent gave the view that 'short and common' phrases were acceptable to use, but in general, there was no suggestion that longer phrases would constitute a higher risk of plagiarism. We set out to try to establish safe 'boundaries' for reusing phrases, assuming that length would have been a particularly important factor, so this finding was somewhat surprising. We have seen that, in the responses to Question 6, fewer respondents felt that phrases containing more than nine words could be reused, and perhaps for pedagogical purposes it might be useful to establish nine words as some kind of maximum and fairly safe 'rule of thumb'.

Respondents also thought about their own experience in using phrases to consider whether a particular usage was acceptable or not, for example: 'Whether I would be likely as a researcher/academic and native English speaker to use these phrases myself and whether I think I have read these phrases by multiple authors'. A strong view was that the boundaries are established by the disciplines and tutors: 'Students should take guidance from the school/discipline/lecturer involved I think to understand the boundaries'. Thus, the advice from respondents is for students to follow their discipline and their tutors, and also engage in learning about phrases, as one respondent concluded: 'The most important point here is that students should collect and reuse such phrases'. This draws attention to the importance of the teaching and learning of phrasal use on EAP programmes and within the disciplines, especially in reading activities.

CONCLUSION

In this small-scale study we set out to understand more about academics' views on the reuse of commonly used phrases and to try to identify the boundaries of where plagiarism begins and ends in relation to a writer's use of these. The main findings can be summarised as follows:

- The overwhelming majority of respondents felt that the advice given to non-native students by Swales and Feak on 'borrowing phrases' could be helpful.
- The majority of respondents felt that it was acceptable practice to recycle phrases with the following characteristics: (i) not containing content words bound to a specific domain; (ii) not having a unique or original construction; (iii) not expressing a clear point of view of another writer; (iv) depending on the phrase, up to nine words in length (though length by itself did not seem to be a major criterion); (v) containing up to four generic content words.

- It was suggested that phrases should not be borrowed from the same text the author is consulting as a source for ideas. On the other hand, common phrases, without specific information or views, from previously read texts, are acceptable.

We acknowledge the limited nature of this research and the fact that the survey responses were made without reference to specific contexts, whether textual or with respect to student level. Nevertheless, this preliminary study has shown that most academics recognise the reuse of common phrases as being an acceptable strategy for students writing academically. There is thus a need to develop materials to increase students' awareness of this important area and this may be a key contribution from EAP to content degrees. More broadly, these findings contribute to the debate about what is acceptable in student writing in terms of reusing words, and clarify our understanding of some boundaries of plagiarism.

REFERENCES

Angelil-Carter, S. (2000). *Stolen language? Plagiarism in writing*. Harlow: Pearson Education.

Bakhtin, M. M. (1981). *The dialogic imagination*. Austin: The University of Texas Press.

Davis, M. (2007). The role of Turnitin in the formative process of academic writing: a tool for learning and unlearning? *Brookes e-Journal of Learning and Teaching*, 2(1). Retrieved from http://bejlt.brookes.ac.uk/article/the_role_of_turnitin_within_the_formative_process_of_academic_writing/

Flowerdew, J., & Li, Y. (2007). Language Re-use among Chinese Apprentice Scientists Writing for Publication. *Applied Linguistics*, 28(3), 440–465.

Handa, N., & Power, C. (2005). Land and discover! A case study investigating the cultural context of plagiarism. *Journal of University Teaching and Learning Practice* 2(3b), 64–86.

Howarth, P. (1998). Phraseology and second language proficiency. *Applied Linguistics*, 19(1), 24–44.

Hyland, K. (2008). Academic clusters: text patterning in published and postgraduate writing. *International Journal of Applied Linguistics* 18(1), 41–62.

McGowan, U. (2005). Does educational integrity mean teaching students NOT to 'use their own words'? *International Journal for Educational Integrity, 1*(1). [Online]. Retrieved from http://www.ojs.unisa.edu.au/index.php/IJEI/issue/view/3

Nattinger, J., & DeCarrico, J. (1992). *Lexical phrases and language teaching*. Oxford: Oxford University Press.

Oxford Brookes University (2011). Plagiarism avoidance. *Library guide*. Retrieved from http://www.brookes.ac.uk/library/skill/plagiarism.html

Pawley, A., & Snyder, F. H. (1983). Two puzzles for linguistic theory: native-like selection and native-like fluency. In J. C. Richards & R. Schmidt (Eds.), *Language and Communication* (pp. 191–226). Harlow: Longman.

Pacquot, M. (2010). *Academic vocabulary in learner writing*. London: Continuum.

Sinclair, J. (1991). *Corpus, concordance, collocation*. Oxford: Oxford University Press.

Swales, J., & Feak, C. (2004). *Academic writing for graduate students* (2nd ed.). Ann Arbor: University of Michigan Press.

Thompson, C. (2005). 'Authority is everything': A study of the politics of textual ownership and knowledge in the formation of student writer identities. *International Journal for Educational Integrity 1*(1). [Online]. Retrieved from http://www.ojs.unisa.edu.au/index.php/IJEI/issue/view/3

University of Manchester (2011). Avoiding plagiarism. *Faculty of Humanities Study Skills Website*. [Online]. Retrieved from http://www.humanities.manchester.ac.uk/studyskills/essentials/writing/avoiding_plagiarism.html

Wray, A. (2002). *Formulaic language and the lexicon*. Cambridge: Cambridge University Press.

APPENDIX: SURVEY QUESTION 6

6. Please tick the appropriate box according to whether you think reusing the word sequences listed below constitutes plagiarism or not.*

* 'reusing': recycling in another piece of writing

	Yes	No
within the field	○	○
The relationship between a diet high in fats and poor health has been widely investigated	○	○
systematically review	○	○
deliberately and incisively debunks such myths	○	○
The research to date has tended to focus on X rather than Y	○	○
a large volume of published studies describing	○	○
the main weakness of this study was the lack of	○	○
However, there are limits to how far the idea of X can be taken	○	○
While a variety of definitions of the term X have been suggested, this paper will use the definition first suggested by	○	○
the findings of this study	○	○
Taken together, these findings suggest a role for	○	○
approximately half of those surveyed	○	○
An issue that was not addressed in this study was whether	○	○
The findings of the current study are consistent with	○	○
These results therefore need to be interpreted with caution	○	○
the majority of respondents	○	○
This discrepancy may be due to	○	○
The single most striking observation	○	○
it has been demonstrated that	○	○
a set of stable energy levels	○	○
A possible explanation for this might be that	○	○
In their insularity and absolutism, both groups scare each other into existence and are reflections of the enemies they create	○	○
The results of this investigation show that	○	○
much of the research up to now has been descriptive in nature	○	○
Dawkins is deaf to theology	○	○
In this paper I argue that	○	○
several possible explanations	○	○
to account for this	○	○
Recent evidence suggests that	○	○
a significant difference between the two conditions	○	○
contrary to expectations	○	○
It has become a catchword used to label and delegitimise political movements	○	○

SECTION III
EAP across the institution

Helen Armstrong and Suzanne Evans

Compulsory EAP classes and social integration networks: helping international students to succeed

Introduction

The rise in international student numbers at UK HE institutions has prompted universities to put internationalisation strategies at the forefront. This has led not only to internationalising the curriculum, but also to looking at improving the international student experience. This paper will discuss how a UK university adopted a holistic approach to internationalisation and, within its English language unit, considered two inter-related aspects of provision: a compulsory in-sessional course and the creation of social integration networks. Montgomery's (2010, p. xii) research into the international student experience took a 'contextualised, wider view of learning at university, emphasising that learning and development in HE is much more than simply what goes on in the classroom, and is embedded in an influential social and cultural context'. This supports the social constructivist view, as social interaction in learning is central, and it suggests that integrating these two aspects of the international student experience will be one way of improving it. Challenges that international students can face include not only culture shock, but also improving their language and academic skills (academic shock) (Ryan & Carroll, 2005; Myles & Cheng, 2003). Dooey (2010, p. 186) suggests that, to help reduce these problems, institutions should 'encourage two-way integration between local and international students to foster a more beneficial learning experience for all students, and ultimately to help them to attain the appropriate skills upon graduating'. This paper will discuss the delivery of the in-sessional course at Teesside University in 2006 to 2008, and show how, in response to low completion rates, changes were made to increase student engagement and to facilitate cross-cultural relationships. It will also discuss the establishment of the English Language Café to enhance home student and international student integration and therefore attempt to reduce academic and culture shock.

Throughout this paper, we use the term 'international' students to refer to students from outside and within the EU who are not native English speakers.

IN-SESSIONAL EAP PROVISION 2006–2008

From 2006 to 2008, the in-sessional EAP course was an optional credit-bearing module. There were very low completion rates during this period: in 2006 the international student intake was 380, 168 of whom enrolled on the in-sessional course at the start of term, with only 20% completing the course. The situation in 2007 and 2008 was similar, with 204 enrolments on the in-sessional course out of a total of 416 international students and a 27% completion rate, and 483 enrolments out of a total of 623, with a 35% completion rate, respectively. It was clear that changes were needed in order to engage the students and ensure they were supported.

The completion rates may suggest that the students perceived the course as ineffective. It could also be said that, because the course was optional, it was potentially seen as less important or in some way additional or extra to core learning, which resulted in students not engaging with the course. However, a consequence of withdrawing from the in-sessional course was an over-reliance on the Drop-In Study Skills Centre (DISSC), which offers one-to-one 30-minute appointments which focus on writing skills and language development. It was found that, rather than attending the English course, many students would use the centre before submission dates. The English language tutors working in the centre found themselves covering the same ground as on the in-sessional course, but the sessions were short and the availability of appointments was limited because of the expense of providing individual tuition. Moreover, many schools throughout the university requested short academic skills courses with the same content as the in-sessional to be set up half-way through the academic year, to support students who had failed in-course assessments in December and January.

THE CURRENT IN-SESSIONAL EAP COURSE (CHANGES MADE FROM 2009)

The main change to the in-sessional course was making it compulsory, with which came greater pressure to make it relevant and manageable for students and staff. It was also made shorter, so that the majority of the course content was delivered in the first term. This ensured the content of the course was delivered in a timely manner alongside their degree course, and was relevant to the students' needs in terms of study skills, which could aid confidence building in the first term, when students may be giving presentations for the first time or speaking in seminars. The students were also able to receive feedback for their written and spoken work from the English tutors early in the first term; this feedback could improve students' degree work. The course was changed to 14 weeks for students with IELTS 6.5 or less (or equivalent) and to 20 weeks for students with lower levels of English proficiency. The course was reduced to a 7-week optional course for students with equivalent to IELTS 7 and above. It was made optional so as not to ignore those students with high levels but who may have limited experience in writing or speaking in

English (Feak, 2009). All students were tested on arrival, which is now an integral part of the enrolment and orientation weekend. This means that the course is seen as a standard university requirement and is supported and marketed by programme leaders in all schools.

Making the course compulsory has led to all international students being aware of and receiving EAP support. Kingston and Forland (2004) propose that due to low attendance there should be a compulsory element to classes, especially by those who need the course the most; although they suggest it to be necessary only in induction week. Bailey (2006) suggests universities need to 'review their curricula to make them more accessible to international students, and build language or study skills training into programmes in such a way that they benefit the maximum number of students'. This was crucial, as an analysis of the attendance patterns on the in-sessional course showed that those who were hardly attending or had withdrawn from the course were students with lower-level English and those who were placed in predominantly mono-lingual classes (due to students attending the course being of the same nationality). A perceived lack of time could be a reason why students do not attend voluntary in-sessional courses, as students often cease to attend optional classes when workloads increase and assessments are set, i.e., when many will need the classes most (Rochecouste, Oliver & Mulligan, 2011). It was observed by Feak (2009) that in her institution students who were considered at a 'just fine' level were not offered courses, yet it was found in Feak's case study that students of higher levels of English would benefit from EAP classes. Students or institutions may not always recognise the

need for further English language development in order to succeed in their studies (Rochecouste et al., 2011; Dooey, 2010) and may perceive an optional support course as unnecessary. Making it compulsory can improve the value or perception of the course and ensures that no student, regardless of their level of English, is ignored or not offered support.

Research into the provision and content of EAP courses has become more widespread, and the debate over subject-specific versus generic EAP courses continues. This was highlighted at the 2009 BALEAP Conference 'English for Specific Academic Purposes', at which Hyland stated it was 'the most central concept in language teaching' (2009, p. 13), and with the emergence of models for ESAP such as the Contextualisation, Embedding and Mapping model (CEM) (Sloan & Porter, 2010). This discussion of generic versus subject-specific EAP is not within the scope of this paper; however, looking at the social and academic context of an in-sessional class, the general EAP classes enable students to meet and work with students from other cultures and disciplines, raising their 'interdisciplinary awareness' (Feak, 2009, p. 43), which is also seen by Hyland (2002) to be of value. As 69% of the total number of Chinese students at Teesside University are currently enrolled in the same school and 85% of all Libyan students are enrolled on the same degree programme, if the classes were subject-specific, there would be more mono-lingual classes. The in-sessional course classes now consist of students from a variety of nationalities, because they are studying different programmes. This is not a change from how it was delivered in 2006, but, as there are more students attending, this provides the variety of nationalities.

This environment promotes the use of English in the classroom and social interaction.

The result of these changes to the course can be seen in an increase in completion rates as well as a reduction of requests from departments for short academic courses across the university. In 2009, 733 out of 852 students enrolled on the in-sessional course, with a 61% completion rate. In 2010, there were 817 enrolments, and a 73% completion rate, representing an increase of 53% from 2006. The number of requests from schools concerning individual students fell dramatically, as did DISSC appointments, which meant those who did attend DISSC could be supported more effectively, as tutors were building on the input given in the in-sessional course rather than teaching it afresh. In the 2009 International Student Barometer, English language support at Teesside University received 93% satisfaction, suggesting that students are engaging with this course and find it relevant.

SETTING UP INTEGRATION NETWORKS: ICH@T

Whereas the in-sessional EAP course facilitates academic integration and focuses on reducing academic shock, we also focused on social integration. It is often seen by lecturers that there is a lack of cross-cultural integration in the degree course classroom. Home students often perceive international students to have a negative effect on their learning experience (Beaver & Tuck, 1999; Harrison & Peacock, 2007). Equally, international students can also have the same experience; for example, it was found by Montgomery (2010) that some

international students consider home students to not take their academic course seriously or that they are more interested in socialising, yet this could be due to cultural or age differences. Montgomery (ibid., p. xiii) suggests that 'learning takes a great number of shapes and forms and often takes place in contexts beyond the classroom and beyond university walls'. Therefore, although the in-sessional course enables integration among international students, it was not providing a setting for home and international student integration.

Social interaction can have a large impact on academic studies. In Rochecouste et al.'s (2011) study, 'mixing with English speakers' as a strategy to improve international students' English was found to have a positive correlation to academic success. Social integration has also been recognised as a crucial issue to be addressed by institutions. In the UKCOSA report, *Broadening Our Horizons* (Merrick, 2004), it was highlighted that 59% of international students said most of their friendships were with co-nationals or other international students. Thirty-two per cent were friends, with a mixture of UK and international students, and 7% were friends with mainly UK students. Suggested reasons include living with friends from the same country and the tendency of certain nationalities to study the same subjects. The benefit of the co-national relationship is that it provides a close support network (Montgomery, 2010), which has been described as a 'community of practice' sharing the same experiences, interests and problems (Wenger, 1998, cited in Montgomery, 2010, p. 17), and which can be emotional support and a relief from the struggle of trying to express oneself (Bailey, 2006). Conversely, UK students cite poor English as grounds for not wanting to integrate with international students (Harrison & Peacock, 2007). Whatever the reason, the lack of interaction between home and international students emphasises the deficit approach which many hold about international students and ignores the mutual benefits which these relationships can have. The deficit model is described by Ryan and Carroll (2005) as the view that international students lack the necessary language and study skills and are inferior to home students, yet they stress that this is unfounded, as international students are often already successful students in their home country universities and can perform well in a foreign environment. However, if the deficit view is held this will, of course, put a barrier up against integration among students. Home students miss the opportunity to experience intercultural relationships which could help prepare them for a global future (Forland, 2006); international students often state that they would like to know more home students to have the opportunity to practise their English and learn more about UK academic and social conventions, again supporting the view that this social interaction can help reduce academic and culture shock.

Consequently, the International Conversation Hubs at Teesside (ICH@T) project was created in 2011 with funding from the Learning and Teaching Innovation Fund with the aim of:

- setting up, facilitating and mediating face-to-face informal settings for home and international and EU students to meet up to promote international integration on campus, develop language skills and share world and cultural knowledge
- improving international students' satisfaction with their engagement

with native English speakers, and also helping to develop cultural awareness and international communication skills in all students

The main social aspect of the project is the language café. We used the model of another language café on campus which had already been running for a year for Spanish, French and German. This was already successful and is host to both foreign and home students as well as members of the local community. The English Language Café was established and piloted successfully in the spring of 2011 with pre-sessional students and tutors. It was opened up to all students from the end of October 2011 with four two-hour sessions per week and has been well attended by both home and international students.

In order to encourage home students to attend, this scheme is also connected to mentoring modules in different schools and the university's volunteering scheme, which encourages attendance and is mutually beneficial to students; those who volunteer can gain official volunteer certification for their participation. We have seen that this is a popular route and many international students who feel confident to be mentors or facilitators at the café can also volunteer formally and receive certification. It has been found that mentoring can support international students academically and socially (Kingston & Forland, 2004; Beaver & Tuck, 1999; Partridge, 2008). Twenty-nine per cent of 154 institutions in the UK had mentoring schemes in 2008, 52% of which said they were successful (Partridge, 2008), and so this is an area which will be promoted more throughout the next year. The English Language Café is growing in popularity, yet this has taken time.

Attendance of the pre-sessional and international foundation-year students at the café is embedded into their timetables, and this has meant there are always students present as well as staff. The presence of home student volunteers has led to a more social and relaxed atmosphere, as students may have felt it more like a classroom environment with tutors present.

CONCLUSION

To improve the international student experience and reduce academic and culture shock, changes were made to the in-sessional EAP course and the English language Café was created. These changes have fostered social interaction and this has also increased retention rates and centralised the support we offer as a department. We recognise that in-sessional classes will differ between HE institutions in terms of length of course, whether they are credit bearing or not and whether the course is subject-specific or generic; however, ways in which academic shock and culture shock can be reduced within the in-sessional class or in other social environments must not be ignored and social interaction should be encouraged.

REFERENCES

Bailey, C. (2006). Supporting international students in UK Higher Education: key issues, and recommendations for further research. CELT Learning and Teaching Projects 2005/2006, University of Wolverhampton. Retrieved from http://wlv.openrepository.com/wlv/handle/2436/7590

Beaver, B., & Tuck, B. (1999). *The adjustment of overseas students at a tertiary institution in New Zealand.* Paper presented at HERDSA Annual International Conference, Melbourne, 12–15 July 1999.

Dooey, P. (2010). Students' perspectives of an EAP pathway program. *Journal of English for Academic Purposes, 9*(3), (2010), 184–197.

Feak, C. (2009). Culture Shock? Genre Shock? In S. Etherington (Ed.), *Proceedings of the 2009 BALEAP Conference.* Reading: Garnet Education.

Forland, H. (2006). *The international student learning experience: bridging the gap between rhetoric and reality.* Paper presented at Going Global 2, the UK's international education conference, Edinburgh.

Harrison, N., & Peacock, N. (2007). Understanding the UK student response to internationalisation. *Worldview Summer, 2007.* Retrieved from http://www.ukcisa.org.uk/files/pdf/world_views/uk_student_response.pdf

Hyland, K. (2002). Specificity revisited: how far should we go now? *English for Specific Purposes, 21*(4), (2002), 385–395.

Hyland, K. (2009). Discipline and divergence: evidence of specificity in EAP. In S. Etherington (Ed.), *Proceedings of the 2009 BALEAP Conference.* Reading: Garnet Education.

ISB. (2009). *International Student Barometer Entry Wave 2009 i-graduate international insight.*

Kingston, E., & Forland, H. (2004). *Bridging the gap in expectations between international students and academic staff – 'At home the teachers feed me with knowledge, but in the UK they help me pick up the spoon and learn to feed myself!'* Paper presented at the European Conference on Education Research Post Graduate and New Researcher Pre-Conference, University of Crete, 20–21 September 2004. Retrieved from www.leeds.ac.uk/educol/documents/00003751.htm

Merrick, B. (2004). *Broadening Our Horizons: International students in UK universities and colleges.* London: UKCOSA.

Montgomery, C. (2010). *Understanding the International Student Experience.* Basingstoke: Palgrave Macmillan.

Myles, J., & Cheng, L. (2003). The social and cultural life of non-native English speaking international graduate students at a Canadian university. *Journal of English for Academic Purposes, 2*(3), (2003), 247–263.

Partridge, C. (2008). *Mentoring schemes for international students: A practical guide.* London: UKCISA.

Rochecouste, J., Oliver, R., & Mulligan, D. (2011). English language growth after university entry. *International Journal of Educational Research, 53*(1), 1–8.

Ryan, J., & Carroll, J. (2005). 'Canaries in the coalmine': International students in Western universities. In J. Ryan & J. Carroll (Eds.), *Teaching international students: Improving learning for all* (pp. 3–10). Oxon: Routledge.

Sloan, D., & Porter, E. (2010). Changing international student and business staff perceptions of in-sessional EAP: Using the CEM model. *Journal of English for Academic Purposes, 9*(3), 198–210.

Jackie Dannatt

Reformulation, noticing and the development of L2 academic writing

Introduction

The provision of effective and efficient feedback on academic writing is an important part of the role of a teacher of academic writing. It allows the teacher to provide the students with a 'reader reaction' and 'targeted instruction' (Hyland & Hyland, 2006, p. 206), whilst attempting to convey 'an understanding of the expectations of the communities they are writing for' (ibid.). My experience, on the English Language Centre's pre-sessional course at the University of Bath, however, has been that some students, particularly those with a lower level of proficiency in L2 writing, seem to be less than motivated by feedback on their writing in the form of a correction code, and are often unable to correct errors, perhaps because of insufficient grammatical knowledge to do so (Lee, 1997), a lack of understanding of the terminology of the code (ibid.) or maybe because they prefer to deal with errors in discussion with the teacher, rather than

alone. I was keen, therefore, to revisit my feedback methods and to find a way of engaging the students in the learning process whilst being able to transfer implicit knowledge, which is often culturally rich, and which often makes the difference between an L1 and L2 writer. I decided to make use of a model to help them to understand what their writing should resemble if it were to achieve native-like fluency and accuracy in the appropriate academic style.

Reformulation of the students' texts

As I had been working increasingly with student output as a starting point for input, I decided that the 'model' I would use would be a reformulation of their own text – that is, a rewrite by me of what they wanted to say but using my knowledge as an L1 writer to express that content in an appropriate way. In seeing their ideas expressed in this way, the students have the opportunity to notice features of the target genre, whether grammar, lexis and syntax, or the deeper issues of style and cognition. I had been interested in studies which had used this technique (Levenston, 1978; Cohen, 1982, 1983; Allwright, Woodley & Allwright, 1988; Thornbury, 1997; Swain & Lapkin, 2002; Adams, 2003; Yang & Zhang, 2010), and I wanted to see if the students could see the differences between their original text and my reformulation and, if so, what features they would actually notice. I was also keen to see if these features were then put into use in their subsequent attempts at writing. My few attempts at reformulation had been well received by the students and I believed it had validity in terms of their needs. Alexander, Argent and Spencer's comment (2008, p. 8), that the focus of the EAP classroom should be 'what the student is trying to do in the future … rather than what the student can do now', seemed to address the issue of raising awareness of the gap to bridge between their own non-native and the required native-like performance expected for their future undergraduate and postgraduate courses.

NOTICING WITHOUT A DISCUSSION STAGE

Noticing is an essential part of the reformulation technique. It is the ability to see where the native-writer text differs from the original, to see what it is that makes the difference, in order to attempt to transform this into linguistic intake and subsequent use. Noticing has been seen as the 'cornerstone of the whole reformulation strategy' (Allwright et al., 1988, p. 238), and many of the reformulation studies done previously

have included some form of discussion stage, with a native speaker available to guide the student in the noticing phase, which Thornbury (1997, p. 332) refers to as an exercise to ascertain whether 'input and output are matched' or a method to 'highlight mismatches'. Course timetable constraints, however, dictated that there would be no opportunity for a discussion phase, and the aim of this study was to determine whether the students could study both their own and the reformulated texts alone, without guidance, and whether they could notice any 'mismatches' without prompting. If this proved to be the case, it would be a valuable and motivating feedback option, which could empower students in the development of their writing.

ENGAGING THE STUDENTS IN THE PROCESS

As time was short, I planned a small-scale study, to last six weeks, in the third term of the academic year – a time when students are becoming acutely aware of achieving the level of writing required for their future courses. The study group consisted of ten students, two undergraduates and eight postgraduates, who were writing with a degree of fluency that demonstrated an awareness of organisation, yet required broadening in terms of vocabulary, consolidating in terms of grammar and developing in terms of academic style. Seven nationalities and a variety of learning backgrounds were represented within the group. I decided to give the students one writing task every week for six weeks, which I then reformulated and gave back to them. The students responded well to the fact that I had taken the time to rewrite their work and readily agreed to take on the follow-up 'noticing' exercise. The writing tasks were simple essays on subjects familiar to the students, such as family, work and education. After I had reformulated their texts, the 'noticing' tasks took place every week in class, and the students wrote down the differences they were able to see between their own text and mine. I collected and analysed each student's notes throughout the six weeks by categorising items noticed into language areas to see if what they had noticed had influenced their writing. They were not required to redraft their original text at this point. What follows is an example excerpt of one student's writing, week by week, with my reformulation of that writing, and then the student's 'noticing' notes. The complete texts would be too long to include in this paper, but I have included the student's feedback comments for the whole texts, in order to give a broader picture of the language features being noticed by the student overall. Indicators of the student's country, city or nationality have been removed for anonymity purposes.

EXCERPTS FROM THE WEEKLY WRITING, REFORMULATION AND NOTICING PROCESS

Excerpt from the original text by Student [001] – Week 1

> *During last tow deceit people have been become spent there time on things are not important. Consequently, people have lack in there free time spatially with family. There is several factors lead to lacking human time such as obviously technology.*

Reformulated version by the teacher – Week 1

> *During the last two decades, time has been increasingly spent on non-essential activities. Consequently, people seem to lack time for their families. Technology has contributed to this.*

Noticing notes from the student – Week 1

> *Obviously my writing has poorly words in other words teacher has good academic words. There are some grammar weakness such as passive – word order. My writing is not direct. Too long.*

Excerpt from the original text by Student [001] – Week 2

> *The main aim is to write about the role of (…) family which it has affected to the (…) society. First of all the (…) family has range approximately 4 to 9 family members. Consequently, the society has an extended family, that obviously happened in (…) wedding the number of visitors about 600 to 1000 people.*

Reformulated version by the teacher – Week 2

> *The role of the (…) family has influenced (…) society. The (…) family has typically 4 to 9 members. Consequently, (…) society has extended families, which, at times of weddings, can mean a total of 600 to 1000 guests.*

Noticing notes from the student – Week 2

> *I have to make my sentences more simple. Poor vocabulary. Grammar problem in writing structure.*

Excerpt from the original text by Student [001] – Week 3

The aim of this writing is to discus one of the biggest issues in (…) about unemployment situation. During last few years (…) government has been became increasingly worried about unemployment because the percentage of them rose to more then one million.

Reformulated version by the teacher – Week 3

The unemployment situation is a significant issue in (…) and, in recent years, the (…) has become increasingly concerned about the number of unemployed, which has risen to more than a million.

Noticing notes from the student – Week 3

- *Vocabulary – 'biggest' – 'significant', 'urgent' – 'problem', 'Given' – 'award'.*
- *There are some weakness on writing structure – 'built' – 'construction' 'aimed'.*
- *Useful linking – 'one of these', 'urgent action', 'Another is the'*

Excerpt from the original text by Student [001] – Week 4

During last two decades (…) national education has been developed the education system. This essay will discuss that the advantages and disadvantages of education system in (…).

Reformulated version by the teacher – Week 4

The (…) system has been undergoing development in the last two decades. This essay will discuss its advantages and disadvantages.

Noticing notes from the student – Week 4

- *New words – 'undergoing', 'curriculum', 'struggle', 'across different regions'*
- *I learned to avoided the sentences.*

Excerpt from the original text by Student [001] – Week 5

Recently, in (…), it has become an extremely controversial issue that improving the public transport system in the main cities such as (…). Therefore, for purposes of this essay I will confine the discussion to some strengths and weaknesses on the subject of (…) public transport system.

Reformulated version by the teacher – Week 5

Improving the public transport system in the main cities, such as (…) has recently become an extremely controversial issue in (…). Therefore, this essay will discuss the strengths and weaknesses of the public transport system in the country.

Noticing notes from the student – Week 5

- *New words – 'built along', 'wide avenues', 'private ownership', 'for instance'.*
- *I did not write conclusion.*
- *I feel my writing has improved in writing structure and word order.*
- *There are still some vocabulary weaknesses.*

Excerpt from the original text by Student [001] – (final) Week 6

Recently, in many countries around the whole world, it has become an extremely controversial issue that national health organisation has been done a several scientific approaches to improve the healthcare system. However, some countries have significant facilities …

I relied on my teaching experience to interpret the comments made by the students in order to categorise them into aspects of language. This student noticed vocabulary and structure, both at sentence and text level. On analysis of the student's texts week by week, these features appeared to be reflected in actual performance and the greatest improvements seemed to be in vocabulary and cohesion, followed by grammatical accuracy and fluency. A brief breakdown of the noticing and actual performance of all the students in the group can be found in Appendix 1, and an overview of this information is represented in Table 1.

Table I An overview of the incidence of noticing and actual progress in the students' writing, according to vocabulary range and accuracy, organisation and coherence, and grammatical accuracy and fluency, over the six-week period (the shaded cells indicate where a student has both noticed and made progress in a particular language area)

Student	Vocabulary range and accuracy		Organisation and coherence		Grammatical accuracy and fluency	
	N (noticed)	P (progress made)	N	P	N	P
001	✓	✓	✓	✓		✓
002	✓	✓	✓	✓		✓
003	✓	✓	✓	✓	✓	✓
004	✓		✓			
005	✓	✓	✓	✓		
006	✓		✓			✓
007	✓		✓			
008	✓	✓	✓		✓	✓
009	✓		✓		✓	
010	✓	✓	✓	✓		✓

OBSERVATIONS ON THE PROCESS

Progress in the students' writing was measured by analysing the texts in detail for the number of errors occurring in the language areas identified in Table 1. These areas, along with task achievement, correspond to the English Language Centre's marking criteria. If there was a reduction in the number of errors of this type in the text overall, then progress was seen to be made. Table 1 shows that two participants – [003] and [005] – showed progress in all areas noticed. Three participants – [001], [002] and [0010] – showed progress in two areas noticed, but also in grammatical accuracy and fluency, which they did not comment on in their noticing feedback. On the other hand, participants [004], [006], [007] and [009] noticed areas of difference but made no apparent progress. These students could have been exercising agency by deciding that they needed other areas of language at this point in the course, rather than those presented in the reformulated texts (Yang & Zhang, 2010). For example, Student [006] noticed organisation and coherence but made progress in grammatical accuracy and fluency. This student was particularly challenged in grammar and, therefore, could have simply taken in what was required at this stage of acquisition (Johnson 1988, cited by Thornbury, 1997). Student [007] had presented a challenge, being considered somewhat fossilised in his development. Although this student noticed vocabulary, organisation and grammar features, there was no clear evidence of progress in any area. Student [009] had made slow progress in previous terms, attributed partly to a lack of confidence. Of the ten students, four were identified as 'conscious learners' (Cohen, 1982, p. 17), namely students [002], [003], [005] and [0010]. These were students who Cohen would have identified as being very aware of language. All four made progress in all areas noticed. Student [001] made similar progress and, although not readily appearing to be a 'conscious learner', was a confident communicator.

Overall, therefore, six of the ten participants showed progress in at least two areas noticed. Other reasons for not making progress, despite noticing a feature, might be that the gap is too wide between the student's ability and the target language; the student concerned might need longer to assimilate the information; the student might be focusing on another area of presumed need; might have become fossilised; or may lack particular confidence in that area. Of added interest in this table, however, is that, out of the six students making progress in grammatical accuracy and fluency, only two

actually noticed these features. This might suggest that grammar could be addressed incidentally through this feedback method. Future research might seek to explore this.

Specific features noticed by all included the length of the native texts, almost always proving to be shorter than the student's original text, as found by Cohen (1982). It had been a surprise for many of the students that complexity did not necessarily mean lengthy sentences. They had, it seemed, associated advanced writing ability with longer texts. Of significance for me was simply the fact that 'noticing' had taken place and writing progress appeared to have been made. The study cannot claim that one is the result of the other, but there seemed to be enough incidence of progress made in areas noticed to perhaps warrant further investigation.

What the current study does show, however, is that, even though the students were asked to 'notice' alone, rather than in a discussion phase, the outcomes of the noticing were similar to previous studies, in terms of the type of student it tended to suit, namely 'conscious learners' (ibid., p. 17), and the area of language that seemed to benefit most, namely cohesion and coherence (ibid.). This suggests that the discussion phase might be an important enhancer of the process but not the gatekeeper to it. The length of the study and the size of the sample are undoubtedly limitations, and reformulation takes a considerable amount of time and effort on the part of the teacher, but a post-study group discussion with the students revealed that they had enjoyed the exercise, as had I. They would have preferred more time in the 'noticing' sessions, but they did believe, overall, that their writing had benefited.

TAKING THE PROCESS FORWARD

I now incorporate reformulation into my feedback methods, and it is greatly appreciated by the students receiving it. I often only reformulate one paragraph or, for lower-level students, a couple of sentences, as it is a time-consuming process and, in whole-text form, can be overwhelming. The students are now familiar with the method and, as a review exercise at certain intervals in the term, I ask students to redraft their own texts, with an attention to both surface features and style. It has re-energised writing classes and seems to have empowered the students, giving them greater autonomy and agency in the learning process. It has provided a positive, rather than a deficit, approach to feedback and allows the students to access and focus on what they believe they need at any given time. In so doing, the teacher is provided with a valuable insight into the nature of those needs.

Several implications for future research have arisen from this study. As 'conscious learners' (Cohen, 1982, p. 17) responded well in terms of progress, an investigation into which student profile is best served by the method could be an area of future study. It would also be interesting to investigate whether nationality or other affective variables influence the outcome. Likewise, greater investigation could be conducted into language proficiency and the optimum L2 proficiency level required in order to optimise the benefit of this feedback method. In addition, longitudinal studies could establish whether attitudes towards reformulation change over time as a result of students becoming more proficient at noticing.

CONCLUSION

Finding the optimum feedback strategy is a challenge, and the concepts of reformulation and 'noticing' are not new. I have found, however, that students respond well to this form of feedback at certain times in their writing development. The extent and timing of this input depends, in my experience, on the students' willingness and confidence to engage in the process. Reformulation is student-centred, it is scaffolded (Reid, 1994, cited by Tardy, 2006, p. 62), and it exploits the teacher's rich store of culturally-informed writing experience, whilst maintaining the identity and value of the students' content and ideas. Retaining their ownership through the content has been a motivating factor for the students. The blend of student and teacher expertise enables the student voice to emerge and the text to be redrafted to align more closely to the target academic community – both key skills in preparation for university study. As they have become aware of the potential of the skill to notice and have been encouraged to work independently to transfer what is 'explicit' into 'implicit knowledge' (Thornbury, 1997, p. 326), my students have increasingly enjoyed the process. The technique has become a key part of my feedback strategy in the development of L2 academic writing, and, with apparent success without a discussion phase in the noticing, it has become a key part of my students' move towards learner independence.

REFERENCES

Adams, R. (2003). L2 output, reformulation and noticing: Implications for IL development. *Language Teaching Research*, 7(3), 347–376.

Alexander, O., Argent, S., & Spencer, J. (2008). *EAP Essentials: A teacher's guide to principles and practice*. Reading: Garnet Publishing Ltd.

Allwright, R. L., Woodley, M-P., & Allwright, J. M. (1988). Investigating reformulation as a practical strategy for the teaching of academic writing. *Applied Linguistics*, 9(3), 236–56.

Cohen, A. D. (1982). Writing like a native: The process of reformulation. Paper presented at the 16ᵗʰ Annual TESOL Convention, May 1–6, Honolulu, Hawaii. (REIC Document Reproduction Service No. ED224338).

Cohen, A. D. (1983). Reformulating second-language compositions: A potential source of input for the learner. The Hebrew University of Jerusalem: The School of Education. Revised version of a paper presented at the 17th Annual Convention of Teachers of English to Speakers of Other Languages, Toronto, Ontario, 15–20 March 1983. (For related document, see REIC Document Reproduction Service No. ED224338).

Hyland, K., & Hyland, F. (2006). Contexts and issues in feedback on L2 writing: An introduction. In K. Hyland & F. Hyland (Eds.), *Feedback in second language writing: Contexts and issues*. New York: Cambridge University Press.

Lee, I. (1997). ESL learners' performance in error correction in writing: Some implications for teaching. *System*, 25(4), 465–477.

Levenston, E.A. (1978). Error analysis of free composition: The theory and the practice. *Indian Journal of Applied Linguistics*, 4(1), 1–11.

Swain, M., & Lapkin, S. (2002). Talking it through: two French immersion learners' response to reformulation. *International Journal of Educational Research*, 37(3/4), 285–304.

Tardy, C. (2006). Appropriation, ownership, and agency: Negotiating teacher feedback in academic settings. In K. Hyland & F. Hyland (Eds.), *Feedback in second language writing: Contexts and issues*. New York: Cambridge University Press.

Thornbury, S. (1997). Reformulation and reconstruction: Tasks that promote 'noticing'. *ELT Journal*, 51(4), 326–335.

Yang, L., & Zhang, L. (2010). Exploring the role of reformulation and a model text in EFL students' writing performance. *Language Teaching Research*, 14(4), 464–484.

Appendix 1

Student [001] noticed the following aspects week by week (quotation denotes student's actual words):
(Week 1) Academic words; passive voice; word order; the length of the teacher's text
(Week 2) Sentences need to be more 'simple'; 'poor' vocabulary; grammar for sentence structure
(Week 3) Formal vocabulary; collocation; writing structure; 'useful' linking phrases
(Week 4) New vocabulary; 'learned to avoided the sentences' – learned to be brief?
(Week 5) New vocabulary; collocation; 'didn't write conclusion'; structure and word order improved; 'still some vocabulary weaknesses'
(Week 6) No noticing requested

Student [001]'s greatest 'noticing' was in the areas of vocabulary and structure (sentence and whole text). This seems to be reflected in actual performance over the six weeks, in that the greatest improvements were made in vocabulary and cohesion, followed by grammatical accuracy and fluency.

Student [002] noticed the following aspects week by week (quotation denotes student's actual words):
(Week 1) Nominalisation; useful expressions; academic vocabulary; word order; grammar in general
(Week 2) Word order; structure; lack of formality; connecting sentences; a need to be more concise
(Week 3) Formal vocabulary; collocation; nominalisation
(Week 4) Structure; word order; article 'the'; the need for more academic vocabulary and connectors
(Week 5) article 'the'; appropriate vocabulary; position of adverbs
(Week 6) No noticing requested

Student [002]'s greatest 'noticing' was in the area of vocabulary, followed by structure. The actual performance over the six weeks, indicated cohesion and organisation first, followed by vocabulary. Grammatical accuracy and fluency improved the least.

Student [003] noticed the following aspects week by week (quotation denotes student's actual words):
(Week 1) Position and use of connectors; vocabulary (synonyms); prepositions
(Week 2) Articles; collocation; appropriate vocabulary; nominalisation
(Week 3) Formal vocabulary; collocation; nominalisation; use of relative pronouns
(Week 4) Relative clauses; nominalisation; appropriate vocabulary; articles
(Week 5) Position of 'generally'; conciseness through vocabulary; synonyms; comparison
(Week 6) No noticing requested

Student 003's greatest 'noticing' was in the area of grammar (relative clauses/articles/prepositions), vocabulary (synonyms/more formal) and style (nominalisation). The actual performance over the six weeks, indicated greatest achievement in grammar and fluency, followed by cohesion and organisation. A smaller improvement was made in vocabulary range and accuracy.

Student [004] noticed the following aspects week by week (quotation denotes student's actual words):
(Week 1) Shorter and more effective sentences; appropriate words; new vocabulary
(Week 2) Appropriate words; grammar (sentence structure); detail
(Week 3) Conciseness; new more appropriate vocabulary; grammar (tenses)
(Week 4) Word order; wrong words; more appropriate vocabulary; word order; nominalisation
(Week 5) Appropriate words; sentence order; grammar (tenses); style of reformulated text
(Week 6) No noticing requested

Student [004]'s greatest 'noticing' was in the area of vocabulary and style. However, actual performance indicates no improvement overall in organisation and cohesion, or grammatical accuracy and fluency, and the level of vocabulary range and accuracy actually dropped at times. This might indicate an example of there being too great a gap in level between the student's original text and the teacher's reformulated text for the student to benefit from the exercise.

Student [005] noticed the following aspects week by week (quotation denotes student's actual words):
(Week 1) Sentence; word order; vocabulary; conjunctions; linking; conciseness
(Week 2) Formality; cohesion; tenses
(Week 3) Vocabulary; sentence structure; tense; passive
(Week 4) Vocabulary, pronouns, linking, passive
(Week 5) Noun phrases; sentence structure
(Week 6) No noticing requested

Student [005]'s greatest 'noticing' was in the areas of sentence structure and lexis, which this particular student associated with conciseness. Actual performance indicated an improvement in vocabulary, followed by cohesion. There was no apparent improvement in grammatical accuracy and fluency.

Student [006] noticed the following aspects week by week (quotation denotes student's actual words):

(Week 1) Paragraphing; passive; phrases; linking
(Week 2) Phrases (collocation); sentence structure; word order
(Week 3) Vocabulary range; sentence structure
(Week 4) Word order; vocabulary range
(Week 5) Noun phrases; vocabulary range; collocation
(Week 6) No noticing requested

Student [006]'s greatest 'noticing' was in the area of phrases, vocabulary range and sentence structure. Actual performance showed improvement in grammatical accuracy and fluency, but not in the other areas.

Student [007] noticed the following aspects week by week (quotation denotes student's actual words):

(Week 1) Vocabulary range; passive
(Week 2) Tense; subordinate clauses; vocabulary; word order
(Week 3) Vocabulary; complex sentences; grammar (tense formation)
(Week 4) Conciseness
(Week 5) No data available for noticing
(Week 6) No noticing requested

Student [007]'s greatest 'noticing' was in the area of vocabulary and sentence formation. Actual performance indicated no change throughout the investigation period in all areas of analysis. Interestingly, this student had presented a challenge to the Department long before this current study was conducted, and had appeared to have fossilised, having been with the department for the entire year to date, without showing any real improvement over this period. The student was not available for the noticing session in Week 5, but it was felt that enough information was available to build a picture of what was being noticed and used from the other weeks' work.

Student [008] noticed the following aspects week by week (quotation denotes student's actual words):

(Week 1) Vocabulary range; repetition of nouns
(Week 2) Conciseness; paragraphing; grammar and vocabulary
(Week 3) Grammar; time phrases; vocabulary; conciseness
(Week 4) Introduction; academic style and expression
(Week 5) Conciseness; complexity of sentences; repetition
(Week 6) No noticing requested

Student [008]'s greatest 'noticing' was in the area of vocabulary, grammar, style and conciseness. Actual performance showed the greatest improvement in vocabulary range and accuracy, and grammatical accuracy and fluency. No progress was recorded overall in the area of cohesion.

Student [009] noticed the following aspects week by week (quotation denotes student's actual words):
(Week 1) vocabulary; academic style
(Week 2) organisation; style; grammar (articles); vocabulary
(Week 3) vocabulary; collocation; noun phrases
(Week 4) collocation; grammar (prepositions); passive
(Week 5) vocabulary; collocation
(Week 6) No noticing requested

Student [009]'s greatest 'noticing' was in the area of vocabulary and style. Actual performance showed progress was made in task achievement, whereas no particular progress was evident in other areas.

Student [0010] noticed the following aspects week by week (quotation denotes student's actual words):
(Week 1) passive; academic style
(Week 2) phrases; collocation; vocabulary
(Week 3) vocabulary; collocation
(Week 4) vocabulary; phrases; academic expression
(Week 5) noun phrases; linkers; vocabulary
(Week 6) No noticing requested

Student [0010]'s greatest 'noticing' was in the area of vocabulary, and style. Actual performance showed the biggest improvement in cohesion, followed by vocabulary range and accuracy and then grammatical accuracy and fluency.

FRANCINE ROUSSEL

MULTICONCORD AND THE EAP TEACHER AND LEARNER

FINDING THE WORD THAT FITS THE CONTEXT

One difficulty in using a foreign language is to find the word or phrase that not only matches one's thought but also fits the context. This is difficult enough in everyday situations, and much more so in academic activities such as writing up an essay or a paper, doing a translation, drafting an application letter or simply writing an e-mail to a tutor.

Dictionaries sometimes fail to provide the contextual information we would hope for, although they have greatly improved in this respect. In such cases, we choose somewhat arbitrarily among the list of items proposed, not always making a felicitous choice. Like one of my students who described Mark Twain as a 'comical writer', when he meant 'a comic writer' (as dictionaries do not mention that 'comical' implies 'making people laugh unintentionally, sometimes even at one's own expense'). Or like an English colleague of mine, who made us smile when he asked in the staff room, 'Qui accepterait de me servir de cochon d'Inde, pour une expérience?' (unaware that the English word 'guinea-pig' is rendered by 'cochon d'Inde' only in the literal sense, and by 'cobaye' in the context of an experiment). Or like a French academic who wrote 'Guten Tag' or 'Guten Nachmittag' (to translate 'Bonjour') at the beginning of his e-mails to German colleagues, when Germans regularly use 'Hallo' (an option which is not offered by French/German dictionaries – whether on paper or online).

Such problems arise because the choice of words is context-dependent – in other words, one must respect 'the company that words keep', to take up Firth's phrase (1957) – and there is only a limited and fairly unpredictable degree of overlap across languages. The limitations on our memory span, added to the fact that instances of a given word or structure can be relatively few and far between, often make it difficult for us to grasp the kind of context(s) which fit(s) this feature and make(s) it an apt candidate in a translation.

The purpose of this paper is to show what sort of help can be brought, in the field of EAP, by 'parallel concordancing', an approach which could be defined as 'the comparative exploration of the way in which a given language point is realised in L1 and in L2' – (possibly also in L3, with a 'multilingual parallel concordancer').

After a brief presentation of MultiConcord, a multilingual concordancer conceived with the language learner and teacher in mind, we shall discuss some implications and applications of this approach, but also some possible limitations, and see how these can be (partly) overcome.

MULTICONCORD AND PARALLEL CONCORDANCING

MultiConcord is a multilingual parallel concordancer which benefited at first from European Union funding and from the collaboration of ten partner institutions in the Lingua Multilingual Concordancing project. Thanks to additional funding from Université de Nancy2, which is now part of UDL (Université de Lorraine, France), and which had initiated and coordinated the original project, a Java version of MultiConcord is now available,[1] with a copyright-free database of parallel texts in twelve languages: English, French, German, Italian, Spanish, Portuguese, Modern Greek, Dutch, Danish, Finnish, Swedish and Russian; (these languages can be paired at will).

Of course we want biotechnology's applications to go **hand in hand** with complete safety for working people and consumers.	*Nous voulons bien sûr que les applications de la biotechnologie aillent de pair avec une sécurité absolue pour le travailleur, mais aussi pour le consommateur.*
Then we can work **hand in hand** and reduce energy consumption through coordinated action.	Nous pourrons alors travailler de concert et réduire la consommation d'énergie par des actions cohérentes.
We must operate **hand in hand**.	*Nous devons agir la main dans la main.*
Evacuation and disarmament must go **hand in hand**.	*Évacuation et désarmament doivent aller de pair.*
It is all the more worrying, to my mind, in that it goes **hand in hand** with a resurgence of racism and antisemitism in Poland	Elle est d'autant plus inquiétante, selon moi, qu'elle s'accompagne d'une résurgence du racisme et de l'antisémitisme en Pologne.
These two services go **hand in hand** and cannot be separated.	*Ces deux services vont de pair et sont indissociables.*
We must also be realistic with regard to the problems of the illegal immigrants in the European Union, because these problems too, which often go **hand in hand** with discrimination, will have to be pinpointed by the authorities.	Nous devrons également appeler les choses par leur nom lorsqu'il est question des problèmes des clandestins dans l'Union européenne, car ces problèmes, souvent accompagnés de discrimination, devront être pris en compte par les pouvoirs publics.
It deleted the reference to the fact that measures aimed at improving convergence go **hand in hand** with the promotion of growth and employment in the medium term.	*Il a également supprimé toute référence au fait que les mesures destinées à améliorer la convergence sont indissociables de la promotion de la croissance et de l'emploi à moyen terme.*

Figure I Excerpt from an English/French concordance of 'hand in hand'

[1] For further information on MultiConcord and a demo of the program see: http://ceres.univ-lorraine.fr/contentId%3D9272, or contact Francine.Roussel@univ-lorraine.fr.

Like other parallel concordancers, MultiConcord does not translate. It retrieves from a vast corpus[2] of well-translated texts the list of contexts of a given language item – word, part of word or phrase – in language X, and displays, in a parallel column, the corresponding translations into language Y (or Z) produced by professional translators. The parallel concordance (Figure 1) is an excerpt from an English/French concordance of the phrase 'hand in hand'. The 6 citations (out of a total of 19) come from files of parliamentary debates.

SOME PEDAGOGICAL ASSUMPTIONS BEHIND THE PARALLEL CONCORDANCING APPROACH

The parallel concordancing approach is based on a number of pedagogical assumptions. First, that *performance* is to be preferred to *prescription*, and real data to what is familiarly referred to as 'cooked' data; second, that the technology should be used to help the learners discover how the foreign language works, but it should also help them pass more easily from one code to another; and finally, that it should help them avoid interference from their mother tongue.[3]

DATA-DRIVEN LANGUAGE LEARNING
Even such a short excerpt from a parallel concordance as the one in Figure 1 challenges us: we start wondering why the phrase 'hand in hand' is translated 'la main dans la main'

or 'de concert' (the two phrases suggested by bilingual dictionaries) only in citations 3 and 4. We realise that in French these metaphors cannot be used when the subject is inanimate. They can express *collaboration* (with an animate subject), but other phrases are used for *concomitance*: 'aller de pair', 's'accompagner de', 'être indissociable de'. We can see how the parallel concordancer can enable us, and give us an incentive, to exert our heuristic abilities from the observation of real data, in other words, to promote 'Data-Driven Language Learning (DDLL)', to take up Tim Johns' phrase (Johns, 1988).

We can speak of real data in the case of such parallel concordances because the corpus is made up of original texts – debates, letters, e-mails, *The Adventures of Alice in Wonderland*, *Methods and Sources*, a Michelin tourist guide, etc., – which were not written for language learners, and of translations, which may be faulty in places, but which were proposed by various professionals. It is precisely this latter concern that prompted the Lingua multilingual concordancing project. In the first parallel concordance-based study I did 20 years ago (Roussel, 1991), using Tim Johns' monolingual concordancer Microconcord[4] (Johns & Scott, 1993), many translations were mine and therefore reflected my idiolect. Others had been retrieved from the Canadian Hansard corpus, but this proved a very time-consuming task.[5] A new tool was needed to make this retrieval easier and faster.

---

[2] Several million words.
[3] For more information on this point see Roussel, 2009.
[4] MicroConcord was the first interactive monolingual concordancer for the PC. It is a DOS program, which was commercialised by Oxford University Press. It is now available from www.amazon.co.uk.
[5] The concept of the parallel concordancer MultiConcord was expounded in the conclusion to the above-mentioned article: 'Given sets of cross-indexed texts, a program which could, in addition to producing concordance output from one set of texts, also identify the equivalent citations in the alternative set of texts, would make the production of [parallel concordances] considerably easier' (Roussel, 1991, p. 83).

WORD COUNT

One question which often comes to a learner's mind is whether a given L2 item is frequent or not. If one looks up 'de pair', for instance, MultiConcord shows there are 24 citations of this phrase in the Debate corpus, mostly in connexion with the verb 'aller'. So it is safe to use this phrase in argumentative speech.

Reading a *Tintin* album in Spanish, I was once struck by the use of 'de que' in the sentence: '¿Estás seguro de que Tintin está en Shanghai?' ('Are you sure that Tintin is in Shanghai?'). I wondered whether it was frequent and after what sort of words it was to be found. MultiConcord produced 2,200 citations and showed that it could come after an adjective, but also a noun, a verb or a subordinating conjunction (see Figure 2, in which the left context appears in bold followed by the research item).

TWO-WAY LEARNING IN PAIR WORK

Parallel concordances often have a two-way interest. If you have speakers of two different languages in a class, they can work in pairs and puzzle out oddities through mutual help. In Figure 3, for instance, an English speaker may wonder whether it would be possible in French to say *'Elle l'entendit murmurant' or *'Je vous vois secouant la tête' (the answer being 'only the infinitive is acceptable in French'). And the French learner might ask his English partner whether it is regular with the verb 'to say' to have 'she heard him say …', and not 'she heard him saying …'.

Sea cual sea la cifra definitiva, hemos **de asegurarnos de que** el dinero se utilice además para ayudar a los productores de
- (FR) _ Las iniciativas comunitarias son uno de los instrumentos, al margen de los Fondos estructurales (FEDER, FSE, Fondos
Sobre todo, una voz y un minuto para afirmar que el problema radica en esa quiebra de la demanda, en la orientación de la
Acabamos **de enterarnos de que** la República Serbia ha creado un propio tribunal de guerra para juzgar a los sospechosos de
- (EN) _ En la última CIG, los gobiernos de los Estados miembros no consiguieron convencer a los ciudadanos **de Europa de**
Lamentablemente nuestra experiencia nos dice que este dinero se destina al mantenimiento de la energía nuclear y a dar una
Naturalmente, hemos **de felicitarnos de que** los otros trece Estados miembros no se conformasen, dado su apoyo a nuestro
La indemnización queda subordinada a la condición **de hecho de que** se hayan aceptado la idoneidad y la cuantía de los
Compartimos la opinión **de Hoppenstedt de que** la Comisión no debe decidir en materia de concesión de licencias, ni tener
Especialmente grave en este contexto es la información que se puede ver en la prensa **de hoy de que** la televisión —y aquí se
Tengo el gusto **de informar de que**, en respuesta al llamamiento lanzado desde Palermo, las autoridades israelíes han
Únicamente empleando dos números E diferentes se ofrece a los consumidores la posibilidad de comprobar en la lista **de**
Señor Presidente, me estoy dando prisa, pero si desea de mi un comentario sobre las enmiendas, no podré atenerme al tiempo
En lo relativo a mi pregunta sobre los Fondos Europeos de Desarrollo, ¿tiene conocimiento el Sr Wynn de los temores que los
Soy plenamente consciente -no acabo de llegar **de Marte- de que** no le es posible contestar a doscientas enmiendas, el tener
Comparto la idea, expresada por el ponente en la exposición **de motivos, de que** relativamente pocos Estados miembros de la
La Comisión es decididamente de la opinión -ya he dicho el porqué en multitud **de ocasiones- de que** no queremos abandonar

Sea cual sea la cifra definitiva, hemos **de asegurarnos de que** el dinero se utilice además para ayudar a los productores de novillas para carne que, con el régimen actual, no reciben primas	Whatever the final figure is, we must ensure that this money is also used to support the producers of heifer beef who, under the

Figure 2 Excerpt from a Spanish concordance of 'de que', sorted on the left context

I can **see a trend developing**.	*Je vois se dessiner une tendance.*
I want to **see biotechnology operating** within a firm European framework.	*Je voudrais voir la biotechnologie évoluer à l'intérieur d'un cadre européen bien établi.*
If we look at the history we **see rapid action following** the oil shock in 1973.	*Si nous revenons sur le passé, nous constatons que la réaction a été rapide à la suite du choc pétrolier de 1973.*
Do I **see you shaking** your head?	*Vous secouez la tête?*
'No room! No room!' They cried out when they **saw Alice coming**.	*"Pas de place! Pas de place!" s'écrièrent-ils en voyant arriver Alice.*
Just then she **heard something splashing about** in the pool a little way off, and she swam nearer to make out what it was: at first she thought it must be a walrus or hippopotamus, but then she remembered how small she was now, and she soon made out that it was only a mouse that had slipped in like herself.	*A ce moment précis, elle entendit patauger, non loin d'elle, dans la mare, et elle nagea dans cette direction pour voir ce qui se passait: elle pensa d'abord que ce devait être un morse ou un hippopotame, mais ensuite elle se rappela sa taille minuscule, et elle ne tarda pas à s'apercevoir que c'était tout simplement une souris qui avait glissé dans la mare, tout comme elle.*
And she **heard it muttering to** itself 'The Duchess! The Duchess! Oh my dear paws!	*Alice l'entendit marmonner: "La Duchesse! La Duchesse!*
As they walked off together, Alice **heard the King say** in a low voice, to the company generally, 'You are all pardoned.'	*Tandis qu'elles s'éloignaient ensemble, Alice entendit le Roi dire à voix basse à l'ensemble du groupe: "Vous êtes tous grâciés."*

Figure 3 Excerpt from an English/French concordance of 'see', 'saw' and 'heard' in the context of '*ing' (within 3 words to the right)

SERENDIPITY LEARNING

There may be yet a further 'bonus' in this approach: in doing a search, we may notice in the parallel concordance an interesting feature we had not been looking for; for instance, the phrase 'non loin d'elle' in Figure 3, or 'Nous devrions appeler les choses par leur nom' in Figure 1. This triggers our interest in further searches. This bonus is what Tim Johns calls 'serendipity learning' (ibid.): we embark on a succession of searches fuelled by our curiosity.

SOME ADDITIONAL ADVANTAGES OFFERED BY A MULTILINGUAL CONCORDANCER

In today's world, the need for communication is such that learners are urged to learn several foreign languages. A multilingual concordancer can be useful to help them avoid some pitfalls and develop greater ease in switching from one code to another.

REMEDIAL EFFECT IN CASES OF INTERFERENCE FROM A PREVIOUSLY LEARNED L2

In some cases, foreign language learners make mistakes because of interference from another foreign language they have learnt. A Danish *lectrice* at my university pointed out to me the problems her French students had with the Danish preposition 'for' in time complements, because they tended to associate it with the English preposition 'for', when in fact it means 'ago'. A quick look at the concordance of this Danish preposition 'for' and of its translations into English (Figure 4) can put an end to this interference. It also shows that the word 'siden' systematically appears at the end of this time complement in Danish. The important thing is to let the learners discover the underlying pattern by themselves.

MULTILINGUAL LEARNING FOR POLYGLOTS

For multilingual learners, a further advantage presented by a multilingual concordancer such as MultiConcord is that it can give them an overview of a given language point in various languages.

- _ (DE) _ Fru formand, **for et kvarter siden** forlod mange parlamentsmedlemmer salen	- _ (DE) _ *Madam President, many Members left the Chamber a quarter of an hour ago.*
Vi drøftede også dette spørgsmål **for et år siden.**	*We discussed this matter also a year ago.*
Hvis arbejdsløsheden kunne »snakkes ihjel«, havde vi gjort det **for længe siden** - men det kan man ikke.	*If unemployment could be 'talked out of existence' we would have got rid of it here a long time ago - but that is not possible.*
For blot ti år siden skete det.	*It happened only ten years ago.*
Derfor fik nogle et forklaringsproblem **for 10 år siden.**	*That is why some people had some problems explaining themselves 10 years ago.*
For 46 år siden var for Robert Schuman og mange andre den europæiske enhed den eneste løsning med henblik på at sikre freden og genopbygge den ødelagte økonomi.	*For Robert Schuman and many others 46 years ago, European unification was the only solution for securing peace and rebuilding the destroyed economy.*

Figure 4 Excerpt from a concordance of the Danish time preposition 'for' and of its translations into English

The following concordances, run from a corpus of e-mails (Figures 5 and 6), can help, for instance, English-speaking learners express their thanks in Italian and in Russian. As the twelve languages available in MultiConcord can be paired at will, one can see that the program can be of use to polyglots of various language backgrounds.

Thanking you in advance, X	Ringraziandola fin d'ora. X
This get-together will give us the opportunity to show our friendship and **thanks to X,** (**whose** post as ''Maître de Langues'' has come to an end), by giving him a little something to remember Nancy by.	Questo incontro sarà l'occasione per esprimere la nostra riconoscenza e la nostra amicizia a X, il cui lavoro come 'Insegnante di lingue' è giunto al termine, e per consegnarli un piccolo ricordo del suo passaggio a Nancy.
Just a quick one to all those who contributed to the presents given to Sandrine and Michelle from Scolarité as a token of **thanks for all the** work they are doing for us, often outside their normal hours. I managed to buy them two items made of Daum molten glass, which were given to them yesterday at the beginning of a meeting which several of us attended	Vorrei semplicemente dire a tutti coloro che hanno preso parte ai regali per Sandrine e Michelle della Scolarità in ringraziamento di tutto il lavoro che fanno per noi, molto spesso anche al di fuori dell'orario di lavoro, che ho acquistato due oggetti in pasta di vetro Daum e che li abbiamo dati loro ieri all'inizio della riunione che vedeva riuniti molti di noi.
I think they were deeply touched by what we did and they asked me to **thank you all, hence** this email!	Credo siano state molto commosse dal gesto e mi hanno chiesto di ringraziarvi, cosa che faccio con questa mail …
We would be **grateful if you could** let us know if you can come along to the drinks party and maybe even make one of your specialities	// Vi ringrazio in anticipo se darete conferma della partecipazione e se, eventualmente, preparerete una vostra specialità.

Figure 5 Excerpt from an English/Italian concordance of 'thank'* (the wild card [*] corresponding to any letter(s) ending this word) and *grateful*

Thanking you in advance, X	Заранее благодарю Вас. X
This get-together will give us the opportunity to show our friendship and **thanks to X**, (whose post as professor of Languages has come to an end), by giving him a little something to remember Nancy by.	На этой встрече мы, пользуясь случаем, сможем выразить наши дружеские чувства и нашу признательность Шиамале, контракт которой заканчивается, и вручим ей небольшой подарок в память о пребывании в Нанси.
Just a quick one to all those who contributed to the presents given to Sandrine and Michelle from Scolarité as a token of **thanks for all the** work they are doing for us, often outside their normal hours. I managed to buy them two items made of Daum molten glass, which were given to them yesterday at the beginning of a meeting which several of us attended.	Я только хотела сказать всем, кто принимал участие в подарках, преподнесённых Сандре и Мишели из отдела Внешних связей за всю работу, которую онм для нас делали и часто в нерабочее время, что я смогла купить две хрустальные вазы работы Баккара и что мы их вручили вчера в начале собрания, на котором многие из нас присутствовали.
I think they were deeply touched by what we did and they asked me to thank you all, hence this email!	Я думаю, что это их очень тронуло, они просили меня вас поблагодарить, что я и делаю этим мейлом …
We would be **grateful if you could** let us know if you can come along to the drinks party and maybe even make one of your specialities.	Пожалуйста, скажите нам, сможете ли Вы прийти на вечер и если да, приготовите ли Вы одно из ваших любимых блюд.

Figure 6 Excerpt from an English/Russian concordance of 'thank'* and *grateful*. The examples come from an e-mail corpus

ADDITIONAL RESOURCE FOR A CLASS INCLUDING STUDENTS OF DIFFERENT NATIONALITIES

Very often, an EFL class, or a FLE class (cours de Français Langue Etrangère) is made up of students from different language backgrounds. A multilingual concordancer can be a useful resource if it is made available on self-access, for some difficult language items, as in Figure 7.

It seemed to us illogical that we should run the risk of further ambiguity, **however small that risk** might be, in a report which was itself devoted to the clearing-up of ambiguity.	*Es schien uns unlogisch, in einem Bericht, der der Klärung von Zweideutigkeiten gewidmet ist, das Risiko einer weiteren Zweideutigkeit einzugehen, so gering dieses Risiko auch sein mag*
However that may be, I believe these problems are on the way to being solved.	*Wie dem auch sei, so befinden sich diese Probleme meiner Meinung nach auf dem Wege einer Lösung.*
But some sections of the House set very little store by this, which is really most regrettable, because if you want to have such a committee, it is because you expect it to be independent and neutral, but you must then be prepared to accept its decisions, **however much you might** disagree with them.	*In diesem Fall gilt dann eine solche Erkenntnis relativ wenig in Teilen des Parlaments, und das ist eigentlich bedauerlich. Denn wenn Sie so einen Ausschuß fordern, dann wollen Sie ihn doch, weil Sie ihm eine gewisse Objektivität und Neutralität zuschreiben, und dann sollte man auch akzeptieren, wenn die Erkenntnisse nicht dem entsprechen, was man selbst will.*
However that may be, as from 1 July 1997 – at least according to the information I have available – passports will be issued as follows: Hong Kong Special Administrative Region passports to people who have not asked for British Overseas National status, and people currently holding a Hong Kong Certificate of Identity.	*Wie dem auch sei, werden ab 1. Juli 1997 - zumindest ebenfalls den mir zur Verfügung stehenden Informationen zufolge - Pässe mit folgenden Bezeichnungen ausgestellt: _ Hong Kong Special Administrative Region _ an Personen, von denen der Status _ Britisch National Overseas _ nicht beantragt wurde, sowie an Personen, die heute Inhaber einer _ Hong Kong Certificate of Identity _ sind.*
Those were not just formal engagements, **however important those may** be.	*Es handelt sich dabei nicht nur um förmliche Treffen, so wichtig diese auch sein mögen.*
However right it may be to say that every refugee is entitled to get his home back, it is equally true to say that many of those homes that are still intact have long ago been taken over by other refugees.	*So richtig es ist, daß jeder Flüchtling das Recht hat, in seine Wohnung zurückzukehren, so wahr ist es auch, daß viele der noch intakten Wohnungen längst von anderen Flüchtlingen belegt sind.*

Figure 7 Excerpt from an English/German concordance of 'however' followed by 'may' or 'might' (within three words to the right)

LIMITATIONS OF THE PARALLEL CONCORDANCING APPROACH AND POSSIBLE SOLUTIONS

One can quickly see how an enthusiastic learner may feel tempted to use the parallel concordancer as an autonomous learning tool. But some problems need to be pointed out.

THE SIZE, SPREAD AND REPRESENTATIVENESS OF THE CORPUS

The corpus attached to MultiConcord contains several million words and it covers various genres, as has been mentioned above. Still, as it has to be copyright free, it is bound to be limited. For the program to be useful to a wide variety of users, a facility has been implemented to enable the importation of parallel files at will, thanks to two companion programs, FOXALIGN and

FOXMARK, devised by Eugène Faucher, from Université de Nancy 2, and Gérard Scheurer.

THE RETRIEVAL OF SOME SYNTACTIC OR PRAGMALINGUISTIC FEATURES

Lexical searches are straightforward. But some syntactic or pragmalinguistic features may be less easy to search for with a concordancer. Some facilities have been added to the program to remedy this: the possibility of searching for an item in the context of another item (as in Figures 3 and 7); and the possibility of searching for suffixes. For instance, in order to retrieve polite requests (for action or for information) from a French letter corpus, one may call up conditional endings: *~rais, ~rait, ~rions, ~riez, ~raient*, as in Figure 8.

Je joins un exemplaire d'un rapport provisoire que j'ai rédigé récemment, et je vous **serais reconnaissant pour tout** commentaire ou suggestion que vous pourriez m'apporter.	*I enclose a copy of a provisional report which I have recently completed, and I would be grateful for any comments or suggestions you might be able to make.*
Je vous **serais très reconnaissant si** vous pouviez faire la promotion de ce cours auprès de tous les enseignants d'EFL, parmi vos connaissances, qui seraient susceptibles d'être intéressés.	*I would be most grateful if you could advertise this course among any EFL teachers you know who might be interested.*
Si nous avions du mal à nous procurer des exemplaires de la version française de S. A., vous **serait-il possible de** le faire pour nous en France et de déduire le montant correspondant de notre allocation totale?.	*If we had difficulty ordering copies of the French version of S. A., would you be able to do it for us in France and deduct the requisite amount from our total allocation?*
Y **aurait-il un moment** qui vous conviendrait pendant la deuxième quinzaine d'avril?	*Would some time in the last two weeks of April suit you?*
Pourriez-vous me donner davantage de précisions lorsque vous serez plus avancés dans l'organisation de cette rencontre?	Perhaps you could let me have further details as planning proceeds.
Que **diriez-vous du 18** au 21 avril, ou dans ces parages ?	*How about 18th to 21st April or thereabouts?*
Pourrais-tu lui traduire le texte joint en annexe à ce message (il travaille actuellement sur un projet de recherche).	*He is currently working on a research project and was therefore wondering if you could translate the document attached to this email for him.*
Je **voudrais savoir s'il** vous serait possible de me fixer rendez-vous dans les jours prochains, de préférence après 18h.	*I was wondering whether it would be possible to arrange a meeting in the next few days, preferably after 6pm.*

Figure 8 Excerpt from a French/English concordance of French conditional endings in a letter corpus

THE RISK OF BEING SUBMERGED BY LONG CONCORDANCE LISTS

Having too few results can be a problem; having too many can also be disturbing, not to say off-putting, if one has not been prepared for it.

The answer to this problem is partly in the hands of the pedagogue, and partly provided by the technology. It is probably best for the teacher to start by getting learners to develop an interest in concordancing (through graded and guided activities), before letting them run concordances on their own. But the concordancer itself must provide facilities to make the teacher's and the learner's task fast and engaging.

MultiConcord offers the following options:

a) to set a limit on the number of citations for a given search

b) to highlight the left context (as in Figure 2) or the right context (as in Figures 4 and 5), and then to do an alphabetical sort so as to make collocations stand out

c) to classify interesting citations into sets, and delete unwanted citations with one click

d) to save results in Word and present them as a table

THE NEED TO INTRODUCE VARIETY AND 'PEP' INTO CONCORDANCE-BASED TEACHING MATERIAL

The concordance output may sometimes be turned into a quiz, or some sort of challenging activity, as in Appendices 1 and 2 (on English translations of the French word 'déjà'). Otherwise it may be regarded as repetitive and boring by less motivated learners.[6]

If, as a conclusion, we come back to the example of confusion, mentioned at the outset, between the adjectives 'comic' and 'comical', what enabled me at the time to supply useful information to my student were the bulky paper volumes of monolingual concordance lists of the Brown and the Lobbe corpora, compiled in the 1960s on Unix machines. The years that have elapsed since then have made it much easier to benefit from this promising approach, first, thanks to the monolingual concordancer for the PC, and now, thanks to the multilingual concordancer, usable on various platforms, which is a sort of polyglot informant, always at the user's beck and call.

ACKNOWLEDGEMENT

I take this opportunity to express my gratitude to my Nancy research team, I.D.E.A., to Eugène Faucher and Philip King, and to all my LINGUA partners,[7] particularly to our regretted Tim Johns, who inspired this project and to whose memory the program is dedicated.

[6] More suggestions on pedagogical uses of parallel concordance-based material are to be found in Roussel 1996, 2000 and 2003.
[7] My Lingua partners: Tim Johns, Philip King, Paula Chicken, David Woolls, Joseph Rézeau, Marie-Madeleine Kenning, Kiersten Wølch Rasmussen, Dieter Wolff, Margherita Ulrych, Roberta Alessandro, Andrew Thompson, George Kokkinakis, Ana Gimeno, Kari Sajavaara.

REFERENCES

Firth, John R. (1957). *Papers in Linguistics 1934–1951*. London: Oxford University Press.

Johns, T. F. (1988). Whence and whither classroom concordancing? In Bongaerts, T. et al. (Eds.), *Computer Applications in Language Learning*. Dordrecht: Foris.

Johns, T. F., & Scott, M. (1993) MicroConcord, (a monolingual concordancer operating on IBM PCs, first published by Oxford University Press and now available from amazon.co.uk).

Roussel, F. (1991). Parallel concordances and tonic auxiliaries. In T. F. Johns & P. B. King (Eds.), *Classroom Concordancing* (pp. 71–101). Birmingham: E.L.R. Journal, 4.

Roussel, F. (1996). *Multilingual concordance-based exercise types*. Paper given at the TALC (Teaching and Language Corpora) Conference, Lancaster (unpublished).

Roussel, F. (2000). El programa MultiConcord: una ayuda para la enseñanza, el autoaprendizaje y – ahora también – para la traducción de lenguas extranjeras. In M. P. Battaner & C. López (Eds.), *VI Jornada de Corpus Lingüístics. Corpus lingüístics i ensenyament de llengües* (pp. 77–86). Barcelona: Institut Universitari de Lingüística Aplicada, Universitat Pompeu Fabra.

Roussel, F. (2003). Explorer les profondeurs linguistiques avec le concordancier parallèle MultiConcord. In C. Stévanovitch & R. Texier (Eds.), *Surface et Profondeur* (pp. 109–132). Nancy: Publication de l'AMAES, Collection Grendel n°7.

Roussel, F., (2009). Les concordances parallèles et l'étude du lexique. *Enseigner et Apprendre le Lexique* (pp. 35–43). Paris: Les Langues Modernes, APLV.

APPENDIX 1: QUIZ

QUIZ: TRANSLATIONS OF THE FRENCH WORD ....:

➜**Imagine the way you would translate these sentences into French.**
What word is common to all the French translations of these five sets of sentences?

SET 1
1. I've told you dozens of times!
2. Sarah, I've told you not to play with toothpaste!
3. This seems unrealistic. I personally find it difficult enough to visualise three-dimensional space!

SET 2
4. Life's hard enough as it is.
5. I dislike the soaps because I think real life is interesting enough as it is and I would rather live it than watch it.
6. It is a phrase often repeated, that 'the business of government is difficult enough as it is'.
7. The family is in enough trouble as it is without cutting off a whole generation.

SET 3
8. Have you ever ridden a delivery bike before?
9. Number 28 Vicarage Lane – you've been there before.
10. He had been up to the Head's office twice before.

SET 4
11. Have you finished it yet?
12. I wonder if he has come yet.
13. Have they made up their minds yet?

SET 5
14. Have you ever seen him drunk?

SET 6
15. They arrive late. The film they wanted to see has already begun.
16. We already know many of the properties it must have.
17. 'It's spitting already!'

APPENDIX 2: (WHICH CAN SERVE AS A KEY TO THE EXERCISE IN APPENDIX 1)

HIDE AND CHECK TRANSLATION!

SET 1	
1. Je te l'ai **déjà** dit cent fois.	I've told you dozens of times.
2. Sarah, je t'ai **déjà** dit de ne pas jouer avec du dentifrice!	Sarah, I've told you not to play with toothpaste!
3. Personnellement, j'ai **déjà** assez de mal à visualiser l'espace à trois dimensions!	I personally find it difficult enough to visualize three-dimensional space!
SET 2	
4. La vie est **déjà** assez dure **comme ça**!	Life's hard enough **as it is**!
5. La tâche de gouverner est **déjà** assez difficile **comme cela**.	The business of government is difficult enough **as it is**.
6. La famille connaît **déjà** assez de difficultés sans qu'on aille supprimer toute une génération!	The family is in enough trouble **as it is** without cutting off a whole generation!
SET 3	
7. Es-tu **déjà** monté sur un vélo de livraison?	Have you ever ridden a delivery bike **before**?
8. C'est pour le 28 Allée du Presbytère. Tu y es **déjà** allé.	Number 28 Vicarage Lane – you've been there **before**.
9. Par deux fois **déjà**, il était monté dans le bureau du directeur.	He had been up to the Head's office twice **before**.
SET 4	
10. Tu as **déjà** déjeuné?	Have you had breakfast **yet**?
11. As-tu **déjà** vu la Simili-Tortue?	Have you seen the Mock-Turtle **yet**?
12. Ils ont **déjà** signé?	Have they signed **yet**?
SET 5	
13. Tu l'as **déjà** vu ivre?	Have you **ever** seen him drunk?
SET 6	
14. Ils arrivent tard. Le film qu'ils voulaient voir a **déjà** commencé.	They arrive late. The film they wanted to see has **already** begun.
15. Ils reviennent **déjà**?	Are they coming back **already**?
16. Il tombe **déjà** des gouttes!	It's spitting **already**!

Jianying Du

Integrating teacher feedback in the L2 writing classroom

Background

In L2 writing literature, teacher-corrective feedback is frequently documented, and the discussions about its effectiveness seem everlasting. A radical disagreement is seen in the continuing debate between Truscott (1996, 1999, 2004 and 2007) and Ferris (1999, 2004 and 2006). Teacher-corrective feedback is normally provided in written form and rather linguistically oriented. As pointed out by Ellis (2009a, p. 3), corrective feedback 'takes the form of a response to a learner utterance containing a linguistic error'. It is believed that this type of feedback has positive impact on the learners' L2 writing accuracy. However, two issues are noteworthy: writing is far more than a matter of linguistic accuracy (Williams, 2007, p. 13), and the L2 writing class can be more effective if the learners are engaged in the entire process of teaching, rather than merely revising their writing in strict accordance with teacher feedback.

It is also unclear whether the feedback is fairly delivered, since it is based on the teacher's own understanding of the learner's writing (Knoblauch & Brannon, 1984). Nor is there a guarantee that the feedback is correctly perceived and effectively processed by the learner (Hyland & Hyland, 2006). The insufficiency or incompleteness of teacher-student interaction may account for the failure of teacher-written feedback in tackling learners' metacognitive process involved in writing (Hyland, 2003).

In the light of teacher feedback as a form of formative assessment, and learner development as the long-term goal of teaching, we propose in this paper an integrative model of L2 writing instruction. In this model, L2 writing instruction is a recursive and interactive process, in which both the students and the teacher are consistently at the centre. The model was applied in an L2 writing program at a Chinese university to investigate whether and how this model enhances the effect of teacher feedback, hence L2 writing instruction. The study aims to answer the following two questions:

- Whether and how the integrative model generates rich opportunities for teacher-student interaction?
- Whether and how the teacher-student interaction in the integrative model facilitates L2 writing?

LITERATURE REVIEW

This section consists of two parts: teacher feedback in process models of L2 writing instruction, and the theoretical framework of the integrative model of teaching L2 writing. The former indicates the need for a pedagogical framework encouraging consistent teacher-learner interaction, while the latter serves as the theoretical support of the integrative model proposed in the paper.

TEACHER FEEDBACK IN PROCESS MODELS OF L2 WRITING INSTRUCTION

Process methods (Flower, 1989; Hyland, 2003) are widely practiced in L2 writing teaching. Although sequences in the process approach are regarded as recursive and non-linear, teacher-student interaction occurs only in stages of topic selection, response to drafts and evaluation. In teaching reality, the L2 writing course module is rather linear and follows a traditional process of teacher presentation, student practice, teacher feedback and student response (see Figure 1 below).

At the presentation stage, the teacher introduces knowledge and skills involved in writing. The students then perform given tasks, which normally end up with writing. Response is optional, since the students are not always required to reproduce L2 writing

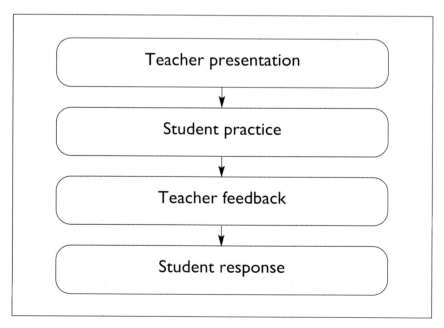

Figure 1 Linear process model of L2 writing teaching

after receiving teacher feedback. The linear pattern of L2 writing instruction indicates insufficient interaction between the teacher and the learner.

Despite the linear process of teaching, teacher feedback in the L2 writing classroom is normally accuracy oriented. According to Ellis and his colleagues' typology (Ellis, 2009b; Ellis, Loewen & Erlam, 2006), the main functions of teacher feedback include indentifying, explaining and correcting the linguistic errors, whereas the students are left to self-revision or self-reflection. The effect of this type of feedback on learner development in L2 writing is questioned by Hyland and Hyland (2006). Hyland (2006) even concludes that teacher-corrective feedback may hinder L2 development because:

- focusing on linguistic error indicates that L2 writing is a matter of linguistic accuracy
- correction (explicitly or implicitly) and evaluative comments may convey the message that the teacher as arbiter and supervisor is the sole source of standard
- the rarely practiced teacher-student interplay in corrective feedback fails to maintain the authenticity and validity of classroom assessment

The lack of teacher-student dialogue reduces the effectiveness of teacher feedback, while the discrepancy between the substantial effort and time investment in teacher feedback and limited up-take by each individual learner gives rise to the issue of efficiency (Goldstein, 2004; Hyland & Hyland, 2006). Constructing a teaching model with maximized teacher-student interaction may be worth the effort.

INTEGRATIVE MODEL AND THE UNDERPINNING THEORIES

The literature reviewed previously suggests that the linear process model fails to provide sufficient opportunity for teacher-student dialogue; the approach hence reduces the effectiveness and efficiency of teacher feedback. An integrative model (see Figure 2 overleaf) is constructed to enhance the dual engagement of, and interaction between, the teacher and the learner. Our hypothesis is that the integrative model can be considered as effective and efficient if it facilitates learner development in L2 writing while reducing teacher workload outside the classroom.

The integrative model is designed as a combination of Butler and Winne's (1995) self-regulated learning framework, Butler's (2003) framework of teachers' professional development and Hyland's (2003) recursive and interactive L2 writing teaching model. The teacher and the students are concurrently at the centre of instruction.

In the integrative model, each goal set involves joint decisions made by the teacher and the students. Student engagement at this stage helps to clarify the teaching objective and facilitates correct interpretation of, and response to, teacher feedback. As another feature of the integrative model, the teacher, as a group member, joins in student group discussion and writing tasks. This method of participation allows the teacher to maintain closer observation on, and richer evidence of, learning. As such, a friendly atmosphere is generated for the students to interpret and respond to teacher feedback. The roles of the teacher and the learner also interchange at the reflection stage: the students may have their say about the form and content of classroom activities, whereas the teacher may speculate on teaching from a learner's perspective.

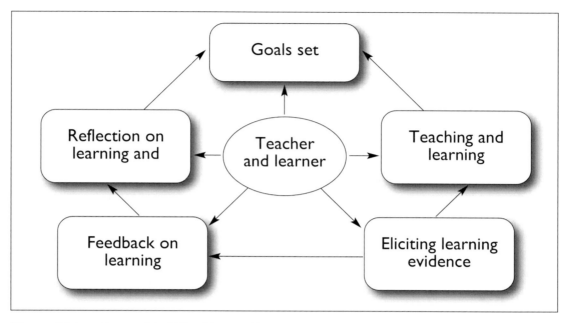

Figure 2 Integrative model of L2 writing teaching

The integrative model is underpinned by theories of formative assessment, models of self-regulated learning and teaching and the hypothesis of ZPD (zone of proximal development). Behind these theories is the belief that learning is a process of self-regulation. The process is facilitated by interaction and targeted at cognitive development.

Formative assessment is widely accepted as an effective way of facilitating teaching and accelerating learning (Rea-Dickins, 2001). It is, therefore, normally seen as assessment *for* learning rather than *of* learning. Teacher feedback addresses active teacher-student communication and achieves formative purposes of assessment. It is defined by Ellis (2009a, p. 12) as 'an instructional and interactive phenomenon' and 'a potential tool for acquisition'. It is therefore categorized as a subset of formative assessment (Sadler, 1998; Black & William, 2009). This suggests that teacher feedback should concern not only the strengths and the weaknesses of students, but also the appropriateness and effectiveness of instruction.

While formative assessment theories explain the function of teacher feedback, self-regulation frameworks (Butler & Winne, 1995, and Butler, 2003) suggest the significance of interaction triggered by teacher feedback. According to the framework of self-regulated learning (Butler & Winne, 1995), teacher feedback indicates the gap between the learner's current aptitude and the target proficiency, hence helping the learner to justify the learning goal. A model of self-regulated teacher development (Butler, 2003) is proposed later, suggesting that feedback also benefits teaching. According to this model, teachers develop their knowledge of learning and teaching, and modify teaching goals and strategies. In this sense, both teaching and learning are a series of contextualized decision making, in which consistent teacher-student interactions are vital.

Another theoretical support for the integrative model relates to students' cognitive development as the ultimate goal of education. Vygotsky's (1978) hypothesis on the zone of proximal development has long been interpreted as learners' improvement in performing and perceiving abilities (e.g., Bruner, 1986; Tharp & Gallimor, 1998; Gillen, 2000). A reinterpretation of ZPD has recently been proposed by Chaiklin (2003), who distinguishes learning from development and interprets ZPD as the learner's cognitive development. He also suggests that only assistance aiming at psychological maturity brings about qualitative change. In regard to language teaching with L2 writing instruction included, the long-term goal should be learners' learning and thinking abilities rather than the accurate use of language.

The theories above underpin the integrative model in terms of the function and the goal of teacher feedback. Effective teacher feedback is in close association with profound teacher-student interaction. Teaching should be directed at learners' cognitive development, in which active engagement of the learner plays an important role.

PEDAGOGICAL APPLICATION OF THE INTEGRATIVE MODEL: A CASE STUDY

The integrative model proposed in this paper has been applied to an L2 writing course at Huazhong University of Science and Technology. It is hypothesized that the model, especially with various forms of teacher-student interplay, enhances opportunities for learner development and reduces teacher workload.

PARTICIPANTS AND THE COURSE DESIGN

Teacher participants include two L2 writing tutors. One teacher is responsible for course design, teaching and marking, whereas the other, as the program advisor, is mainly involved in marking students' work. Student participants are 19 English-majored postgraduate students registered for the course. As revealed by the entrance examination held by the postgraduate office at the university, these students' English language proficiency level is upper-intermediate. The course is titled as advanced L2 writing in the postgraduate school curriculum. Running for eight weeks with three hours per week, the course is expected to help the learners to indentify principles and features of academic writing and to develop their L2 writing abilities for effective learning and communication.

Linguistic accuracy is not particularly emphasized in the course. This is mainly because of the course objective and the students' English language proficiency. In addition to teacher presentation and student practice in traditional L2 writing teaching processes, extensive teacher-student conferences and group discussions feature in the integrative programme. Desks and chairs in the classroom are set in the round-table style, suggesting the equal status of the teacher and the students, so as to encourage teacher-student interplay in a relaxed and harmonious atmosphere.

METHODS

The L2 writing course module introduced in this paper is rather a tentative application of multi-formed teacher-student interaction. Both qualitative and quantitative data are collected and applied for the study with students' unanimous agreement.

Qualitative data are obtained from the teacher's portfolio and learners' portfolios. The former includes the teacher's record of mini-workshops, in-class discussions, teacher-student conferences and e-mails between the teacher and the students. The latter consists of notes taken about in-class learning and after-class reading, L2 writing tasks and learner diaries. The teacher checks each student's portfolio regularly (i.e., once to twice per week) and provides written feedback individually.

Quantitative data comes from scores provided through students' self-assessment and teachers' marking. A set of assessment criteria is constructed with mutual agreement of the teachers and the students at the beginning of the course. As shown in Table 1, student writing is assessed in terms of language, content, and structure. Each student essay is rated by three markers: the student writer him/herself and the two teacher participants in the program. It is believed that this way of marking may help to maintain the credibility of the study.

Students' essays at the beginning (i.e., week one), the middle (i.e., week four) and the end (i.e., week eight) of the course are rated by themselves and the two teachers with the criteria shown in Table 1. The scores are analyzed with a non-parametric test since the subject number in this study does not meet the requirement of parametric statistics (i.e., $n \geq 30$).

RESULTS

The purpose of the evaluation is two-fold: to assess students' improvement in L2 writing in the integrative classroom and to measure students' self-evaluation abilities facilitated in the programme.

Table 1 Assessment criteria in L2 writing

Overall structure: 2 points	Language use: 4 points	Content: 4 points
completeness: 1 point	vocabulary: 1 point	clarified theme: 1 point
proportioning: 1 point	appropriateness: 1 point	coherence: 1 point
	syntax: 1 point	reasoning: 1 point
	tense: 1 point	referencing: 1 point

Data presented in Tables 2 and 3 suggest inaccurate self-assessment of the students before they develop a better understanding of good L2 writing. Asymptotic Significance (2-tailed) (i.e., p value) in Table 2 and Table 3 are .000 (i.e., p < 0.5), indicating a significant distance between students' self-scoring and teachers' scoring. The students over-rate their L2 written product (M=7.74 versus M=5.32 as teacher scoring) before the program, and become unconfident (M=4.16 versus M=6.63 as teacher scoring) about their writing when the assessment criteria are introduced formally in the classroom.

A remarkable increase in student self-assessment abilities can be seen in Table 4. According to data collected at the end of the programme (i.e., week eight), students' self-scoring (M=7.84) is very close (p=.69>.05) to that of the teacher (M=7.79).

Table 2 Student self-scoring and teacher scoring in Week 1

	N	Mean	Std. Deviation	Man-Whitney U	Asymp. Sig. (2-tailed)
Student self-scoring	19	7.7368	.80568	6.500	.000
Teacher scoring	19	5.3158	.67104		

Table 3 Student self-scoring and teacher scoring in Week 4

	N	Mean	Std. Deviation	Man-Whitney U	Asymp. Sig. (2-tailed)
Student self-scoring	19	4.1579	.68825	.000	.000
Teacher scoring	19	6.6316	.67104		

Table 4 Student self-scoring and teacher scoring in Week 8

	N	Mean	Std. Deviation	Man-Whitney U	Asymp. Sig. (2-tailed)
Student self-scoring	19	7.8421	.50146	168.500	.686
Teacher scoring	19	7.7895	.71328		

In L2 writing classrooms, it is never easy for the teacher to explain the assessment criteria and their respective values. Due to their abstract nature, it is doubted that these criteria can be clarified through a teacher's written comments and corrections. In the integrative programme, the students are involved in the overall assessment process, including setting the criteria, scoring their own writing, studying teachers' rating and reflecting on differences between self- and teacher-assessment results. These activities aim to improve L2 writing by an increased awareness of linguistic and stylistic features in various written products. A student participant reported in the journal his understanding of the use of hedging in L2 writing:

> I rarely noticed hedging and thought using big words and complex sentences would definitely reflect the author's talent of writing until the teacher pointed out the negative effect by comparing her writing with ours on the same topic. I then quickly pay special attention to hedging in my own writing.

The positive impact of the interaction between self-evaluation and L2 writing learning is also seen from students' progress in written performance. Table 5 provides scores of students' writing assessed by teachers at three stages of the programme. Students' L2 writing has improved significantly (Chi-Square=35.09, p=.00<.05) from 5.32 before the program to 7.79 at the end.

DISCUSSION

The results displayed in Tables 2, 3, 4 and 5 indicate students' improvement in L2 writing, as well as a positive relationship between students' L2 writing and their self-assessment abilities. Therefore, it may be safe to argue that the integrative model, with students' involvement in most (if not all) stages of teaching, is effective in enhancing L2 writing. However, it is not yet known whether the integrative model is more effective than other L2 writing models, including the linear process model.

The integrative model is characterized by multiple opportunities of teacher-student interaction. The interaction takes place as e-mails, group discussions, seminars and workshops, etc. These interactions may also be interpreted as a variety of forms of teacher feedback. Students are therefore provided with more channels to explore principles and problems in L2 writing. The students can either discuss with the teacher through e-mails or bring their doubts to seminars and workshops. In fact, a major advantage of the integrative model lies not in the rich interactional opportunities but the comfortable atmosphere it generates for learning. As a student put in her journal, the class is more like a forum of discussions and discoveries in L2 writing:

> The class is more like a forum, which is a kind of flexible according to the real setting. The form of our teacher's teaching writing gives us

Table 5 Teacher scoring in Weeks 1, 4 and 8

	N	Mean	Std. Deviation	Chi-Square	df	Asymp. Sig.
Week 1	19	5.3158	.67104			
Week 4	19	6.6316	.59726	35.086	2	.000
Week 8	19	7.7895	.71328			

a complete new experience. Various kinds of problems arise and are dealt with effectively, and we don't feel bored or tired.

…

When our writing problems are discussed in teacher-student conference, I never felt that I am personally criticized. Instead, I focus on mistakes made by me and my classmates. We then work on effective ways to correct them.

Students' active engagement in various forms of interaction leads to their cognitive growth. In the integrative L2 writing programme, the learners are encouraged to develop a critical view of learning and teaching. They are encouraged to analyze, question, and reflect on teacher or peer feedback, so as to establish their own learning targets and strategies. Although cognitive maturity is far greater than students' self-assessment abilities and their self-reflections on learning L2 writing, it can be viewed as a good start and an indispensible component of learner development.

The issue of efficiency stands out continuously in the programme. As mentioned in the literature review section of this paper, the integrative model is expected to reduce teacher workload outside the classroom. Group discussions and other classroom interactions enable a few students to receive teacher feedback on their individual work. A majority of the participants still willingly hand in their L2 writing for teacher comment. This can hardly be seen as a decrease of teacher workload, not to mention e-mails and other electronic messages waiting for replies.

CONCLUSION

The paper proposes an integrative model of L2 writing instruction. The rationale behind the model is that teaching is an interactive process and that various forms of teacher feedback should be performed as an integral part of classroom instruction. For advanced learners, L2 writing teaching should aim at their cognitive development rather than accurate use of the target language. Opportunity for learning and thinking should therefore be prioritized in teacher-student interaction.

Results of the pedagogical practice introduced in this paper confirm the feasibility of the integrative model as well as its effectiveness in teaching L2 writing. However, there has been no sign of reduced teacher workload in or outside the classroom.

REFERENCES

Black, P., & Wiliam, D. (2009). Developing the theory of formative assessment. *Educational Assessment, Evaluation and Accountability, 21*, 5–31.

Bruner, J. S. (1986). *Acts of meaning*. Cambridge, MA: Harvard University Press.

Butler, D. L. (2003). *Self-regulation and collaborative learning in teachers' professional development*. Paper presented at the 2003 annual meeting of the European Association for Research in Learning and Instruction.

Butler, D. L., & Winne, P. H. (1995). Feedback and self-regulated learning: A theoretical synthesis. *Review of Educational Research, 65*(3), 245–281.

Chaiklin, S. (2003). The zone of proximal development in Vygotsky's analysis of learning and instruction. In A. Kozulin, B. Gindis, V. S. Ageyev & S. M. Miller (Eds.), *Vygotsky's educational theory and practice in cultural context* (pp. 16–39). Cambridge: Cambridge University Press.

Ellis, R. (2009a). Corrective feedback and teacher development. *L2 Journal, 1*(1), 3–18.

Ellis, R. (2009b). A typology of written corrective feedback types. *ELT Journal, 63*(2), 97–107.

Ellis, R., Loewen, S., & Erlam, R. (2006). Implicit and explicit corrective feedback and the acquisition of L2 grammar. *Studies in Second Language Acquisition, 28*, 339–368.

Ferris, D. R. (1999). The case for grammar correction in L2 writing classes. A response to Truscott (1996). *Journal of Second Language Writing, 8*, 1–10.

Ferris, D. R. (2004). The 'Grammar correction' debate in L2 writing: Where are we, and where do we go from here? (and what do we do in the meantime …?). *Journal of Second Language Writing, 13*, 49–62.

Ferris, D. R.(2006). Does error feedback help student writers? New evidence on the short- and long-term effects of written error correction. In K. Hyland & F. Hyland (Eds.), *Feedback in second language writing: Contexts and issues* (pp. 81–104). Cambridge: Cambridge University Press.

Flower, L. (1989). Cognition, context and theory building. *College Composition and Communication, 40*, 282–311.

Gillen, J. (2000). Versions of Vygotsky. *British Journal of Educational Studies, 48*, 183–198.

Goldstein, L. (2004). Questions and answers about teacher written commentary and student revision: Teachers and students working together. *Journal of Second Language Writing. 13*(31), 63–80.

Knoblauch, C., & Brannon, L. (1984). *Rhetorical traditions and the teaching of writing.* Upper Montclar, NJ: Boynton/Cook.

Hyland, K.(2003). *Second language writing.* Cambridge: Cambridge University Press.

Hyland, K. (2006). *English for academic purposes.* London: Routledge.

Hyland, K., & Hyland, F. (2006). Feedback on second language students' writing. *Language Teaching, 39*, 83–101.

Rea-Dickins, P. (2001). Mirror, mirror on the wall: Identifying process of classroom assessment. *Language Testing, 18*, 429–462.

Sadler, D. R. (1998). Formative assessment: Revisiting the territory. *Assessment in Education, 5*(1), 77–84.

Tharp, R., & Gallimore, R. (1998). A theory of teaching as assisted performance. In D. Faulkner, K. Littleton, & M. Woodhead (Eds.), *Learning relationships in the classroom* (pp. 93–109). London: Routledge.

Truscott, J. (1996). The case against grammar correction in L2 writing classes. *Language Learning, 46*, 327–369.

Truscott, J. (1999). The case for 'The case against grammar correction in L2 writing classes': A response to Ferris. *Journal of Second Language Writing, 8*(2), 111–122.

Truscott, J. (2004). Evidence and conjecture on the effect of correction: A response to Chandler. *Journal of Second Language Writing, 12,* 96–104.

Truscott, J. (2007). The effect of error correction on learners' ability to write accurately. *Journal of Second Language Writing, 16,* 255–272.

Vygotsky, L. (1978). *Mind in society.* Cambridge, MA: Harvard University Press.

Williams, J. (2007). *Teaching writing in second and foreign language classrooms.* Beijing: World Publishing Corporation.

GAMZE ONCUL

EAP READING: A MEANS TO AN END

INTRODUCTION

In an EAP course students should be learning to use the language as a means to an end – to reach an academic purpose – and this means that EAP materials and tasks should represent the possible challenges of real academic life and aim to teach students how to meet these challenges by themselves. Reading instruction, with its various purposes, means and ends, is an invaluable component of EAP courses, because carefully chosen reading material not only gives students the context, the content and the need to practice a variety of skills required in real academic life, but also offers various models of writing and turns the course into a meaningful experience. This kind of approach to EAP reading might require a more focused needs analysis in an English for Specific Academic Purposes (ESAP) context (Hyland, 2006), but within the boundaries of English for General Academic Purposes (EGAP) it is possible to talk about a set of skills and strategies fundamental to EAP reading instruction.

Grabe (2009, p. 332) proposes nine 'key components of reading curriculum' to define various means and ends of reading instruction:

1. promote word recognition skills
2. build a large recognition vocabulary
3. practice comprehension skills
4. build awareness of discourse structure
5. develop strategic reading
6. practice reading fluency
7. promote extensive reading
8. develop motivation
9. integrate both reading and content-learning expertise

Taking Grabe's curricular principles for reading instruction as its guide and with reference to actual classroom practice and students' end-of-semester reflections in a first-year EAP course at Bilkent University in 2010 Fall semester, this paper explores ways to turn EGAP reading instruction into the real training for the real challenges of academic life through a careful choice of authentic material and proper task design.

The discussion will comprise the importance of setting a meaningful purpose and pre-, while- and post-reading strategy training.

SETTING A MEANINGFUL PURPOSE

Grabe's 'combining content and language learning' and 'promoting extensive reading', which will make the rest of his key components of a reading curriculum possible to achieve, deserve a place at the top of this proposed list of strategies for EAP material choice and task design. This can be realized when a meaningful purpose reflecting and/or serving real needs is set.

Real-life academic reading always has a purpose, whether it be revision for an exam or reading to write an academic assignment; likewise, it requires certain skills, which is why EAP reading tasks should represent real-life experiences and should bear a real purpose. This can be achieved with a real context and real content that might trigger real needs because real needs ease learning; the more meaningful the purpose is, the more effective the reading experience will become.

A content-driven EAP course designed within the framework of Content-Based Instruction (CBI), where students read authentic reading material, such as academic articles or book chapters brought together around a topic, will give way to extensive reading practices: CBI will provide students with both the content and the context mirroring real-life academic experiences with real-life purpose and real need to practice academic skills; it will also give the EAP instructor the frame to combine content and language. In an EAP course, this combination is important because learning requires meaning because meaning nurtures

need, and need in turn feeds learning; this will promote motivation for reading, will give students the opportunity to practice reading fluency and comprehension skills, while promoting word recognition skills and strategic reading, as Grabe proposes.

PRE-READING STRATEGY TRAINING

The schema theory of reading advocates the need for activating existing schemata prior to reading. Accordingly, if the reader can make necessary connections between the text and his/her existing schemata, the reading experience might gain ease and speed and become more effective. Making predictions about the text prior to reading is a skill serving not only the activation of the existing schemata but also real academic needs, like scanning text to identify and/or filter information to make suitability and reliability decisions. That is to say, the academic reader often has to make choices of the right sources according to a pre-set aim, which often requires quick reading, during which the reader makes some guesses about the content, scope and quality of the text to determine whether it really is worth close reading.

Therefore, students need to know about such strategies as guessing what the text is about to see its relevance for their purpose; what the main idea is; what the main points are; or to identify the writer's stance. These involve reading the title, reading an abstract (if available), subtitles and captions (if any). This might be followed by quick scanning of the introduction and conclusion to see the writer's main argument and, by reading first and last sentences of paragraphs, to see the outline of the text. At the end, the student can make use of this sort of knowledge to decide how relevant the text is for the set purpose(s) and at the same time get ready for a closer reading.

- The title in real-life reading is usually a short-cut for decisions on what to read. The title usually gives the reader the first clue on whether it is what s/he is looking for. Making guesses about the content and the scope of the text with the title, checking the value and/or accuracy of the predictions and turning this into a constant practice will help students with their reading.

- The abstract is a genuine time saver for the academic reader. A well-written abstract helps to make quick decisions. Likewise, the abstract will give the students the main question the writer is trying to answer, possibly his or her answer to that question, and how he or she has reached that answer, which is important for two purposes: to make right choices and to get ready for a closer reading.

- The author and the publisher of a book, book chapter, journal or an article can easily give the academic reader an idea about the credibility, reliability, scope and even the language of the source. Similarly, finding more information about the writer and the source might help the students with their predictions while they are preparing to read an article. A simple Google search about the writer to find more on his or her field and works, and finding out more on the publisher, should be practiced in class always with an emphasis on the possible value of the information gathered.

- Subheadings help the reader see the outline, the structure of the text. Seeing the structure can make it easier to make reliable guesses on what is going to be read. Providing students with relevant practice to show how valuable subheadings are and how well they work will give them the awareness of their value in both choosing the right material and getting ready to read.

- Pictures, figures, graphs and captions give the reader clues on what the text is going to be about. Practice with real articles, making predictions about the scope and content by looking at the pictures, figures, graphs and/or captions will give students the chance to see the value of the graphic material as a prediction tool, when available.

- The introduction and conclusion help to make more predictions about the content and the structure of the text. The writer sets out his or her purpose, gives the main question he or she is trying to answer and his or her answer to that question in the introduction, and he or she may repeat or extend it to make it clearer in the conclusion. Students should be taught the value of being able to see the writer's purpose before closer reading, and reading the introduction and the conclusion before detailed reading should be offered as another prediction strategy. With constant practice with authentic reading material, they can see how an introduction and/or the conclusion can serve the right purpose, and ideally they can take this as a model that they can carry into their writing.

- The first and/or last sentence of each paragraph gives the reader the chance to guess more about the scope, content and structure of the text. A well-organized paper will give hints about its structure and content with the first and/or last sentence of each paragraph. EAP reading instruction should give the students the awareness and opportunities to see and practice how well it works.

In brief, EAP reading instruction should give students the awareness of the value of making predictions and the opportunity to practice prediction strategies and make use of suitable prediction tools. It is clear in two students' end of semester reflections below, that making predictions prior to reading makes their work easier, faster and more effective and so 'promote[s] motivation for reading', as Grabe proposes:

> I haven't read that kind of long readings [before], it is not easy but thanks to you I learned how to read and how to make it easy (subheadings, scanning); I did not use prediction before but now I do use it. At the weekend I did my homework, I had to read a lot of articles, all very long but thanks to the strategies, I coped with the difficulty and wrote my essay easily.

> Yes, [I] improved my reading in actually fast reading long articles I have to read. Reading the first sentence, it helped me in difficult times. I used some of the strategies, my vocabulary was an obstacle, I changed some of your strategies and used them. Highlighting I used a lot with my first quick reading and this helped me a lot with my second reading.

WHILE-READING STRATEGY TRAINING

In real situations, academic reading requires close reading and record-keeping. EAP reading instruction should give students the awareness that academic reading is not something like 'read and put it aside', and that they will need the text in the future. Then, they need to learn and practice leaving the right traces on the text and record-keeping for any future need. The metaphor I am offering for this stage is taking an X-ray of the text – identifying, highlighting and labeling the key points, which entails the following:

SEE THE MAIN QUESTION

An academic article should have a purpose, which is usually in the form of an answer to the main question, and this main question is usually given in the abstract (if available), the introduction and/or in the conclusion. Seeing the main question is important for getting ready to read and for double-checking its suitability for the set purpose.

SEE THE MAIN ARGUMENT

When there is a question to answer, the text will have its answer, its main argument, the writer's stance, which is again most probably given in the abstract, the introduction and/or in the conclusion. Seeing the main argument, identifying the writer's stance helps the reader to understand better the writer's overall purpose and the text structure. Raising students' awareness and giving them opportunities to practice will help them with their reading.

See the key point for each paragraph

It is important to convince students that every paragraph in a text should have a purpose and a key point somewhere within. Constant modeling and practice in identifying and highlighting the key point will help raise students' awareness and confidence in making marks on the text for any future use

Label the text

The highlighted key point of the paragraph should help the reader to give that paragraph a label. In cases where there are no subheadings in the text, this sort of labeling might turn into giving subheadings to the text. When students are convinced that the subheadings offer good help to see the outline of the text, which is crucial in identifying and filtering the information, they can realize how fast and easy their second/third reading will become, and this will raise their motivation.

Make a chart/mind-map

It is perfectly fine to annotate, just to make marks on the text, but especially for visual learners, who like to see the big picture at the end, forming a chart or a mind-map with the help of what has already been done will work better. For this reason, it is a good idea to show students sample annotations, charts and mind-maps and guide them through their own choice.

To conclude, any effort used to find out more about the text structure will help students 'build an awareness of discourse structure' as Grabe recommends. Seeing the whole picture, taking an X-ray of the article will make reading easier, quicker and more effective. When students are convinced they should employ these strategies while reading academic articles, they can see that their

reading improves. Student comments below show how they feel about this practice:

> Before I took this course I used to read every page four times, when I came to the end or the middle I used to not remember the beginning, it was overwhelming. Taking margin notes, finding the key sentence, the topic sentence are really helpful. Like a very big city, you can't see everywhere with just one short visit, look at all and build a parameter divide it and will be easier to understand.
>
> [while] reading in English I was very slow last year. Reading this much helped me a lot. The subheading idea helped me a lot. Last two readings were very long, I would forget what I read if I didn't use the subheadings.
>
> I have learned some strategies on how to read an article, long article, when I have short time. I learned those strategies and also I improved my vocabulary. I use giving subheadings after finding key points. This is good because you forget.

Post-reading strategy training

In real academic life, we often read for a written or spoken end product. The end product for reading in an EAP course should represent real-life end products of reading. Krathwohl's (2002) adaptation of Bloom's taxonomy for 'Higher Order Thinking Skills' offers a realistic framework for task design:

Remembering

Pre-reading strategy training represents this first level of thinking skills.

Understanding

Raising awareness of the clause structure of academic grammar, working on complex grammar and vocabulary by re-stating the key points through closer analysis of the key points will give students an opportunity to 'practice comprehension skills that combine awareness of grammar, main idea identification, and comprehension strategies' as Grabe (2009, p. 332) proposes.

APPLYING

Offering authentic academic texts as models for writing and giving opportunities where students can practice these models in their own writing in terms of organization, source integration, building and supporting an argument, refuting and/or accommodating an argument will offer real-life practice with application as a higher-order thinking skill.

ANALYZING

Locating, comparing, or simply gathering information, opinions, or evidence on a chart or mind-map, and/or writing an analytical summary of the text or an analysis of a specific situation within the text and/or with reference to the text will give the students real opportunities for analysis.

EVALUATING

Writing a critical summary, an evaluation or writing a response to the whole or a piece of the text will offer real-life evaluation practice.

CREATING

Writing a literature review, or an argument-led essay based on the articles read will suitably give way to real academic practice.

Student comments below show how reading tasks designed with this logic helped them to deal with and better understand the articles, to learn better about the topic and to improve their reading and thinking, and made it easier to prepare to write:

> *I learned how to look at the article, find what I need to find search for what I am looking for. I can understand complex words complex sentences.*

> *When I read a complex sentence, I didn't used to try hard, I used to give up reading, but now, I know how to find the object, subject, and I try to understand.*

> *Especially the first one [the reading chart where all relevant arguments about the essay question brought together] I found really beneficial. I had everything I needed for the essay on the sheet = everything I have to think. You can't write without understanding.*

CONCLUSION

Grabe's 'Key components of a reading curriculum' offer a logical, practical and effective approach to EAP reading instruction. Meaningful reading material, exploited with meaningful tasks and constant focus on meaningful modelling, and the practice of reading strategies develop students' motivation for reading, which is well indicated in my students' reflections on their reading and their use of reading strategies, where reading faster, feeling more confident about vocabulary and complex grammar were the common points raised.

According to Grabe (2009, p. 335), we can develop strategic reading through 'consistent modeling, scaffolding, extensive practice and eventually independent use of those strategies'. Tasks modeling reading strategies and giving students a chance to practice those strategies will work well for this purpose. Tasks guiding students through reading, helping them to look for what they need and modeling reader/writer-friendly ways of record keeping will be of great value. Modeling reading strategies like prediction, highlighting the key points, taking margin notes, keeping note cards, mind-mapping, using grids, graphic organizers or using the text as a model for writing will help students improve their reading. It will also be useful to offer enough practice opportunities to students and to persistently scaffold the model to aid the students' improvement.

REFERENCES

Grabe, W. (2009). *Reading in a second language: Moving from theory to practice*. New York: Cambridge University Press.

Hyland, K. (2006). *English for academic purposes: An advanced resource book*. Abingdon: Routledge.

Krathwohl, D. R. (2002). A revision of Bloom's taxonomy: An overview. *Theory into Practice, 41*(4), 212–218.

Chitra Varaprasad

English for Specific Academic Purposes: a balancing act?

Introduction

An EAP classroom teacher who is teaching writing may feel caught between teaching a set of general English writing skills which could be applied to different academic contexts (Zhu, 2004) and adopting an ESP approach with a focus on specific literacy skills closely tied to the features of specific academic disciplines. This issue is made even more challenging for the classroom teacher who has to deal with students from varied disciplinary backgrounds. Student diversity in the classroom is a reality that teachers have to contend with (Hyland & Hamp-Lyons, 2002). One way to rise to the challenge would be to teach students the required general writing skills and at the same time sensitize them to the conventions specific to their discipline (Dudley-Evans & St John, 1998).

This paper reports on a classroom-based study, involving a group of graduate students at the National University of Singapore, which focused on raising their awareness of the general and specific academic writing features and conventions. The first section briefly discusses the different perspectives on the general/specific dichotomy in EAP, followed by the rationale for the study and its research objectives. Data collection methods and findings will then be presented, the latter in the context of the three research questions that the study set out to address (presented in Section 3).

The general-specific distinction in EAP

In the ESP literature, and in particular in EAP contexts, a distinction is drawn between English for General Academic Purposes (EGAP) and English for Specific Academic Purposes (ESAP). 'EGAP refers to the teaching of skills and language that are common to all disciplines; ESAP refers to the teaching of the features that distinguish one discipline from others' (Dudley-Evans & St John, 1998, p. 41). The issue of specificity in the language classroom has thus gained attention among both researchers and teachers, not only in target texts but also in the area of pedagogy.

However, there are different schools of thought about the focus of specificity expressed in the literature. Halliday, Mackintosh and Strevens' (1964) original conception of ESP centred on the language and activities appropriate to particular disciplines and occupations. By contrast, Hutchinson and Waters (1987), Blue (1988) and Spack (1988) believed that the focus should be on learners and learning rather than on target texts and practices. Others believe that there is evidence that academic discourses represent a variety of specific literacies (Candlin & Plum, 1999; Hyland, 2000, 2002a; Johns, 1997; Prior, 1998). Hyland (2002a) has argued that effective language teaching in the universities involves taking specificity seriously, as professional communities have their own particular practices, genres and communicative functions.

Teachers are aware of these different schools of thought and 'have also come to acknowledge that teaching those who are using English for their studies differs from teaching those who are learning English for general purposes only' (Hyland & Hamp-Lyons, 2002, p. 2). They realize that the approach advocated by Hyland (2002) to focus on discipline specifics in teaching academic writing would be the ideal path to take, but that the reality of the curriculum, with its many demands, and the classroom diversity pose different challenges to them. Hyland and Hamp-Lyons (2002, p. 5) themselves concede that there are 'obstacles to putting specificity into practice' and that it involves 'juggling institutional constraints'. In the context of this study there were curriculum requirements to contend with and also the need to cater to students' academic and language needs from a variety

of disciplines. In the interest of the students, we as teachers have no choice but to devise teaching methods that would enable us to strike a balance in teaching the general and specific aspects of academic writing.

SUGGESTED CLASSROOM APPROACHES

Several pedagogical recommendations have been offered by researchers. Hutchinson & Waters (1987, cited in Dudley-Evans & St John, 1998) and Blue (1988, cited in Dudley-Evans & St John, 1998) argued that EGAP should be focused on EAP teaching and that ESAP can be acquired by students through individual project work. Dudley-Evans and St John (ibid., p. 42) elaborated further that 'the common-core EAP work makes more sense and is more relevant if it is supplemented by specific work'. A combination method is advocated in the literature, which means that teachers should first help students develop core academic skills with more specific work to be accomplished later, perhaps with the help of subject specialists.

Attempts have also been made to team-teach or co-teach by language teachers with subject specialists. Dudley-Evans & St John suggest three-level cooperation for subject-specific work: Cooperation, Collaboration and Team-teaching. *Cooperation* involves the language teacher taking the initiative to find out the workings of the discipline and *collaboration* requires the language and subject teachers to work together outside the classroom. The third level, *team-teaching*, refers to both language- and subject-teacher cooperating inside the classroom. However, this level may not always be feasible due to administrative constraints, such as timetabling, especially if the classroom involves students from varied disciplines. Thus, while collaboration is seen as an attractive proposition, working beyond cooperation may be problematic or prevented by institutional constraints.

RATIONALE AND OBJECTIVES FOR THE STUDY

This project was designed for graduate students on an academic writing module (ES5001A) at the National University of Singapore. In order to strike a balance between teaching EAP general skills and raising students' awareness of discipline specific writing conventions, it was decided to focus on the common-core EAP work and supplement it by specific work in the form of a project: *Research Project on Academic Writing Conventions*. Appendix A provides a sample of the questionnaire. For the project, students were asked to select and analyze a research article for the different general academic writing conventions covered in the classroom and, further, to identify other conventions that differed from those covered in the classroom with reference to their specific discipline. In the course of analyzing a discipline-specific research article for these conventions, it was hoped students would become aware of the writing conventions in their own disciplines. This is how work pertaining to the specific disciplines was incorporated with the teaching of general academic conventions.

A classroom-based study was undertaken to ascertain the effectiveness of the project in terms of students' learning by observing their ability to identify general academic features and conventions specific to their discipline. The study aimed to explore the extent to which students' awareness could

be raised in the project writing process by obtaining their feedback on the project.

The study addressed three research objectives:

1. to discover the extent to which students were able to identify the general academic writing conventions pertaining to the organization and language that were taught in the classroom
2. to discover the extent to which the project helped to raise students' awareness of discipline-specific writing conventions
3. to survey students' perceptions about the pedagogical process of writing a project

METHODOLOGY

THE MODULE

ES5001A is an intermediate-level writing module for graduate students. Before being assigned to the module, students take a Diagnostic English Test which also determines placement into either a basic or an intermediate-level writing module. The focus of these modules is mainly on writing, with students covering three writing tasks: summary writing, writing a critique and data commentary. The module textbook *Advanced Writing for Graduate Students* (Swales & Feak, 2004, – hereafter referred to as AWG) focuses on academic writing conventions and organization pertaining to the different curriculum writing tasks. The book was chosen because it is one of the few that focus on academic writing conventions for graduate students, providing both explanations and sample classroom activities. Activities from the book contributed to the common core EAP work, while the module's project constituted the specific work.

PARTICIPANTS

Twenty-seven students from two tutorial groups participated in this study. Students were from several disciplines including Engineering, Science, Medicine, Mathematics and Pharmacy. This diversity in student discipline was the main reason that the focus of the module had to stay on general conventions in academic writing. Two of the students were 'coursework' students, who were not required to write research papers, while the others were focused on obtaining their Masters solely through research work.

RESEARCH DESIGN

Data was collected in two ways. First, the project required the students to analyze the writing conventions in a self-selected journal article (of between five and ten pages) representative of their field, using a framework discussed in class. Table 1 shows a sample of the analytic concepts or tools that students were given to analyze their selected article. Secondly, they had to report their findings at three points during the semester, that is, at the end of Phase 1 (Week 5), Phase 2 (Week 7) and Phase 3 (Week 11).

Table 1 Tools for Analysis

Phase 1 analysis: language	Phase 2 analysis: organization (IMRD)	Phase 3: written report framework (IMRD)

Formal Vocabulary:
   Verbs
   Nouns
	Introduction (I)
	Methods (M)
	Results (R)
	Discussion (D)
		Introduction
		Methods
		Results
		Discussion

Structures of Comparison/Contrast:
   Adjectives
   Expressions of comparison
   Expressions of contrast
	Text Types
	   General–Specific
	   Problem–Solution
	   Problem–Process–Solution	

Academic Style
General Conventions:
   No contractions
   Formal negative forms
   Limited use of 'run-on'
   expressions (*so forth*, etc.)
   Avoidance of 'you'
   Use of indirect questions
   Adverbs in mid-position		

Reporting Verbs: Objective versus evaluative verbs Weak versus strong verbs		

Evaluative Language:
   Nouns
   Verbs
   Adjectives
   Adverbs		

In Phase 1, the students focused on the academic conventions relating to vocabulary, grammar, academic style and flow. In Phase 2, the focus moved to the organizational structures used in a research article. In this phase students had to identify and explain the use or lack of use of the IMRD (Introduction, Methods, Results, Discussion) (Swales & Feak, 2004) pattern of organization. In addition, they needed to analyze the organization patterns of the different sections of the article, based on the functional patterns covered in class, such as the General–Specific text type. In Phase 3, students had to construct a report. To guide their construction, students were also asked to read Unit 7: *Constructing a Research Paper* (ibid., pp. 215–241) and Appendix 4: *Writing up a Small Research Project* (ibid., pp. 315–322) in the book.

Students' input from the three phases such as their worksheets from Phase 1, their journal article analysis of organization from Phase 2 and their report from Phase 3 provided qualitative data for this study. In addition, data was also collected by asking students to respond to a questionnaire to obtain their perceptions about the project after the completion of the three phases. Through the questionnaire, they were asked to rate the different phases of the project on a scale of 1–4 (1 being least useful and 4 being extremely useful). They were also asked to state the general and specific writing conventions they had learnt. Appendix B provides a sample of the questionnaire.

DATA ANALYSES

Data was analyzed both qualitatively and quantitatively. Students' output from the three phases was qualitatively analyzed to address Objective 1. Students' identification of the organizational and language elements and their explanations were analyzed. Table 1 shows some of the academic language features or categories used for examining students' data. Similarly, students' analyses of the organizational features of the journal article (Phase 2) were carefully assessed for their identification of organization patterns given in Table 1.

Objective 2, on awareness of disciplinary conventions, was evaluated in two ways. Students' analysis of the journal article, their report in Phase 3 and their answers to one of the questions on awareness of disciplinary conventions in the questionnaire were qualitatively analyzed.

For the third research question on students' perception about the project, data from the questionnaire was quantitatively and qualitatively analyzed. Students' rating responses to the various phases of the project were counted and percentage scores tabulated for quantitative evidence and their comments for qualitative support.

FINDINGS AND DISCUSSION

To address Objective 1, students' analyses of the journal article and report in Phase 3 were analyzed for their understanding of the different organization patterns mentioned earlier. It was found that almost all students were fairly competent in identifying the macro IMRD pattern of organization and other patterns of organization discussed in class. Students' input from their Phase 3 reports reproduced below can be considered to be representative of their understanding:

> *Several organization patterns were identified: General–Specific pattern in the introduction section …, Problem–Solution in section 2.4 …,*

Problem–Process–Solution in section 3.2 … Research papers in Computer and Civil Engineering follow the typical IMRD and Problem–Solution pattern.

As for students' understanding about the various academic language features, their worksheet in Phase 1 and their research report in Phase 3 were carefully examined for their awareness of these features. Reproduced below are a few samples of students' comments, which are representative of many such comments made by most of the students.

Several academic writing conventions such as placing adverbs in mid position, avoiding contractions, using phrasal verbs (e.g., 'conducted ' instead of 'carried out') and summary words were used.

Some unused conventions found were reporting verbs, evaluative language (scientific paper, so no literature review) and indirect questions. The last contributed to a very informal style.

Found use of passive voice in process descriptions, modal verbs to indicate probability.

What is encouraging is that, in addition to identifying features of academic language, students were also able to provide reasons for why some of these features were not found, as shown in this student's comment:

All conventions with regard to vocabulary and style are followed except for evaluative language. This is because this is a technical paper and there is no need to review studies.

To address Objective 2, students' research reports in Phase 3 and their answers to the open-ended question in the questionnaire about what they had learnt about discipline-specific conventions were examined. While most of the students were able to identify the similarities between the general and discipline-specific writing conventions pertaining to organization and language, there were also students who commented on the differences. Reproduced below are a few such comments representing this aspect of students' understanding. These students were from different disciplines: Materials Science and Metallurgy, Electrical and Electronics Engineering, and Science.

The article organization did not follow the IMRD pattern. It had the following pattern: Introduction, Visual Examination, Experimental Results and Conclusion. This is because it is written for industrial scientists and specialists. Discussion was part of the results. There was a separate conclusion section. (Materials Science and Metallurgy)

Reporting and summarizing phrases were not found as we always commonly use a reference number for this purpose. We follow the conventions laid out by IEEE (Institute of Electrical and Electronics Engineering).

The Chemistry and Biology articles were organized differently: Biology: Results first, followed by the introductory section, followed by Results and Discussion and summary of methods. Chemistry: traditional IMRD format, with Results and Discussion combined, followed by a Conclusion section.

Comparison and contrast phrases used, but phrases in Chemistry more quantitative and in Biology more qualitative as the article dealt more with theories than experiments. (Science)

To address Objective 3, students' rating responses to the various phases of the project were counted and percentage scores tabulated.

Of the 25 who responded to the questionnaire, 76% found Phase 1 (Language) of the project 'very useful', while 24% found the project 'useful'. As for Phase 2 (Organization) of the project, 84% found the project very useful and 16% found the project useful. Since none of the students stated that they found the project 'somewhat' or 'least' useful, and since all students combined found it 'useful', it can be safely concluded that all students perceived that they had benefited from Phases 1 and 2 of the project with regards to both organization and language.

With regard to Phase 3 (Research Report), 20% found writing the research report 'very useful', 72% found it useful, while 8% found the project 'somewhat useful'. One finding that needs to be highlighted for Phase 3 is that the numbers for 'extremely useful' had dropped considerably to 20% as compared to Phases 1 and 2 (76% and 84% respectively). One reason could be that writing a research report in the format of a journal article had direct relevance only to a few students at that point in time. A couple of these students even mentioned this in their responses to the questionnaire (see students' comments below). This could also be the reason why 72% of the students found writing the research report 'useful', as they would be expected to produce research papers in the near future. Two students who mentioned that Phase 3 of the project was 'somewhat useful' could have been the two coursework students (mentioned earlier), who were not expected to write research papers.

In addition to the above findings, descriptive comments from students in their questionnaire responses (exemplified below) attest to the usefulness of the project for raising their awareness of general and specific academic writing conventions.

This project has helped me to become familiar with general academic writing conventions and with conventions in my own discipline. Both are important for writing research papers in my discipline.

I have learnt the importance of organizing my paper in a logical manner and also to use formal writing conventions when writing academic articles.

IMPLICATIONS FOR TEACHING, LEARNING AND RESEARCH

Several implications for teaching and learning can be drawn from this study. It can be claimed that the suggestion by Hutchinson and Waters (1987, cited in Dudley-Evans & St John, 1998) and Blue (1988, cited in Dudley-Evans & St John, 1998) that EGAP should be focused on EAP teaching and that ESAP can be acquired by students through individual project work has been put into practice in this study. This augurs well for a combination method advocated in the literature, which means that teachers should first help students develop core academic skills with more specific work to be accomplished later, via a project, as is the case in this study.

This classroom-based study has also shown that teachers grappling with common-core curriculum and varied disciplinary backgrounds have to be creative and devise ways of addressing the 'common-core academic' and 'subject-specific work' debate in their own classrooms. While it may not be possible to teach students discipline-specific conventions, given the different classroom constraints, it is still possible to raise their awareness of how academic writing conventions across disciplines can be both similar and different. This project attempted to give students some structured analytical tools for each of the phases with which to raise their awareness and measure their ability and response to using these tools.

While it may not be possible to transfer the methodology used in this study to all classrooms, it is still possible to apply some of the concepts, such as getting students to analyze a piece of text for writing conventions pertaining to language and organization. Students' comments also reveal that they have been engaged in the learning process about core academic writing conventions. The project helped confirm certain conventions pertaining to language and organization that students were exposed to in the classroom. It also enabled some other students to highlight the differences in academic conventions in their disciplines. All this helped students to consolidate their own understanding and learning. This is a cause for optimism for the teaching and learning of these conventions in the classroom.

As for research, small classroom-based studies such as these can help confirm the usefulness of such projects and even make suggestions for fine tuning them. For example, two students mentioned in their comments that the Phase 1 worksheet tried to cover too much ground by including all the language elements and that the number could be reduced by prioritizing the more important language items. Similarly, students commented that:

> One research article is insufficient to fully understand the writing conventions in a particular area. (Civil Engineering Student)

While the comment about the number of language elements can be fine-tuned in future studies, adding additional research articles would have to be undertaken as an independent study task, as it is beyond the scope of a classroom-based study.

Another student commented that:

> This project was a good starting point to learn to write an academic article. However organization will vary based on the purpose and the audience reading the paper. So several articles in the field should be considered. (Mechanical Engineering Student)

This comment echoes the thinking of this researcher.

The student quotes reported here show that students have developed an awareness of the features of academic writing and some pertaining to their discipline. In the case of the former, whether they were able to translate this awareness into their writing is an area that future studies can explore, as it was not the objective of this study. In the case of the latter, it would involve some discipline-specific writing, which was not included in this curriculum. It is another area into which future studies can venture.

CONCLUSION

The three objectives of this study were to explore students' identification of general academic writing conventions taught in the classroom, to also raise their awareness of writing conventions specific to their discipline and to examine students' perceptions of the research project. It represents a small effort to balance the teaching of the general and discipline-specific academic writing conventions. Based on the findings and discussion, it is possible to conclude that the balancing act has been successful to a large extent.

If curriculum and classroom time permit, incorporating students' suggestions as part of another classroom-based study can help throw further insights on balancing the teaching of the general and discipline-specific academic writing conventions.

REFERENCES

Blue, G. (1988). Individualising academic writing tuition. In P. Robinson (Ed.), *Academic writing: Process and product* (pp. 95–99). ELT Documents, 129.

Candlin, C. N., & Plum, G. A. (1999). Engaging with challenges of interdiscursivity in academic writing: researchers, students and teachers. In C. N. Candlin, & K. Hyland (Eds.), *Writing: texts, processes and practices* (pp. 193–217). London: Longman.

Dudley-Evans, T., & St John, M. J. (1998). *Developments in English for specific purposes.* Cambridge University Press, Cambridge.

Halliday, M., Mackintosh, A., & Strevens, P. (1964). *The linguistic sciences and language teaching.* London: Longman.

Hutchinson, T., & Waters, A. (1987). *English for specific purposes.* Cambridge: Cambridge University Press.

Hyland, K. (2000). *Disciplinary discourses: social interactions in academic writing.* London: Longman.

Hyland, K. (2002a). Specificity revisited: how far should we go now? *English for Specific Purposes, 21*(4), 385–395.

Hyland, K., & Hamp-Lyons, L. (2002). EAP: issues and directions. *Journal of English for Academic Purposes, 1*(1), 1–12.

Johns, A. M. (1997). *Text, role and context: developing academic literacies.* Cambridge: CUP.

Prior, P. (1998). *Writing/disciplinarity: A sociohistoric account of literate activity in the academy.* Mahwah, NJ: Erlbaum.

Spack, R. (1988). Initiating ESL students into the academic discourse community: How far should we go? *TESOL Quarterly, 22*(1), 29–52.

Swales, J. M., & Feak, C. B. (2004). *Academic writing for graduate students* (2nd ed.). Ann Arbor: University of Michigan Press.

Zhu, W. (2004). Faculty views on the importance of writing, the nature of academic writing, and teaching and responding to writing in the disciplines. *Journal of Second Language Writing, 13*, 29–48.

APPENDIX A

RESEARCH PROJECT ON ACADEMIC WRITING CONVENTIONS

Although there are writing conventions that are universally observed in academe, variations occur among the different fields. In ES5001A we focus on the general conventions in academic writing. However, you need to be familiar with the specific conventions in your own academic field.

The main aim of the ES5001A research project is to familiarize you with these specific writing conventions.

Briefly, the project requires that you compare the writing conventions of a chosen journal article in your field with the conventions we have studied in ES5001A. You will report your findings at three points during the semester, that is, at the end of Phases 1, 2 and 3.

This project may be done in pairs or in a group of three. At the beginning of the semester, you will be encouraged to find students from the same field to work together on the project. **Each student will analyse his/her chosen journal article, but the reports will be written jointly by both/all students.** The grade awarded for the project will be the same for both/all students.

You will receive feedback on your work during Phases 1, and 2. At the end of the term, the final research report (submitted at the end of Phase 3) will be awarded a grade. This final report constitutes 15% of your Continuous Assessment grade.

PREPARING FOR THE PROJECT

1. Select one journal article from your field (about 5–10 pages in length). You should choose articles you would consider to be representative of those in your field. Show the articles to your tutor in Week 2 to confirm that they can be used for this project.
2. Read *AWG*, Unit 7: *Constructing a Research Paper 1* (pp. 215–241) and Appendix 4: *Writing Up a Small Research Project* (pp. 315–322).
3. Follow the detailed guidelines on page 2 of this handout.

DEADLINES FOR SUBMISSION

Phase 1: Week 5
Phase 2: Week 7
Phase 3: Week 11

DETAILED GUIDELINES

Phase 1 – General Academic Conventions
Analyse the **writing conventions** used in your article. Use Worksheet for Phase 1. After you complete Worksheet for Phase 1, select six academic conventions that characterize your journal article as a text written in a formal style. Choose **2 conventions** from each group – Group 1: Vocabulary, Group 2: Grammar/Style, and Group 3: Flow. Highlight these conventions on your journal article itself, and provide at least two examples for each convention in your report. Answer the following questions in a 2–3 paragraph report to be **submitted in Week 5.** Do the writing conventions in your article follow those prescribed in the *AWG*? Which of these conventions are **not** followed? Why do you think the conventions in your field are different? In your own academic writing, how will you deal with these differences?

Phase 2 – Organization
To analyse the **organizational structures** used in your article, answer the following questions: How is the article organized? Is the IMRD framework explicitly used or is it modified? If it is modified, describe the modification. What information is presented in the Introduction section of your article (e.g., findings from previous research, purpose of the present research, other information)? How is this information organized? Find two examples of each of the following patterns of organization in your journal article. (Highlight these sections on your journal article itself.) General–Specific Problem–Solution Problem–Process–Solution Write up your findings in a 2–3 paragraph text to be **submitted in Week 7.**

Phase 3 – Final Report
Write your final report on this project, according to the following guidelines. Write a report using the IMRD framework to present your research. The texts you wrote for Phase 1 and 2 should be used as the first draft of your Findings and Discussion sections. Add to these a brief introduction, description of methodology, and finally a conclusion. To help you do this, review *AWG*, Appendix 4: *Writing Up a Small Research Project*, pp. 315–322, and use the attached Template for Phase 3. Add the copy of your article which you worked on as Appendix 1. Format your report according to the ES5001A Style Sheet, and **submit the entire document in Week 11.**

WORKSHEET FOR PHASE I

ACADEMIC CONVENTIONS IN VOCABULARY, GRAMMAR AND STYLE, AND FLOW

Use this worksheet to help you complete Phase 1 of the research project.

Below is a comprehensive list of the academic conventions we shall be discussing in this course. They have been grouped in terms of vocabulary, grammar and style, and flow.

Your task is to determine whether or not these conventions are followed in your journal article. If they are followed, write 'YES' in Column 2 next to the convention. Then highlight the examples of this convention in your article and copy 1–3 examples of each in Column 3 below. If they are not followed in your article, write 'NO' in Column 2.

I	2 Yes/ No	3 (Examples)
VOCABULARY		

Formal Vocabulary:
    Verbs
    Nouns
    Other parts of speech		

Structures of Comparison/Contrast:
    Adjectives
    Expressions of comparison
    Expressions of contrast		

Reporting Verbs : Objective versus evaluative verbs		
Weak versus strong verbs		

Evaluative Language:
    Nouns
    Verbs
    Adjectives
    Adverbs		

GRAMMAR/STYLE		

General Academic Conventions:
    No contractions
    Formal negative forms
    Limited use of 'run-on' expressions (*so forth*, etc.)
    Avoidance of *you*
    Use of indirect questions		

Adverbs in mid-position Conciseness		

Problem, Process & Solution Descriptions:
    Indirect questions
    Use of passive voice in process descriptions
    ~*ing* clauses of result
    Mid-position adverbs		

Definitions:
    Use of articles (definite, indefinite, zero)
    Restrictive relative clause reductions		

Qualifications and Strength of Claim (Hedges):
    Modal verbs (probability)
    Distancing to show data is 'soft'
    Generalization
    Use of weak/strong verbs
    Qualifying the subject
    Citing exceptions		

Summaries: Nominal *that* clause		

Critiques:
    Past unreal conditionals
    Present unreal conditionals
    Inversions
    Scare quotes		

FLOW		
Punctuation Summary words Summary reminder phrases *this* + summary words Time adverbials Participle used as adjective Linking words and phrases		

TEMPLATE FOR PHASE 3

FINAL REPORT GUIDE

INTRODUCTION

Discuss the background and aims/objectives of the research project. What did you hope to learn about academic writing in your field by completing this type of research?

METHODS

What types of information did you gather? What methods did you use to gather your data? What exactly did you do to get this information? State the procedures for Phase 1 and Phase 2 briefly and clearly.

RESULTS

What did you find out about academic writing in your field? Which general conventions of academic writing did the authors of your article use? Which common organizational structures were employed? Were there any elements that you could not find in the article you chose? State your findings clearly.

DISCUSSION

Having analyzed your data, what conclusions can you draw about academic writing in general and specific writing conventions in your discipline? How are the general academic conventions presented in AWG similar/different to those in your discipline? Did you note any limitations in your study, for example, the need to analyze more research articles to draw generalizations about your findings?

CONCLUSION

How has this assignment helped you to become familiar with academic writing conventions in general and those in your particular discipline? What recommendations can you make for writers/researchers in your field? What related area(s) would you suggest for further study?

APPENDIX B

RESEARCH PROJECT: PHASES 1, 2 AND 3

Input from Students
Tutorial Groups R15/R16
Faculty/School _____

(The objective of this simple questionnaire is to gather feedback to improve the research project. I appreciate your time and effort very much).

Kindly circle the answers of your choice and do not worry about language. Where required, you may write in point form.

(1=not useful at all; 2=somewhat useful; 3=useful; 4= very useful;)

1a. On a scale of 1–4, how would you rate the usefulness of the research project?

    1_____2_____3_____4

1b. Give two reasons for your choice.

    _____

    _____

2a. On a scale of 1–4, how would you rate the usefulness of Phase 1 of the research project?

    1_____2_____3_____4

2b. Give two reasons for your choice.

    _____

    _____

2c. What did you learn about academic writing conventions in general? Mention any three features.

    _____

    _____

2d. What did you learn about conventions specific to your discipline? Mention any three features.

_____

3a. On a scale of 1–4, how would you rate the usefulness of Phase 2 of the research project?

1_____2 _____3 _____4

3b. Give two reasons for your choice.

_____

_____

3c. What did you learn about organization of research articles in general? Mention any two or three features.

_____

_____

3d. What did you learn about the organization of research articles in your own discipline? Mention any two or three features.

_____

_____

4a. On a scale of 1–4, how would you rate Phase 3 of the research project?

1_____2 _____3 _____4

4b. Give two reasons for your choice.

_____

_____

4c. What did you learn about research writing from this phase of the project? You may mention learning points about research writing that you learnt at this phase.

_____

_____

_____

_____

5. Kindly give us suggestions on how we can improve the research project. Please write 3–5 suggestions.

_____

_____

_____

_____

_____

Thank you very much.
Dr Chitra Varaprasad

SECTION IV

EAP assessment and academic argument

Jenny Kemp and Glenn Fulcher

Performance decision trees: developing domain-specific criteria for teaching and assessment

Introduction

English for Specific Purposes (ESP) is an increasingly broad field, with specialisms ranging from Law and Engineering to Tourism and Marketing. Even EAP pre-sessional courses are now being divided up, with one course for Business Studies, another for Media students or Economists, for example. Testing the language ability of these students is thus a little different from testing General English, or even English for General Academic Purposes, as what is important is 'contextualised communicative language ability' (Douglas, 2000, p. 1). Yet there is a tendency to merely adopt or adapt existing general tasks and criteria for these specific contexts of language use.

But what of validity? As practitioners, we should be asking the following important questions:

- Does our test really test what we want it to test?
- Do we know what the scores mean?

- Can the results be extrapolated to the target discourse domain? In other words does the score really tell us what the student will be able to do on their academic course?
- Do we really know what goes on in the target discourse domain, or are we relying on intuition and limited information and experience?
- Would a content specialist consider the same characteristics important as the ones we have focused on?

Such questions are important when developing any test. For us, these questions led to the development of performance decision trees (PDTs), a new means of assessing productive language ability firmly based in linguistic analysis (Fulcher, 2010; Fulcher, Davidson & Kemp, 2011). PDTs attempt to capture more of the interactive and communicative nature of speech than is currently possible in traditional linear rating scales. As a result, PDTs can be constructed to help define and assess language use, give diagnostic feedback and develop ESP syllabuses. Their use would also strengthen the inferences we are able to make about student ability. This paper will first discuss the theory behind PDTs. It will then illustrate the value of this approach, as well as the procedure, with reference to the development of a prototype PDT for one specific domain, that of travel agency discourse, using original data and with reference to the relevant literature from the fields of both marketing and discourse analysis. The authors aim to show how PDTs might be useful in EAP and ESP practice.

THEORETICAL FOUNDATIONS

Our starting point was research done into data-based approaches in the 80s and 90s. The earliest attempt to use language production as a basis for assessment criteria was Fulcher's work (1987; 1996) on data-based rating scales, where descriptors were based on the analysis of actual speech. However, the level of detail in the descriptors was rather complex for raters, who need to assess a sample of language in real time (Fulcher, 2003). Another important innovation was the development of empirically-derived, binary-choice, boundary-definition scales (EBBs) by Upshur and Turner (1995). While not based on as rich a description of discourse data as was Fulcher's scale, EBBs are easier to use, since raters judge performance by answering a series of binary 'yes–no' questions. Performance Decision Trees build on both these methodologies, combining 'thick description' (Fulcher, 1996) with practicality.

There are various principles underlying performance assessment. Firstly,

communication occurs within a context; it is therefore essential that tasks assess a student's ability to communicate within a specific context which pertains to the real world (Douglas, 2000). What is being measured is not success in achieving a task but rather the knowledge and command of the elements that make up a communicative performance, including the interplay between language and specialised content knowledge (ibid.). In the target domain, test takers will be expected to perform professionally, with particular associated patterns of language and behaviour (Skehan, 1984). Thus 'indigenous assessment criteria' (Jacoby, 1998, cited in Douglas, 2000, p. 68) are of great importance – that is, the criteria used by specialists in the field. In order to reflect these criteria, tasks need to be authentic – both in terms of the situation and the interaction – with enough features of the domain to ensure appropriate discourse is used. To achieve this, both tasks and assessment criteria should be based on observation and description. Finally, it is essential to have a practical and meaningful scoring mechanism – one that is useable by non-specialist raters, but which reflects the indigenous, domain-specific assessment criteria.

However, despite the importance of the above factors, many practitioners are still using general rating scales, the most popular of which at the moment is the Common European Framework of Reference (CEFR). In these measurement-driven approaches (see Fulcher, Davidson & Kemp, 2011, for discussion), language proficiency is traditionally perceived as linear and hierarchical. This is partly because performance data is only considered *after* a scale has been constructed, not as integral to its development. Yet the acquisition of the language and communication skills that are necessary to perform well in an academic environment is not, as Westhoff (2007, p. 678) put it, 'climb[ing] the CEFR ladder'. As practitioners, we are well aware of the difficulty of scoring performance on such scales, where a criterion mentioned at one level may not be mentioned at the next, requiring a judgement to be made which can seem arbitrary.

This and other concerns led to the development of the PDT, a performance data-driven approach which 'escape[s] from the illusion of linear development in language use' (Fulcher et al., 2011, p. 2), and which prioritises the principles mentioned above. The PDT described here was developed to assess speaking ability within one particular service encounter context, that of a travel agent (hereafter TA). Although it has been established that context and interaction are particularly important in the assessment of speaking (Jacoby & McNamara, 1999; Jacoby & Ochs, 1995), partly as a result of the socially-constructed nature of discourse (Swain, 2001), this has not heretofore been reflected in the scoring of performance.

DEVELOPING A PDT

The starting point of the process of developing a PDT is a detailed description of the discourse domain. This is approached from two perspectives: a detailed analysis of original data, and a survey of related literature – for our purposes, recordings of

TA discourse and a review of research carried out within the fields of the travel industry and marketing, as well as within discourse studies. These areas of investigation were explored separately, producing a rich description of the target domain, *before* the findings of the literature review were compared with the original discourse data and the PDT constructed. However, to show how these feed into the scoring model it is suggested that the reader refer to the PDT in Appendix 1 throughout.

The analysis of the discourse domain includes a detailed description of interaction in the specific context – here, interaction between a TA and client(s).[1] Three elements of interactional competence can be identified: *discourse competence, competence in discourse management* and *pragmatic competence*. Discourse competence (Canale & Swain, 1980) is dependent on familiarity with a particular genre and script, and refers to the ability to recognise and act within these constraints. For example, understanding the obligatory elements of a service encounter and having the ability to articulate these elements. Figure 1 shows the typical discourse elements of a TA service encounter, according to our research. Understandably, it shares features with Hasan's (1985) Generic Structure Potential (GSP) for service encounters. This is closely linked to context and is how we recognise the genre; but it is also associated with specific language and language functions such as greetings, and asking and responding to questions. Thus the ability to articulate the basic obligatory

---

[1] For this study, five recordings were made in travel agencies in the East Midlands. Further details regarding data collection and analysis can be found in Fulcher et al. (2011).

Greeting

(optional element: *Sale Initiation*)

Need (i.e., *Sale Enquiry or Request*)

Compliance   } **The Service** (which frequently involves multiple exchanges and is not unlike Mitchell's 'investigation of the object of sale' (1957/1978, p. 175)

Resolution (Client decides whether or not to buy/course of action)

(optional elements: *Pay, Goods Handover*)

Closing sequence

Figure 1 Description of the discourse domain: discourse elements of a TA service encounter

elements of a TA service encounter is the first criterion for evaluation on the PDT.

However, participants must also have the ability to move the discourse through the stages of the script. The five main criteria we found for managing this type of discourse are:

1. (elicitation of) identification of purpose + provision of an explicit response
2. identification of participant roles
3. use of backchannelling
4. marking of transition boundaries
5. management of closings

These can all be found on the PDT in Appendix 1. The first is the identification of purpose and provision of an explicit response, which constitute the articulation of the Need and Compliance. This may be elicited through a Greeting, or a phrase such as 'Can I help you?' Elicitation may also be non-verbal. Here is an example from our data (see Appendix 2 for transcript notation):

```
TA:        ((looks up from
           computer))
Client:    Do you do airline
           tickets?
TA:        We do, yes Sir.
```

Here, the roles of service provider and client are established early on. It is important that roles are clearly defined, and Coupland (1983) argues that this is most clearly achieved through explicit interrogatives. Once roles are established, listenership is usually indicated through the use of backchannelling (McCarthy, 2003):

```
TA:        I can make a note to
           check sort of mid
           November=
Client:    =Mm [mm]
TA:        =  [and] then I can
           give you a call
```

Topic transition boundaries should also be marked (Coupland, 1983). Most proficient speakers do this lexically, using what are commonly referred to as 'discourse markers' and other 'signposting language':

```
TA:        Right okay. We can
           also order currency
           and things like that
           for you.
```

Boundaries may also be marked implicitly through filled pauses. However, extended pauses may lead to communication breakdown and therefore the occurrence of filled pauses is important.

TA discourse differs from many other types of service encounter in that there may not be a sale first time; in other words, it may involve a series of visits. Nevertheless, there is *potential* for sale and consequently the closing stage is very important in order to ensure a return. A successful TA will manage this stage carefully (ibid.). Competent speakers perform an extended pre-closing sequence, followed by leave-taking and ending with a single-item bridge (such as 'OK' or 'Fine'. See Fulcher et al. (2011) for an extended example). These are reflected in the PDT.

Our third element of communicative competence is pragmatic competence, which concerns the relational aspects of the discourse; in the current context, this involves the elements of TA communication that are used to make the interaction both successful and pleasant. These interpersonal elements are 'non-obligatory' in Hasan's terms, and have been seen as 'side-sequencing' by some discourse specialists (e.g., Ventola, 1987), as participants seem to step outside the servicescape script temporarily. However, the very term 'small talk', often used to describe such interaction, is misleading (Coupland, 2000; McCarthy, 2003); it is a mistake to ignore these frequently occurring elements as irrelevant (Ylänne-McEwen, 2004).

This is an example of where much can be learnt from the subject specialists, by looking at their indigenous assessment criteria. Here it is clear that the use of small talk is 'economically consequential' (Clark, Drew & Pinch, 2003, p. 25). We learn from the marketing literature that a TA service encounter is not considered purely transactional and that it is vital the service provider builds up a relationship with the customer as a way of achieving their other goals more effectively (Grönroos, 1993; Gutek, Bhappu, Liao-Troth & Cherry, 1999). Thus, customer loyalty is rated highly. Customer satisfaction is partly dependent on *rituality* (Chandon, Pierre-Yves & Philippe, 1997), which includes courtesy and confidence; but another key aspect is *rapport*.

By looking at the notion of rapport in more detail, we can see how the indigenous assessment criteria can cast light on the data collected. Rapport is defined in the marketing literature as 'a customer's perception of having an enjoyable interaction with a service provider employee, characterized by a personal connection between the two interactants' (Gremler & Gwinner, 2000, p. 92). It involves the following: warmth and humour, a good and harmonious relationship, personal interest and care, closeness, bonding and similarity, and echoing.

Our recordings were examined for evidence of these. The following example comes 7 minutes into a 12-minute encounter. The client has enquired about flights to Barcelona for a conference. The Need and Compliance have been completed, as has the Resolution: the client must decide if her dates are fixed, and whether or not to buy, and she says she will decide and contact the TA. The TA has reminded the client of other services available, such as booking

accommodation – thus, the next stage would logically be a pre-closing sequence.

(See Fulcher, 2011 for an online recording.)

There is a wealth of data here, but we will just pick out a few key elements. The TA asks: 'Have you been to Barcelona

```
TA:      Have [you been] to Barcelona=
Client:       [Er::m]
TA:      =↓before.
Client:  ↓No:::.
TA:      It's a fantastic city, you'll [love it.]
Client:                              [No, I] haven't done.
TA:      Brilliant- If you love art, you'll love Barcelona.
Client:  U::m yes I do.
TA:      Yeah. [You'll love it.]
Client:        [I do. And ] erm my sister's been but I haven't [(.) so::]
TA:      Liked it. All the Gaudi and=                          [I re]ally
Client:  =Yeah=
TA:      =It's just beautiful. (.) Lovely. [(          )]
Client:                                    [Yeah. She's]=
         = shown me lots of pho[tos before and (it's beautiful)=
TA:                            [Yeah. (.) It's lovely (.)=
Client:  =and (.) the architecture's (.) (seems amazing)]
TA:      =There's (w-) definitely have a couple of days shopping] because(.)
         er sightseeing because it's lovely. (.)It's really [nice.]
Client:                                                      [And shopping.
TA:      Shopping yeah. ((laughter)) Well that's a must isn't it. I mean we
         are female. ((laughter)) That's just got to ↑be. ((laughter))Yeah
         it's a great city.
Client: [Great.]
TA:     [Really] really [nice.]
Client:                 [Okay] Well (.) thank you very much [for(.) all
        your]=
TA:                                                         [That's o↓kay.]
Client: =↓help.
```

before?' It is a common question, such as a friend might ask, and sounds both natural and friendly. Thus the TA is here projecting herself as a friend, as a fellow traveller. She also enthuses about the city, which she seems to have some personal knowledge of, describing it as *fantastic, brilliant, beautiful, lovely, great* and *nice*. This reiteration produces a cohesive lexical chain; but as McCarthy (1991, p. 66) has argued 'reiteration is not a chance event', and the language here is also persuasive. Moreover, it is echoed by the client – a sign of convergence and similarity.

The TA then returns to the topic of sightseeing, and may thus be attempting to return to business. However, she says *shopping* instead of *sightseeing*, a slip of the tongue picked up by the client. The repetition of *shopping* and laughter are both clear signs of similarity, camaraderie and rapport. Amidst this laughter, the TA aligns with the client still further through gender identification. Rapport having clearly been achieved, she sums up: 'Yeah it's a great city'. The client responds by echoing *great*, a sign of agreement and rapport. Moreover, it also acts as a pre-closing signal.

Through relational talk, the TA seems to have been quite successful in building up a service relationship with the client. There are distinct indications of rapport, a key factor in customer relations and the potential for customer loyalty.

We mention that laughter is a sign of rapport. Other non-verbal indicators include eye contact and smiling (e.g., Gabbott & Hogg, 2000). It is also important to fill extended silences, as these have also been shown to create distance and lead to a negative evaluation (ibid.). There are many potential silences when the TA is engaged on a time-consuming task such as looking for

information online. Our data shows these are sometimes filled by the TA, who may give a running commentary of what they are doing, and at other times by relational sequences initiated by the client. Below is an example of both – the TA explains what she is doing, and the client initiates small talk. Such avoidance of silence contributes to a perception of care and to a harmonious relationship:

```
(6.5)      ((TA trying to
           access information
           on computer))
TA:        Can't get on at the
           moment I'm afraid
           (.hhh)
(12.0)     ((TA looking at
           screen, waiting for
           page to upload))
Client:    You haven't been
           open here very long
           have you.
TA:        No just over a month
           now. (.) Where would
           you like to fly
           from?
Client:    Um (.) Somewhere
           local.
```

The above can be related back to our definition of rapport, of which we have seen clear evidence. This and other features found in our description of the discourse domain have been incorporated into the scoring model. Thus the PDT combines the discourse elements we identified and the indigenous assessment criteria valued by specialists in the field.

The PDT is designed for use with a paired role-play activity, such as that devised by Mills (2009, in Fulcher et al., 2011). As some elements of the PDT are more relevant to the TA, the left side (Discourse Competence and Management) could be used to rate both speakers, whereas the right (Pragmatic Competence) would be used only for the TA. Furthermore, the roles are unequal in terms of power. Therefore, depending on the purpose of the test, two tasks could be set, with participants swapping roles.

The TA could receive a score of between 0 and 19. However, as the PDT is not a linear scale, a score of, for example, 10 could be achieved in more than one way. A PDT also allows a diagnostic profile to be created. This would enable test-takers to be given feedback on areas requiring improvement, but would also indicate potential areas of focus for classroom instruction.

CONCLUSIONS: POTENTIAL APPLICATIONS FOR PDTs

The performance decision tree is a means of assessment based on a detailed description of authentic discourse which incorporates indigenous assessment criteria. Thus it is pragmatic (Fulcher et al., 2011) and may be a much more valid and reliable means of assessing ESP students. The PDT would seem to be much simpler to use in a live-rating situation, by both expert and inexperienced raters; however, further

research is needed to investigate its properties and usefulness. An additional advantage is that the PDT is transparent: areas requiring improvement are clear, as are potential areas of focus for classroom instruction. The potential applications within an EAP or ESP setting are varied. This paper has focused on one ESP domain, but PDTs would seem to be suitable for many other domain-specific contexts, such as interaction between a doctor and patient, lawyer and client, teacher and pupil, employer and employee. Other possibilities include assessing interaction in seminars and monologic speech events, such as presentations. Furthermore, their potential for assessing writing ability could be explored.

There are undoubtedly considerations that have yet to be investigated. Our discourse description was based on a native-speaker model, but this may not be appropriate in other contexts. Nevertheless, whatever the chosen model and discourse domain, PDTs represent an innovation in domain-specific scoring that is likely to prove a significant development in the way we assess the contextualised productive language ability of our students.

REFERENCES

Atkinson, J. M., & Heritage, J. (Eds.). (1984). *Structures of Social Action*. Cambridge: Cambridge University Press.

Canale, M., & Swain, M. (1980). Theoretical bases of communicative approaches to second language teaching and testing. *Applied Linguistics*, *1*(1), 1–47.

Chandon J. L., Pierre-Yves, L., & Philippe, J. (1997). Service encounter dimensions – a dyadic perspective: Measuring the dimensions of service encounters as perceived by customers and personnel. *International Journal of Service Industry Management*, *8*(1), 65–86.

Clark, C., Drew, P., & Pinch, T. (2003). Managing prospect affiliation and rapport in real-life sales encounters. *Discourse & Society, 5*(1), 5–31.

Coupland, J. (Ed.) (2000). *Small talk.* London: Pearson Education Limited.

Coupland, N. (1983). Patterns of encounter management: Further arguments for discourse variables. *Language in Society 12,* 459–76.

Douglas, D. (2000). *Assessing Languages for Specific Purposes.* Cambridge: Cambridge University Press.

Fulcher, G. (1987). Tests of oral performance: The need for data-based criteria. *English Language Teaching Journal, 41*(4), 287–291.

Fulcher, G. (1996). Does thick description lead to smart tests? A data-based approach to rating scale construction. *Language Testing, 13*(2), 208–238.

Fulcher, G. (2003). *Testing second language speaking.* London: Longman/Pearson.

Fulcher, G. (2010). *Practical language testing.* London: Hodder.

Fulcher, G. (2011). Performance Decision Trees. A *languagetesting.info* monthly feature for March 2011. Retrieved from http://languagetesting.info/features/ rating/pdts.html

Fulcher, G., Davidson, F., & Kemp, J. (2011). Effective rating scale development: Performance Decision Trees. *Language Testing, 28*(1), 5–29.

Gabbott, M., & Hogg, G. (2000). An empirical investigation of the impact of non-verbal communication on service evaluation. *European Journal of Marketing, 34*(3/4), 384–398.

Gremler, D. D., & Gwinner, K. P. (2000). Customer-employee rapport in service relationships. *Journal of Service Research, 3*(1), 82–104.

Grönroos, C. (1993). Toward a third phase in service quality research: Challenges and future directions. In A. T. Swartz, D. E. Bowen, and S. W. Brown (Eds.), *Advances in service marketing management,* Vol. II (pp. 49–64). Greenwich CT: JAI Press.

Gutek, B., Bhappu, A., Liao-Troth, M., & Cherry, B. (1999). Distinguishing between service relationships and encounters. *Journal of Applied Psychology, 84*(2), 218–233.

Hasan, R. (1985). The structure of a text. In M. A. K. Halliday & R. Hasan (Eds.), *Language, context and text: Aspects of language in a social-semiotic perspective* (pp. 52–69). Victoria: Deakin University Press.

Jacoby, S., & McNamara, T. (1999). Locating competence. *English for Specific Purposes, 18*(3), 213–241.

Jacoby, S., & Ochs, E. (1995). Co-construction: An introduction. *Research on Language and Social Interaction, 28*(3), 171–183.

McCarthy, M. J. (1991). *Discourse analysis for language teachers.* Cambridge: Cambridge University Press.

McCarthy, M. J. (2003). Talking back: 'Small' interactional response tokens in everyday conversation. *Research on Language and Social Interaction, 36*(1), 33–63.

Mitchell, T. F. (1957/1978). The language of buying and selling in Cyrenaica: A situational statement. *Hespèris,* XLIV, 31–71. Reprinted in T. F. Mitchell (1978), *Principles of Firthian linguistics* (pp. 167–200). London: Longman.

Skehan, P. (1984). Issues in the testing of English for Specific Purposes. *Language Testing, 1,* 202–220.

Swain, M. (2001). Examining dialogue: Another approach to content specification and to validating inferences drawn from test scores. *Language Testing, 18*(3), 275–302.

Upshur, J., & Turner, C. E. (1995). Constructing rating scales for second language tests. *English Language Teaching Journal, 49*(1), 3–12.

Ventola, E. (1987). *The structure of social interaction.* London: Francis Pinter.

Westhoff, G. (2007). Challenges and opportunities of the CEFR for reimagining foreign language pedagogy. *The Modern Language Journal, 91*(4), 676–679.

Ylänne-McEwen, V. (2004). Shifting alignment and negotiating sociality in travel agency discourse. *Discourse Studies, 6*(4), 517–536.

Appendix 1

The performance decision tree (PDT) for assessing travel agency interaction

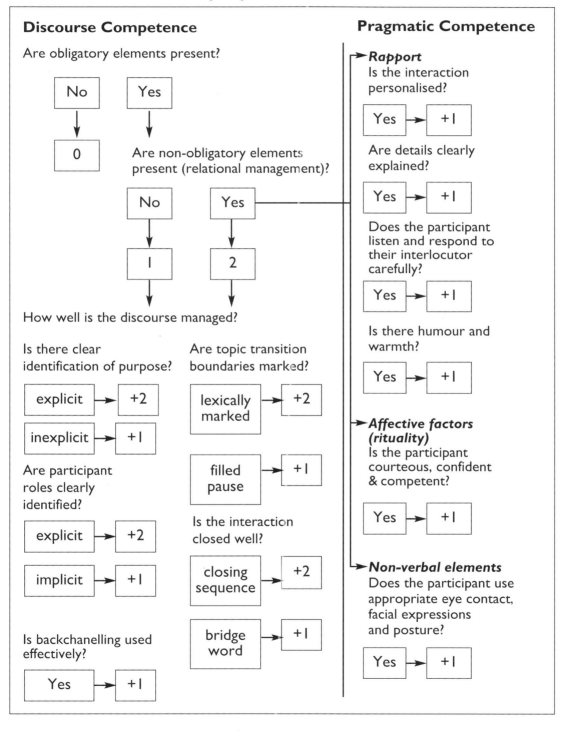

Discourse Competence

Are obligatory elements present?

No → 0

Yes → Are non-obligatory elements present (relational management)?

No → 1

Yes → 2

How well is the discourse managed?

Is there clear identification of purpose?

explicit → +2

inexplicit → +1

Are participant roles clearly identified?

explicit → +2

implicit → +1

Is backchanelling used effectively?

Yes → +1

Are topic transition boundaries marked?

lexically marked → +2

filled pause → +1

Is the interaction closed well?

closing sequence → +2

bridge word → +1

Pragmatic Competence

Rapport
Is the interaction personalised?

Yes → +1

Are details clearly explained?

Yes → +1

Does the participant listen and respond to their interlocutor carefully?

Yes → +1

Is there humour and warmth?

Yes → +1

Affective factors (rituality)
Is the participant courteous, confident & competent?

Yes → +1

Non-verbal elements
Does the participant use appropriate eye contact, facial expressions and posture?

Yes → +1

APPENDIX 2

TRANSCRIPT NOTATION

The transcript notation is based on Jefferson. See Atkinson and Heritage (1984, pp. ix–xvi).

overlapping utterances	[ ]
latching	=
time intervals (seconds)	(4.5)
slight (untimed) pause	(.)
extended sound or syllable	::
abrupt cut-off	-
intonation: marked rise	↑
intonation: marked fall	↓
emphasis	<u>text underlined</u>
audible inhalation	(.hhh)
audible aspiration	(hhh)
other vocalisations	((laughs))
contextual detail	((TA typing noisily))
transcriptionist doubt	( )

Sarah Beaumont and Andy Gillett

An investigation into the role of spoken English competence in an assessed business discussion in an ELF context

Introduction

The Graduate Certificate in Business (GCIB) is a pre-Masters programme run by the University of Hertfordshire Business School. It is a 15-week course, with the aim of preparing students for a range of business-related Masters courses.

In order to achieve its aim, the programme attempts to present the language and content together as an integrated whole. For that reason, the teaching is organised around the subject lecturer and the English lecturer working together. The idea is one of team teaching (Johns & Dudley-Evans, 1980; Dudley-Evans & St John, 1998). Of the several levels of subject-language integration mentioned by Dudley-Evans and St John (1998), team teaching is the final level, since it involves subject and language specialists working together for some of the time in the classroom. However, it goes further than that, in as far as the materials – written and spoken – drawn on by the language teacher are those used by the subject lecturer in teaching the subject. More importantly, the tasks carried out in the language classes are those that are required by the subject lecturer.

There are two main reasons for our choice of teaching method. The first is linguistic, in that, as Hyland (2000) has made clear, disciplines differ in their uses of language. An EAP teacher cannot be expected to be an expert in every discipline, so a team-teaching method seems to be a good way to deal with this lack of expertise. Secondly, given many of the students are primarily interested in developing their business knowledge and skills rather than their language, integrating the language with the content is motivating and leads to increased learning (Brinton, Snow & Wesche, 1989; Hamilton, 2010; Nordmeyer, 2010).

However, Dudley-Evans and St John's belief (1998), that one reason that this kind of teaching is successful is because the roles of the two teachers are clearly defined, does not seem to be realised in practice. In the reality of the classroom, it seems difficult, or impossible, to distinguish between teaching business and teaching the language of business, especially in a subject such as accounting. Language does not exist in isolation, but is strongly connected with what people do with it, with their linguistic practices (Lillis & Scott, 2007). Furthermore, the subject teacher cannot teach the content of the subject without using language.

Our approach sees developing language and business content as two sides of the same coin. This applies equally to the linguistic as well as other skills and practices that the students are expected to develop. As Wingate (2006) has pointed out, it is not possible to separate learning how to study in higher education from the practices of the content subjects, and this needs to be discussed in the context of students' overall academic development. For that reason out-of-context or 'bolt-on' (Bennett, Dunne & Carré, 2000) study-skills courses, as opposed to those that are integrated or embedded, are unlikely to be effective (Wingate, 2006). As well as the problem that these skills form an integral part of the subject practices, there is the danger that these courses 'may not be taken seriously by students, as they are not seen to be relevant to disciplinary study' (Bennett, Dunne & Carré, 2000, p. 166) and instead need to be taught 'within the disciplinary setting' (ibid.). For this reason, our approach is to embed the learning of language and its associated skills into the subject teaching.

This is our basic teaching philosophy. However, although it is clear to us that the subject and language need to be integrated when teaching, it is worth asking to what extent the language, or content, can be separated out in the assessment? Is it possible to test accounting content, in this case, without testing language? Moreover, is it possible to test language without taking into account the content? Bridgeman and Carlson's (1984) survey of subject specialist staff shows that content, answering the question and addressing the topic were the most important in writing tasks. Therefore, English lecturers need to take content seriously when assessing students' performance.

The aim of this study was to investigate the business and language lecturers' marking of the students' oral production and see to what extent the two markers' grades were independent of each other.

BACKGROUND

The course structure of GCIB includes a two-week preparatory block, and the first main teaching block – Block A. This is followed by a reflection and further preparation block and then the second main teaching block – Block B.

In each of the two main teaching blocks, the students study two modules out of a possible three, one is compulsory and one is an option (see Figure 1). Each module has ten hours of class time per week on two days: four hours with a business lecturer and six hours with an English lecturer. The English lecturer attends all the business lecturer's classes and the business lecturer may attend the English classes, but this is not always the case.

Week	Content	
1	Induction for Block A	
2		
3	*Block A: Core*	*Block A: Options*
4	Economic Environment of Business	People Management
5		Managing Accounting Information
6		
7		
8		
9	Preparation for Block B	
10	*Block B: Core*	*Block B: Options*
11	Business Strategy	Introduction to Research Methods
12		Financial Management
13		
14		
15		

Figure 1 Course content

The entrance requirements are a first degree or similar qualification, not necessarily in business. The students are from a range of countries, mainly east and south-east Asia, the Indian sub-continent and central Africa. Most of the students are new to the UK higher education system, but a sizeable minority have undertaken undergraduate work in the UK.

For the last two years, the authors have taught the Block A option module, Managing Accounting Information. Sarah is the business lecturer and Andy the English lecturer.

MODULE CONTENT

The aim of the module is to provide an applied understanding of the role and function of financial information in the decision and communication process of an organisation. It provides an understanding of how accounting data is gathered and how financial information is used to plan, monitor and control the progress of the organisation. Students are expected to apply these techniques to particular industry sectors and organisations.

To reflect the range of assessment activities required of students on a post-graduate programme (Gillett & Hammond, 2009), the GCIB uses a wide range of assessment tasks. The module is wholly assessed by coursework, consisting of an individual written report and a group discussion. For the former, the students write a report interpreting a set of published accounts. For the latter, students work in groups of three to five to prepare a ten-minute discussion on the usefulness and future of budgeting.

The assignments are marked jointly by both the lecturers, with the marks weighted equally. The business lecturer comments on and grades the business content, including knowledge of the subject and use of specific technical language. The English lecturer comments on and grades the language, including fluency of interaction, organisation and coherence, pronunciation and accuracy.

METHOD

In the group discussion element of the assessment of the module described here, students work in multinational/multilingual groups to take part in an assessed discussion on the usefulness and future of budgeting.

This was investigated from two angles: a quantitative comparison of the marks given by the English lecturer and the Business lecturer and a more qualitative comparison between the two lecturers' views of a few selected pieces of conversation between students.

As part of the Managing Accounting Information module in the summer of 2010, a large section of the assessment of this module was a business discussion on the nature of budgeting. The discussion had two components. Firstly the group presented the findings from their research, with each group member contributing a section. This was followed by discussion with other groups. Although there was no independent language assessment, the marking scheme for this business discussion included components for business knowledge and academic skills as well as competence in English. Both these components were rated using rating scales (Upshur & Turner, 1995; Fulcher, 2003) – shown in Table 1 – and recorded on the mark sheet, as shown in Table 2. Each student was given a grade for their performance and comments were made.

Table 1 GCIB Mark Sheet

Content 50%	Grades (F=Fail)	
C1. Demonstrates a thorough knowledge and understanding of the subject gained from wide reading	A B C D F	Shows a weak knowledge and understanding of the subject with limited research
C2. Makes correct use of a wide range of technical vocabulary	A B C D F	Technical terms are not used or are used incorrectly
Language 50%		
L1. Has full command of the language, speaking fluently and confidently; excellent interactive communication	A B C D F	Communicates only basic information with frequent errors of grammar; limited interactive communication
L2. Demonstrates excellent organisation and use of linking devices; excellent timing and pacing	A B C D F	Poor organisation with a lack of linking devices; poor time management
L3. No problems with pronunciation, stress, rhythm and intonation	A B C D F	Weaknesses in pronunciation, stress, rhythm and intonation cause the listener great difficulty
L4. Excellent use of vocabulary and grammatical structures; appropriate style	A B C D F	Unable to use simple language accurately; inconsistent or inappropriate style

As the groups were multilingual, we needed to assess the abilities of the students interacting with each other in this English as a Lingua Franca (ELF) (Jenkins, 2011) situation. We could then compare the business lecturers' assessment of the students' competence in business knowledge and skills with the English lecturers' assessment of their English language ability. From this we could then draw conclusions about the relationship between the two, the difficulties of assessment of the two strands separately, and whether this method of assessment is useful or necessary.

RESULTS

Each student was given a grade for each of the categories C1–2, L1–4. Correlations between the different categories were calculated and these are shown in Table 2.

Table 2 Correlations between individual marks

	C1	**C2**	**C (Total)**	**L1**	**L2**	**L3**	**L4**	**L (Total)**
C1	1.00							
C2	0.87	1.00						
C (Total)	0.97	0.96	1.00					
L1	0.88	0.81	0.87	1.00				
L2	0.78	0.77	0.80	0.79	1.00			
L3	0.80	0.83	0.84	0.92	0.75	1.00		
L4	0.73	0.83	0.80	0.86	0.84	0.87	1.00	
L (Total)	0.85	0.86	0.88	0.96	0.90	0.95	0.95	1.00

The total language mark was plotted against the total content mark, as shown in Figure 2.

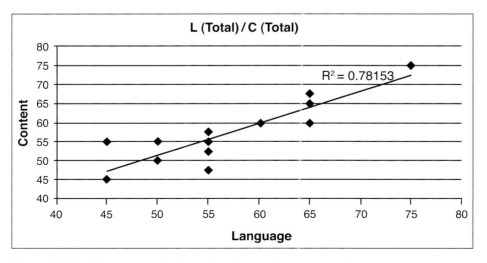

Figure 2 Total language mark plotted against total content mark

The correlation coefficient (C) shows the relationship between the two markers. It can be seen from Table 2 that the coefficients are in the range 0.8–0.97. These show a strong (Cohen, 1988, p. 79–81) relationship between the language marks and the content marks.

The graph shown in Figure 2 shows a good straight-line fit with an R-squared (coefficient of determination) value of 0.7815.

Next we can see some samples of students' oral production with comments from the two lecturers involved. In general, it is difficult to evaluate small individual samples. In practice the overall contribution of each student is evaluated more holistically. Marking is agreed in discussion between the two lecturers.

EXAMPLE 1

VB: I have a question. What do you think if you set up the company, for example, a company they just care about their profits, they don't care about their customer so what do you think about this in your problem?

Sal: Well, most of the companies, they consist on the sales, how much they want to sell because they want to make a profit. They don't care about the people, if they are happy from the goods they sell or not. So only they need to make a high budget through the year. This is the answer. So anyone is going to add?

XQ: Let me continue to answer this question. I think the better budgeting is focus on the cost of the company but not, not, but it doesn't means we don't consider of the company's profits.

COMMENTS ON EXAMPLE 1

Business lecturer:
This interaction shows limited focus on budgeting and some confusion between sales, profits and budgets. The English is not always clear enough to follow the accounting points made.

English lecturer:
Some difficulties but generally conveys the message and the students interact well; effective but limited range and control of appropriate grammatical structures. Adequate range of academic vocabulary and business terms.

EXAMPLE 2

CH: Yeah, erm, so I have some questions. Expanding your companies, but, you have a budget. So what do you think about the limitation?

A: Well, we do have some limitations to a certain extent. But because of technology the companies can forecast furthermore. And then set their budgets, so they do have an idea of what they are actually budgeting, so I think the technology plays an important information, because they can collect more information, they can store more information, they can process the information more quicker.

CH: So what is the important advantage of the better budgeting? What do you think?

COMMENTS ON EXAMPLE 2

Business lecturer:

The question is poorly phrased, but the respondent picks up one point, although he then goes off at a tangent and is not addressing the point about limitations. The point he makes about technology does have some relevance to the material under discussion.

English lecturer:

Some difficulties but generally conveys the message; effective but limited range and control of appropriate grammatical structures. A has a good range of academic vocabulary and business terms. CH's short contribution is accurate and to the point.

EXAMPLE 3

J: I want to ask a question. I've heard that they have not any fixed plan in beyond budgeting. How do you think the beyond budgeting company can win in the marketplace? Because they have any, they have not any fixed plan.

Sak: They can success because they have not a fixed plan because as you know about world business nowsady, nowadays it's not predictable, it's unpredictable, yeah, and because it unpredictable it's almost impossible to plan the long term so let's see the real situation and plan step by step.

COMMENTS ON EXAMPLE 3

Business lecturer:

A good question with a relevant answer, although it lacks depth. The second contribution has insufficient clarity to gain credit for accounting knowledge.

English lecturer:

J is mostly accurate and clear. Sak's contribution causes some problems and does not really convey the message, as it has limited control of appropriate grammatical structures. Adequate range of academic vocabulary and business terms.

EXAMPLE 4

Sum: Yeah, actually I have question for M. And as Sak and you mentioned actually, and it's that managers can decide actually and it's not from the top, it's not coming to down, and they can decide actually whatever they want. And don't you think it's maybe can create to, you know maybe loss, maybe that their decision is not the correct decision actually and they can maybe take the wrong decisions, like because there is no supervision, maybe, or based on your, this one, no supervision from the top? And don't you think that it can lead to loss of the company actually, maybe some losses?

M: I think that when the department has developed authority to handling the real situation, they took, they continue to improve, and it take everything about around it. They may take wrong decision but they have the flexibility to do it and redo it again to without the top managers. But in the …

COMMENTS ON EXAMPLE 4

Business lecturer:
The question reads as rather disjointed, but in live speech it does make sense and is a relevant point addressing the material under consideration. The answer is in the right area and shows some knowledge, although the lack of coherence means it is unclear what the student actually understands.

English lecturer:
Sum has some difficulties but generally conveys the message; effective but limited range and control of appropriate grammatical structures. M is similar. Good range of academic vocabulary and business terms.

CONCLUSION

The results from Table 2 show a strong (Cohen, 1988, pp. 79–81) relationship between the language marks and the content marks. This suggests that there is a degree of dependence between the various categories. It is therefore possible to predict the results obtained in one category from those obtained in another (Gravetter & Wallnau, 1996, pp. 500–505). In other words, the different categories are to some extent measuring the same abilities. If we, for example, believe that pronunciation and business knowledge are distinct abilities, then we would not expect a high correlation between the two scores (Bachman, 1990, p.

259–260; Baker, 1989, p. 58). But as a high correlation is obtained, the business lecturer is – to some extent – assessing pronunciation when marking business content. The same results plotted in Figure 2 again show a high R-squared value, which suggests that the value of one variable can be reliably predicted from the value of another category (Gravetter & Wallnau, 1996, p. 513).

The more qualitative assessment, looking at the comments by the two lecturers, shows similar results. There is a general agreement between the assessment of the business content by the business lecturer and that of the language quality by the language lecturer. This is not surprising, as, if the language is very bad, then the business lecturer would not be able to assess the content and vice-versa.

Our results therefore support our suggestion that language and business content are best seen as two sides of the same coin and cannot be separated. It would be unreasonable to expect high-quality content with weak language or highly competent language that lacks content knowledge. From a summative assessment point of view, then, it would seem that the language lecturer is not contributing much. This is not to say that the language lecturer does not contribute to the assessment because, from a formative point of view, the feedback from the language lecturer is essential.

REFERENCES

Bachman, L. F. (1990). *Fundamental considerations in language testing*. Oxford: Oxford University Press.

Baker, D. (1989). *Language testing: A critical survey and practical guide*. London: Edward Arnold.

Bennett, N., Dunne, E., & Carré, C. (2000). *Skills development in higher education and employment*. Buckingham: The Society for Research into Higher Education and Open University Press.

Bridgeman, B., & Carlson, S. B. (1984). Survey of academic writing tasks. *Written Communication, 1*, 247–280.

Brinton, D. M., Snow, M. A., & Wesche, M. B. (1989). *Content-based instruction*. New York: Newbury House.

Cohen, J. W. (1988). *Statistical power analysis for the behavioural sciences* (2nd ed.). Hillsdale, NJ: Lawrence Erlbaum Associates.

Dudley-Evans, T., & St John, M. J. (1998). *Developments in English for Specific Purposes*. Cambridge: Cambridge University Press.

Fulcher, G. (2003). *Testing second language speaking*. Harlow: Pearson.

Gillett, A. J., & Hammond, A. C. (2009). Mapping the maze of assessment: An investigation into practice. *Active Learning in Higher Education, 10*, 120–137.

Gravetter, F. J., & Wallnau, L. B. (1996). *Statistics for the behavioural sciences* (4th ed.). St. Paul, MN: West Publishing Company.

Hamilton, E. (2010). Motivating students to develop their English literacy skills through science. In J. Nordmeyer & S. Barduhn (Eds.), *Integrating language and content* (pp. 231–240). Alexandria, VA: TESOL.

Hyland, K. (2000). *Disciplinary discourses*. Harlow: Pearson Education.

Jenkins, J. (2011). Accommodating (to) ELF in the international university. *Journal of Pragmatics, 43*, 926–936.

Johns, T. F., & Dudley-Evans, A. (1980). An experiment in team teaching of overseas postgraduate students of transportation and plant biology. In *Team teaching in ESP* (*ELT Documents, 106*, pp. 6–23). London: British Council.

Lillis, T., & Scott, M. (2007). Defining academic literacies research: Issues of epistemology, ideology and strategy. *Journal of Applied Linguistics, 4*, 5–32.

Nordmeyer, J. (2010). Putting content-based second language instruction in context. In J. Nordmeyer & S. Barduhn (Eds.), *Integrating language and content* (pp. 1–16). Alexandria, VA: TESOL.

Upshur, J. A., & Turner, C. E. (1995). Constructing rating scales for second language tests. *ELT Journal, 49*, 3–12.

Wingate, U. (2006). Doing away with study skills. *Teaching in Higher Education, 11*, 457–469.

JOHN SLAGHT

AUTHENTICITY AND NEED IN THE DESIGN OF EAP READING-INTO-WRITING TESTS

There is a compelling argument that students on EAP reading programmes should be tested in a way which most matches their needs on future academic courses, and that assessment measures should simulate the future academic experience as authentically as possible.

Much has been said about authenticity in language testing over the past 30 years. Spolsky (1985, pp. 31–40) went as far as to say that a lack of authenticity led to 'a threat of generalizability' about language proficiency. It seems, therefore, reasonable to suggest that along with reliability, validity, wash back, interractiveness and practicality, authenticity ranks among the six key requirements of a language test. Bachman (1990, p. 300) states that target language use (TLU) is the key to authenticity and that, in order for a test to be authentic, the test writer should harbour 'a sincere concern to somehow capture or recreate in the language test the essence of language use'. Bachman and Palmer (1996, p. 23) defined authenticity in a language test as

'the degree of correspondence of the characteristics of a given language test task to the features of target language use.' In other words, a genuinely authentic test provides the means for interpreting the candidates' performance with correlation to how language is, should or might be used in real world situations. However, as suggested by Spence-Browne (2001), the basic problem is that tests are by their very nature artificial contexts for language use.

In the context of English for Specific Academic Purposes (ESAP) programmes, the level of artificiality can be diluted to a degree by approximating appropriate activities and tasks to those which students might be expected to meet, at least for a range of Humanities/Social Sciences courses. With a reading-into-writing approach, it would seem reasonable to suggest that it is the candidates' academic literacy which is being tested, with a focus on the higher order skills of reading, including some consideration given to the micro-level skills involved in reading. The approach is essentially task-based and conveying meaning is the primary goal, along with the emphasis on real-world activities and the need to achieve the reader's reading purpose. Shaw and Weir (2007, pp. 34–42) investigate validity in testing writing, and, in particular, cognitive validity which would seem to relate to processes such as reading and thinking critically, and processing a range of information for relevance. All processes aim to achieve an authentic writing end purpose while making decisions within a time restriction which are key features of the open-book test introduced below.

The contention is that reading for a real-life purpose is an important element in approximating authenticity in testing reading. It also seems reasonable to agree with Weideman (2006) and the claim that authenticity and task-based testing are conceptually close, at least as far as reading for academic purposes is concerned. It can also be reasoned that, if a task-based integrated approach is adopted, then it is essentially an assessment of academic literacy (i.e., reading-into-writing) rather than reading as a separate language skill which is being tested. Academic literacy is developed later in the text and, with this in mind, a two-strand approach is suggested for the testing of reading. With the changes to the English proficiency assessment system put in place for in-coming international students, this approach may help to direct students towards reading in a way that will encourage them to read widely and actively during pre-sessional courses rather than focus purely on secure English language test (SELT) preparation. It is also hoped that proceeding in this manner will go some way towards convincing the students of the validity of the task-based approach in the testing of reading. It should also have an

appropriate wash-back outcome on teaching and the development of resources for academic reading.

When embarking on university courses at any level, students are met with a number of challenges as far as reading is concerned. They can be faced with literally hundreds of pages of reading per week, depending on their discipline and level of study (Slaght, 1999). Green, Unaldi and Weir (2010) also identify this as a major problem. Arguably reading occupies more time than any other area of academic study. As far as international students are concerned, not only do they have to read a lot, like all students, but they have to grapple with often conceptually difficult ideas and concepts in a foreign language – English. So a major need is learning how to manage lengthy, often dense, texts which display the 'salient' features of the text types that students are likely to encounter in the future (ibid.). Students need to read expeditiously and avoid the pernicious word-for-word deciphering of texts that they can so easily fall into (Slaght, 1999). Urquhart and Weir (1998, p. 131) describe expeditious reading as 'conscious use of strategies to sample a text in the most efficient fashion in line with a particular purpose'.

Students also need to keep their reading purpose in mind and keep reflecting as they read on whether they are indeed sticking to that purpose. They must also learn to bring themselves back on track should they begin to wander away from their purpose. Therefore a thorough understanding of the task must be firmly focused in their minds as they read. Another major skill that is required is being able to read selectively, distinguishing the important from the unimportant. They must have the confidence to reject or skim over the less relevant. Thus students must be able to 'read' critically and 'think' critically about what they are reading. They need to demonstrate in a test that they have the confidence and the competence to 'read the lines, read between the lines and read beyond the lines' (Li Du, 2010) and to perform this expeditiously.

Time management is a further factor. In the digital age, we are confronted with a boundlessness of information, ideas and facts. Being able to assess critically what can be usefully employed to meet one's reading purpose when confronted with such an array of choice is a further cognitive and practical challenge – and students must try to do this rigorously but quickly. They need to apply critical thinking skills in order to judiciously filter information, because the wider the number of options and opinions, the greater the need to evaluate information, data, attitudes, beliefs and opinions critically.

Identifying the most appropriate sources of information in a critical and efficient manner is a further essential skill – in order to make a decision about what sources of information are best fit for purpose. This brings in the need to recognize the style, currency, origin and stance of sources, as well as the relevance of the text. As Leukowicz (1997) suggests, candidates should be working with texts which have sufficient salient features to simulate academic content, style and convention. This is partly down to having sufficiently critical reading abilities and partly down to confidence and a systematic approach. These skills can be demonstrated under certain assessment conditions, which are suggested below.

Once the task has been fully understood, and as decisions about the relevance of the text content are being made, students need to make appropriate notes or annotations to enable them to operationalize their responses to the 'end' task. The end task should be devised in such a way as to encourage students to make best use of the sources they have available and identify what might be selectively summarized, suitably and appropriately paraphrased, or very judiciously quoted.

International students need to be involved in strategic reading at every stage of this process, but they have to have the competence and confidence to do this under challenging conditions. It is the job of the pre-sessional course academic staff and the writers of academic text books and materials for EAP courses to help students to develop the critical faculties, the linguistic competence and the overall confidence needed to perform to their full potential once they have embarked on their future academic courses. Therefore, I feel that the reading test should meet the needs of the international students on pre-sessional courses by encouraging effective pedagogical wash-back practice, and wide and purposeful reading as an overarching pre-sessional component – and as far as possible in an authentic context.

A possible model for this and a means of assessment is the 'open-book' test. The International Study & Language Centre or ISLC (formerly the Centre for Applied Language Studies – CALS) at the University of Reading employed this as an effective assessment measure with an award-bearing Diploma in Language and International Relations course (DELIR) almost a decade ago (Pallant & Slaght, 2002). Unfortunately, the course was dropped after a number of years because of marketing problems, but the following assessment model integrates elements of this test with elements of the topic-based Test of English for Educational

Purposes (TEEP). It is a hybrid of the two measures with added elements. The TEEP is an integrated test of reading-into-writing and listening-into-writing, which is prefaced with a focus task, where candidates are given time to consider the essay title before beginning the topic-linked reading and listening elements. Although the TEEP is the flagship test produced by the testing unit at the ISLC and is well respected in most quarters, it does to a degree suffer from the same artificiality described by Spence-Browne (2001).

Alternatively, or as part of the assessment system, the open-book test has been effectively utilized as a compromise between traditional forms of testing reading and a coursework/portfolio approach to assessment. It may be considered a test of academic literacy rather than reading, as it is difficult to create a task-based reading test which does not involve a certain amount of writing.

Geisler (1994, p. xii) defines academic literacy in part as a form of 'cultural practice identified through the use of genre', i.e., how tests are written and interpreted and in part as the individual's cognitive processing involved in reading and writing.

Hyland and Hamp-Lyons (2002, p. 4) expand this definition as:

> the complex set of skills (not necessarily only those relating to the mastery of reading and writing) which are increasingly argued to be vital underpinnings or cultural knowledge required for success in academic communities …

Figure 1 below outlines the format of the test and illustrates the characteristics of academic literacy as mentioned.

Part 1: focus (15 minutes)

Read and make some notes about the following question:

How can the academic reading needs of international students be most authentically tested?

Part 2: preparation (2 hours 45 minutes)

You have 2 hours 45 minutes to make appropriate use of Texts A–F in order to complete the following tasks to be submitted for assessment by a panel of academic members of staff:

1) Highlight & annotate relevant parts of the texts (10%)
2) Rank in order the relevance of the 6 texts (Swales, J. M. (2009); *JEAP*, Vol. 8:1 (pp. 7–8)) (10%)
3) Complete a set of slides related to the question, which could be used for a presentation (20%)
4) Write a critical review of one of the texts (brief description & comments) of approximately 150 words (20%)
5) Write an answer to the focus question of approximately 350 words (30%) + bibliography (10%)

Part 3: task completion (2 hours)

You have 2 hours to finalize and submit your responses.

Figure 1 Sample open-book test format

The open-book test (OBT) is designed as a whole-day assessment measure: three hours in the morning and two hours in the afternoon. The morning session allows students to read and deconstruct a focus question. This will be the main writing task, i.e., the 'end' task. During this time, students make appropriate notes, etc., from a range of texts, and during the afternoon session they complete a set of tasks using their notes and the texts appropriately. Students are not 'quarantined' during the lunch-break, but all notes and texts are locked away during this period.

Part 1 of the test, the focus task, is there to encourage students to generate ideas they already have about the topic, taken from the course and relevant reading. This part of the test is not graded. Part 2, the preparation stage, is graded in six ways with weighting appropriate to the practical, linguistic and cognitive challenges of each of the six tasks involved. The ability to annotate significant areas of texts and appreciate the relative value of the individual texts is rewarded, but not to the same extent as being able to present relevant key notes in PowerPoint format in an organized and clear fashion, or to write a critical review with comments as well as description. These in turn are not rewarded as highly as the ability to carry out the end task, i.e., answering the focus question.

As for the scoring of the test, it is important to ensure, as far as possible, inter-marker reliability. To this end, the texts are specifically selected or created to ensure a clear rank ordering of relevance. For the third (PowerPoint) stage, students are instructed to use only key ideas from the texts, and inter-marker reliability is achieved through table-top marking and an agreed set of key ideas being compiled or extended during standardization. The critical review content is expected to be drawn from the supplied texts. Any use of assumed knowledge for this will be considered by a principle marker in consultation with the other markers. Assessment of the initial annotation stage is based on a model, but, as with other elements of the test, it is difficult to create a watertight set of appropriate annotations, and decisions can only be made in consultation with a principle marker in certain circumstances.

There is clearly a tension between authenticity and practicality. For example, students on academic courses are unlikely to be expected to carry out such a series of tasks in just five hours. Also, teachers on highly concentrated pre-sessional programmes might argue that the described format simply would not work. Possible objections include an excessive marking load, the difficulty of insuring a rigorous standardization of marking, preventing collusion between candidates during the breaks, ensuring exam security, finding suitable texts, creating suitable tasks, and finally, managing the actual administration over a whole day. There is also the pedagogical argument that none of this tests the lower-order language skills, e.g., identifying referents, dealing with organizational features of a text at sentence level or above, etc. Possibly the most compelling objection is how to develop an appropriate mark scheme and set of descriptors. There is also the problem of the extent to which the writing up of the responses, particularly 4) and 5), is testing writing as much as it is testing reading. However, if the term 'academic literacy' is understood to incorporate both skills, this concern can be nullified. Obviously, the mark scheme and descriptors are carefully plotted, and the training and standardization of markers is crucial.

Open-book tests do mimic to a certain extent the controlled coursework assessment carried out with success in many secondary schools in the UK, where students work on their coursework under supervision, in order to eliminate as much as possible overuse of the internet or the enlistment of outside help. As mentioned, OBTs might be considered a hybrid of portfolio assessment and a topic-based reading-into-writing test such as the TEEP or, to a certain extent, elements of tests such as the Pearson Test of English. There is no reason why an OBT could not be administered in tandem with, say, a one-hour test of reading which tests discrete lower-order reading skills through multiple-choice questions (MCQs), single-answer questions (SAQs), heading banks, paragraph reorganization, etc. It could be that the open-book test format is more useful as a continuous assessment measure rather than an exit test; or, indeed, that the OBT should be combined with a more traditional form of testing reading to provide a greater composite of the candidate's ability, as suggested earlier.

The use made by candidates of texts selected for 'high stakes' tests tends to differ from the use intended by the writers of academic texts written for university-level consumption, because of the limited time frame normally afforded by tests to measure a range of reading processes and skills. The Open-Book Test is aimed at going some way towards encouraging candidates to approach texts in a way more closely resembling actual study practice on degree level courses. The strongest argument, I feel, in support of the OBT is that it is a more authentic test of the type of reading activities that students are likely to face on many academic courses. The test is aimed at measuring more directly the

ability to read and think critically, to manage time, to deal with a range of lengthy texts, to synthesize information from a range of sources, to reference appropriately, etc., – the very skills that students need to put into practice in HE. The format would appear to have strong consequential validity, even if reliability may be considered precarious in certain ways. In the final analysis, in the context of EAP reading, authenticity and need should form perhaps the very essence of any pre-sessional programme of study and the assessment measures that are part of it.

Finally, it is worth appreciating that studies in other academic domains provide interesting support for the use of OBTs as an assessment measure. A study carried out by health scientists (Heijne-Penninga, Kuks, Schonrock-Ademma, Snijders, & Cohen-Schotanus, 2010) focused on the need for students to both use and manage knowledge. This research differentiates between what is termed 'core' knowledge and the 'backup' knowledge, which students need to understand and use properly with the help of references if so desired. The backup knowledge, they claim, is what is deduced from open-book texts and the core knowledge is what the students have already learnt and should be able to apply. Statistical data from 14 such double-subtest open-book tests given to first and second year university medical students were analyzed for two cohorts (N = 435 and N = 449) with multilevel analysis, in accordance with generalizability theory. The reliability of the open-book sections of the separate tests varied between 0.712 and 0.850. Obviously, more extensive research is essential to support the reliability of open-book tests, but from the above there is some strength in support of such a form of assessment.

REFERENCES

Bachman, L. F. (1990). *Fundamental considerations in Language Testing*. OUP: Oxford.

Bachman, L. F., & Palmer, A. (1996). *Language Testing in Practice*. OUP: Oxford.

Geisler, C. (1994). *Academic literacy & the nature of expertise*. Laurence Erlbaum Associates. Hillsdale: New Jersey.

Green, A., Unaldi, A., & Weir, C. J. (2010). *Language Testing*, 27(2), 191–211.

Heijne-Penninga, M., Kuks, J. B. M., Schonrock-Ademma, J., Snijders, T. A. B., & Cohen-Schotanus, J. (2010). Open-book tests to complement assessment programmes: analysis of open- and closed-book tests. *Advances in Health Sciences, Education, 13*(3), 263–273.

Hyland, K., & Hamp-Lyons, L. (2002). EAP: issues and directions. *JEAP 1*(1), 1–12.

Li Du. (2010). Variables influencing the validity of the Reading test. *English Language Teaching*, 3(3).

Leukowicz, J. A. (2000). Authenticity in Language Testing. *Language Testing, 17*(1), 43–46.

Pallant, A. & Slaght, J. (2002). *Integrating Reading & Writing on a pre-sessional course: a consideration of issues involved in materials writing*. BALEAP conference presentation, Southampton.

Shaw, S. D., & Weir, C. J. (2007) *Examining Writing: Research & practice in assessing second language writing. (Studies in Language Testing)*. CUP: Cambridge.

Slaght, J. (1999). *Academic reading: a theoretical overview*. Unpublished paper, the University of Reading.

Spence-Brown, R. (2001). The eye of the beholder: authenticity in an embedded assessment task. *Language Testing, 18*(4), 463–481.

Spolsky, B. (1985). Limits of Authenticity in Language Testing. *Language Testing, 2*, 31–40.

Swales, J. M. (2009). When there is no perfect text: Approaches to the EAP practitioner's dilemma. *JEAP, 8*, 5–13.

Urquhart, S., & Weir, C. J. (1998). *Reading in a second language: process, product & practice*. Longman: London & New York.

Weideman, A. (2006). Assessing academic literacy in a task-based approach. *SAALT Journal for language teaching, 37*(1), 81–101.

Fiona Dalziel and Carole Sedgwick

Argumentation in Second-Language Academic Writing: Teacher and Learner Perspectives

Introduction

This paper will attempt to apply theories of argumentation formulated with reference to a first-language academic environment to the teaching of second-language writing. In particular, it will investigate teacher and learner perspectives on argument in undergraduate essays written as part of a BA in modern languages at the University of Padova in northern Italy. As Andrews (2007, p. 3) affirms: 'Argumentative capacity is the hidden criterion in the assessment of student essays, research papers, critiques and syntheses from about the age of 16 upwards.' The study represents a first, exploratory phase in a research project which aims to address the following questions:

- How prevalent is argument in teacher and learner assessment of academic writing?
- Are there differences in how teachers and learners perceive argument?

- How might argument be fostered in approaches to teaching second language writing?

In order to do this, the authors analysed the peer reviews of 93 essays, comparing these with teacher evaluations. The initial findings would appear to indicate that it is common for both learners and teachers to assess essays in terms of argumentation, which is seen to contribute to the effectiveness of second-language writing, alongside factors such as organisation, register and accuracy.

When students enter a university, they are expected to adopt certain social behaviours, ways of thinking and reasoning expected in an academic environment (Bartholomae, 1985; Johns, 1997). Students are not academics, yet they are often positioned as 'insiders' when work is evaluated (Fløttum, Dahl & Kinn, 2006; Lillis, 2006). One behaviour regarded as integral to life in a university is the ability to take a stance and defend a point of view (Woodward-Kron, 2002; Wu, 2006).

Traditions of argumentation through disputation, and studies of argumentation within the academic discipline of Rhetoric, date back to the early universities of the Middle Ages (Verger, 1992). Andrews (2007, p. 3) summarises the claims made by Habermas (1984) that 'Democratic societies aim to operate via argumentation to explore and resolve differences at personal, local, regional, national and global levels, trying to reach consensus that is a basis for agreed action'. Andrews (ibid., p. 3) further proposes that: 'In continental Europe at postgraduate level, and in the research thesis or dissertation, students have a double responsibility: they not only have to write well on some topic in the field, but they also have to write argumentatively.' Reviews of theories of argument and argumentation that discuss arguments in relation to European traditions (Van Eemeren, Grootendorst & Kruiger, 1987; Tindale, 1999; Andrews, 2005) deal with a range of theories deriving from Aristotelian concepts of logic, a system of argumentation based on: the syllogism – logically connected statements or premises leading to a conclusion; dialectic – defence or refutation of a thesis in debate or discussion; or rhetoric – argument designed to convince an audience of an opinion, or point of view.

The current study was prompted by recent research, adopting an 'ethnographic perspective' (Green & Bloome, 1997) and conducted at postgraduate level, into practices of MA thesis writing on two English studies programmes in two different national locations in Europe, Hungary and Italy (Sedgwick, 2011). 'Rich' data was collected on six MA theses, three in each location. Each thesis was treated as a separate case study. The use of argument was evident as a significant socio-historical practice in the production and evaluation of the theses. Students made claims in the texts for originality, which were promoted and justified through argument. Argument was integral to the process of thesis development and evaluation, ritualised and concretised in the oral defence of the thesis in both contexts. On both programmes students were required to defend their thesis orally. The requirement for argument to be evident in the thesis was stated explicitly in the Hungarian case studies, and in one of the case studies in the Italian location. However, the significance of argument was implicit in all the case studies. Argument determined the structure of five theses and was a strong influence in the sixth.

Given that argument is such a prominent practice at *postgraduate* level, the current study was concerned to explore the extent to which it was already perceived to be a requirement at *undergraduate* level, and, if so, the nature of argument at this level.

CONTEXT

The learners in question were taking a semester-long academic writing course in the third and final year of their studies on the BA language-degree course entitled *Mediazione Linguistica e Culturale,* an alternative to the more traditional degree course focusing on language, literature and philology. As well as studying language and literature, students take courses in subjects such as marketing and law, and there is a strong focus on translation. Wide use is made of the facilities provided by the University Language Centre, with the result that many language courses are blended, with students attending classes at the centre's multimedia laboratories and using various online resources for individual and group activities, such as peer review. One relevant contextual feature is that the majority of Italian university courses involve evaluation by means of oral rather than written assessment, and thus the academic essay is not prevalent as it is in many other countries. However, all students have to produce an 8,000 to 10,000-word dissertation in order to graduate.

In the 2009–2010 academic year, students attending the third-year writing course were required to submit three essays and two pieces of reflective writing regarding their writing skills, one at the beginning and one at the end of the course. The essay writing involved a process of peer review of first drafts before the submission of the final version of the essay. In preparation for each essay, students were given a selection of readings on the topic, took part in brainstorming activities and also attended lectures given by guest speakers, during which they took notes. The essay which will form the focus of the reflections in the following section was the following: 'What may get *lost in translation*? Are there any texts which you consider to be untranslatable? Discuss.' It is important to note here, that before writing this essay, the learners had not received any explicit training in the skills of argumentation.

DATA SET, METHODOLOGY AND INITIAL RESULTS

As regards the data set, in this paper the authors will investigate the peer reviews of the essay mentioned above and the evaluations of two teachers of a representative sample of these essays. A quantitative analysis will be made of the learners' peer reviews, in which terms relating to the concept of argument will be investigated using corpus analysis tools. This will be followed by qualitative analysis of both peer and teacher comments.

ANALYSIS OF PEER COMMENTS

In order to conduct the quantitative analysis, 93 peer comments (one per student) were collected to form a small corpus numbering 14,056 words. There was, however, variation in the length of the comments, which ranged from 33 to 368 words. The instructions for the peer review activity were simply to answer the question 'What could be done to improve this essay?' Thus, learners were not told to focus on argument, or any other specific feature of essay writing. It is therefore interesting to consider how many of the reviews did actually include comments which made direct or indirect reference to this aspect of academic writing. First of all, by means of the concordancing tool of the corpus analysis software AntConc (Anthony, 2011) examples of the noun *argument* and the verb *argue* (including all its inflections) were found. Of the resulting instances, those which consisted of the noun *argument* used with the meaning of *topic* (a 'false friend' for Italian learners of English) or which were direct quotes from the peer's essay were discarded. However, detailed reading of the peer comments revealed there were many ways of referring to the concept of argument without actually using the word itself. For this reason, all phrases found in the comments which made reference to either effective or inadequate argument (expressions such as 'support your ideas', 'logical connection', etc.) were tagged and then searched for in the corpus. Table 1 summarises the results.

Table 1 References to argument in peer comments

References to argument	Instances
Noun *argument*	11
Verb *argue*	3
Other words/phrases	38
Total	**52**

As the results show, 52 out of the 93 students considered argument to be of relevance in evaluating their peers' work. The other prevalent issues addressed in the students' comments regarded the overall structure or organisation of the essay, originality, clarity, appropriacy in terms of register and grammatical accuracy. In their comments, students both congratulated their peers on the good use of argument (in 24 cases) or criticised the lack of it (in 28 cases), as these comments show:

> You developed the argument both making quotations and explaining your own ideas and this is very important!

> [...] what I advise you is to use your sources especially to support your ideas or to put forward an opposite point of view.

ANALYSIS OF TEACHER COMMENTS

The next step was to see whether teachers gave similar weight to argument in their evaluations. One of these (Teacher 1) was a member of staff of the University Language Centre, with many years' experience in teaching general and academic writing skills. The other (Teacher 2) was a research fellow in Applied Linguistics at the Language Department, particularly interested in studying learner language. Thirty essays were given to these two teachers, who were asked simply to provide each with an overall grade (A, B, C or Fail) and a brief comment. No scoring criteria were provided so as not to influence the graders in any way, as the authors were keen to find out what would be spontaneously valued in the essays. As regards the prevalence of argument in teacher evaluations, in the ratings of the first scorer, 14 out of the 30 comments were related in some way to argument, while in the case of the second score the number was 19. However, in other cases, argument would appear to be assumed by graders in cases of highly-valued texts, while in some of the poorly-rated essays, the sole focus of the comments was on the low level of language competence of the student, which impeded comprehension and thus heavily influenced the negative evaluation. The other aspects of writing commented on by the teachers were appropriacy of register, cohesion, grammatical accuracy, clarity, relevance to essay title, originality, use of references and organisation.

There was overall consensus between teachers and students as regards the essays rated highly in terms of argumentation: all 11 essays receiving positive comments from teachers as regards argument were also praised by students. One example is provided below (authors' highlighting in bold):

Teacher comments:
> I enjoyed this essay – **very convincing**. His **quotes and references are very successfully woven into the text**.

> The writer appears to be **engaging with his/her assumed audience, puts forward an argument and attempts to support this in the course of the essay**. He **uses references but also own anecdotal evidence**. There is **evidence of originality/critical thinking** in the essay. The essay is **readable/involving**.

Peer comment:

> *I think that your essay is well structured and written, in addition an appropriate vocabulary and register. As I can see, you know how to use impersonal structures and* **give your point of view**. *The essay is readable and enjoyable, the title used to separate each paragraph is helpful to follow smoothly the text and in this way you give to every of them importance. In my opinion,* **you used few quotation to explain your ideas**, *you need to use the quotes to express contrasting and different point between authors. Finally you write your personal experience and difficulties on a tourist guide translation, and it is an important aspect of the problem, but* **you didn't write if there is a type of text you consider untranslatable and why**. *To sum up, your essay is well done!*

One can note here, however, that in this case the peer comment is slightly more critical than that of the expert raters.

On the other hand, of the ten essays given a poor teacher evaluation in terms of argument, only five were also criticised by their peers. Yet it should be taken into account that for reasons of positive politeness (Brown & Levinson, 1987), students may be hesitant to appear overly critical of their peers' work. One example of consensus follows:

Teacher comments:

> **Introduction seems a long way off from crux of the matter** – *in spite of arousing interest. Writer* **doesn't really put forward an argument** *and the conclusion seems to refute what has been said – i.e., uses references to say that translation is an 'approximation' then says no text can be considered.* **Not sure she got the point or was clear about what she thought**.

> *English OK. Statements need further discussion and exemplifying.* **More quotations than well-argued text.**

Peer comment:

> *I have to point out a couple of things that, in my opinion, are relevant that should improve your essay. I noticed that* **your personal opinion is not clearly explained**, *or you has not gone deeply into your ideas. You made few examples, I mean concrete examples of your personal experiences or about text that you studied or read. Secondly,* **you have not explained your point of view regarding as untranslatable texts. You only quotes someone else's opinion but not write your idea**. *In my point of view you used lot of quotations but few personal ideas, or when you expressed your personal opinion,* **you didn't make examples to support your statements**. *The only advice that I can give to you is to expand your personal opinion despite of quotations.*

Here, it is interesting that both tutor and student agreed on what was required in the text. They expected the student to put forward and defend a point of view, rather than simply supply the views of others.

Overall, in the teacher comments, apart from general statements such as 'well argued' or 'not fully argued', there was appreciation of those texts in which the argumentative intent was clearly stated and then carried through, and criticism of those where it was not, or where there was 'difficulty hitting the nail on the head'. Argument was also referred to as being 'convincing' or 'not (overly) convincing', and in one case 'originality' was mentioned. Poor evaluation was often given on account of claims not being well-supported or connected, in a few cases, the raters felt that the conclusion did not reflect the arguments put forward in the preceding text. The factors leading to praise or criticism in the peer reviews were similar, with students mentioning above all the development of argument, originality and the evidence presented to support claims.

DISCUSSION AND FUTURE DIRECTIONS

Although this study does not claim to be anything but a preliminary investigation, it would appear to confirm the findings of Sedgwick's (2011) research into MA thesis-writing, suggesting that at undergraduate level argument is deemed a salient feature of academic writing by teachers and learners alike. As regards the peer reviews, even though the students in question had not been asked specifically to focus on argument, reference to it can be found in over 50% of the comments. Interestingly, in the majority of these (56%), more effective argumentation was seen as a way to improve the overall quality of the essay. Similar results emerge from the teacher evaluations, where, overall, 55% of comments concerned argument, although the two participants had not been given any guidelines or criteria as to how to evaluate the texts.

There are clearly several ways in which this study could be expanded upon to provide greater insights into how argument is perceived. First of all, more learner data could be collected, including peer reviews on more than one writing task carried out in the course of an academic writing module; this could help to shed light on the process of learning to argue. Secondly, the teachers'

written evaluations could be followed up by interviews, giving them the opportunity to discuss in greater depth what exactly they value in good academic writing and how this relates to argument. Finally, analysis could be carried out on the student texts themselves, to see how argument is constructed in those essays which were highly valued by both teachers and peers.

On a teaching, rather than research level, the results of this exploratory study could encourage teachers to reflect on how argumentative capacity can be fostered in a second-language environment, where stress is often placed on the more formal genre requirements of writing tasks, such as register or paragraph organisation. In relation to first-language setting, Andrews (2010, p. 135) claims that: 'There is remarkable commitment to understanding the function of argument but also a strong sense among students that argument is not addressed – or made explicit by – lecturers.' There follows a number of suggestions as to how this might be done, with particular reference to the Italian context and the findings mentioned above. Teachers could reflect on how to weave activities focusing explicitly on argumentation into a process/genre approach to the teaching of academic writing. For example, a brainstorming activity designed to generate ideas on a given topic could be followed up by one in which students have to make connections between those ideas. This could help learners to follow through their arguments more successfully, which appeared in this study to be a shortcoming in student writing. Moreover, the development of argument, which was found to be lacking in some of the essays in question, could be addressed by involving students in the analysis of argumentative texts written by expert writers in order to see how they take up a position by making claims/propositions, often in contrast to previous arguments (Kaufer & Geisler, 1991), and how the relationship between claims and grounds (as described by Toulmin, 1958) is expressed. Finally, in their peer reviews, students could be asked specifically to consider whether the reader is *convinced* by the writer's arguments, and if not, why not.

Finally, in contexts such as the Italian one, where there is a tradition of oral rather than written examination, it might also be worthwhile introducing other forms of argumentation such as debate into an academic writing course. Experience has shown that, while keen to express an opinion and to try to back it up in an informal discussion context (such as that of the online forum), students frequently interpret the genre requirements of the academic essay as a prohibition of anything resembling their own point of view, resulting in a dry summary of other people's writings. Students, could, for example, be asked to take part in an oral 'argument' about a proposed essay topic, followed up by an exploration of the similarities and differences in the process of argumentation across genres. Alternatively, after the completion of an essay on a given topic, 'regenring tasks' such as those proposed by English (2011) could be suggested. In other words, students could be asked to rewrite their essays in another genre, such as a television debate. Altogether, such activities could help students to acquire a skill which is undoubtedly valued in academia and beyond.

REFERENCES

Andrews, R. (2005). Models of argumentation in educational discourse. *Text, 25*(1), 107–127.

Andrews, R. (2007). Argumentation, critical thinking and the postgraduate dissertation. *Educational Review, 59*(1), 1–18.

Andrews, R. (2010). *Argumentation in higher education.* New York and London: Routledge.

Anthony, L. (2011). AntConc (Version 3.2.2) [Computer Software]. Tokyo, Japan: Waseda University. Retrieved from http://www.antlab.sci.waseda.ac.jp

Bartholomae, D. (1985) Inventing the university. In D. Rose (Ed.), *When a writer can't write: Studies in writer's block and other composing process problems* (pp. 134–165). New York: Guildford Press.

Brown, P., & Levinson, S. (1987). *Politeness: Some universals in language use.* Cambridge: Cambridge University Press.

English, F. (2011). *Student writing and genre: Reconfiguring academic knowledge.* London & New York: Continuum.

Fløttum, K., Dahl, T., & Kinn, T. (2006). *Academic voices – across languages and disciplines.* Amsterdam: John Benjamins Publishers.

Green, J., & Bloome, D. (1997). Ethnography and ethnographers of and in education: A situated perspective. In J. Flood, S. B. Heath, & D. Lapp (Eds.), *Handbook of research in teaching: Literacy in the communicative and visual* (pp. 181–202). New York: Macmillan.

Johns, A. (1997). *Text, role and context*. Cambridge: Cambridge University Press.

Habermas, J. (1984). *Reason and the Rationalization of Society, Volume 1 of the Theory of Communicative Action*, Translated from German by McCarthy, T., Boston: Beacon Press (first published 1981).

Kaufer, D., & Geisler, C. (1991). A scheme for representing written argument. *Journal of Advanced Composition, 11*, 107–122.

Lillis, T. M. (2006). Academic literacies' research as pedagogy: Dialogues of participation. In L. Ganobscik-Williams (Ed.), *Teaching academic writing in UK higher education: Theories, practices and models. Universities in the 21st Century* (pp. 30–45). Basingstoke, Hampshire: Palgrave.

Sedgwick, C. (2011). *Crossing borders: an academic literacies approach to the study of MA thesis writing on English studies programmes in an Italian and a Hungarian university*. Unpublished PhD thesis, Lancaster University.

Tindale, C. W. (1999). *Acts of Arguing: A rhetorical model of argument*. Albany, N.Y: University of New York Press.

Toulmin, S. (1958). *The uses of argument*. Cambridge: Cambridge University Press.

Van Eemeren, F. H., Grootendorst, R., & Kruiger, T. (1987). *A handbook of argumentation Theory: A critical survey of classical backgrounds and modern studies*. Dordrecht, Netherlands: Foris publications.

Verger, J. (1992). Chapter 2: Patterns. In H. De Ridder Symoens (Ed.), *Universities in the Middle Ages* (Vol. 1, pp. 35–76). Cambridge: Cambridge University Press.

Woodward-Kron, R. (2002). Critical analysis versus description? Examining the relationship in successful student writing. *Journal of English for Academic Purposes, 1*, 121–143.

Wu, S. M. (2006). Creating a contrastive rhetorical stance: Investigating the strategy of problematization in students' argumentation. *RELC Journal, 37*(3), 329–353.

Julia Molinari and Anne Kavanagh

'The slippery eel': defining critical thinking for EAP curriculum design and assessment

Introduction

'Critical thinking' is a term that is increasingly referred to in the field of EAP by native and non-native students, EAP practitioners and those teaching in the disciplines (Alexander, Argent & Spencer, 2008; Cottrell, 2005). However, understanding exactly what it means to think 'critically' appears to be equivocal and subjective, and trying to teach and consequently test criticality is an equally 'critical' challenge (Condon & Kelly-Riley, 2004). Despite the academic requirement to be critical, it seemed to us that there was scant, albeit extant, pedagogic guidance on the heuristics of criticality in the EAP literature we examined. Our aims, therefore, were to explore what is meant by 'critical thinking' in the literature and what students and tutors understand it to be, to examine how 'critical thinking' is defined on the web

and in published tasks, and to evaluate the extent to which it can inform our teaching and be formally tested in reading and writing.

Our own teaching of pre-sessional EAP courses has increased our awareness of the need to nurture a more critical approach to reading when the ultimate purpose in higher education is to write. In 2010 we undertook what Hammersley (1998) calls 'practitioner research', which refers to research that has a commitment to best practice and self-reflection, is concerned equally with processes and outcomes, and leads to research-informed teaching. We designed an integrated 'Reading for writing' test, the aim of which was to simulate the target – academic – context, in which students are expected to draw extensively on reading to produce written assignments.

We designed a test that attempted to assess discrete reading skills as well as further a critical understanding of what was being read, the evidence for which culminated in an authentic writing task.[1] Our assessment criteria reflected the prominence we gave to critical thinking tasks (metacognitive) rather than comprehension-checking tasks such as the identification of main ideas (cognitive tasks). In the initial piloting of this test, we encountered a number of issues which still need to be addressed, such as the students' lack of familiarity with our test; in addition, institutional constraints resulted in our pilot cohort being too small to generate significant results. However, one particular difficulty was how to measure students' critical thinking skills and what exactly we considered to be evidence of criticality. As we marked students' writing against our criteria, we began to realise that mapping what the student had written onto our descriptors (which included such evidence as 'demonstrates critical reading and thinking' and 'avoids plagiarism') begged the following questions: 'What is critical thinking?', 'What is the evidence for it?', and 'Why are we reaching different evaluations of the same piece of writing?'.

Critical thinking distinguishes EAP from general ELT because of its specificity to the higher education context (Alexander, Argent & Spencer, 2008; Cottrell, 2005; Thompson, 2001; Yamada, 2009; Wallace & Wray, 2006, and many others). As such, an awareness of and confidence in developing this aptitude, approach, disposition or skill (the literature on how to classify 'critical thinking' is vast – see Siegel, 2008, and Cardew, 2005) need to be at the heart of EAP provision. Yet, this broad term

has many definitions, the relevance of which seems to depend on the discipline and the purpose of the enquiry being undertaken.

As a result of this multi-faceted and context-dependent nature, a number of challenges for the tutor and the student can arise. On the one hand, there is a danger of assessing the same work differently (problem of inter-rater reliability in Weigle, 2002); equally disconcertingly, tutors may be reluctant to deal with critical thinking in their classes because it is hard to manage and measure (see tutor responses to our questionnaire). This in turn could lead to students being inadequately prepared for the demands of their future academic studies.

In this paper, we show that critical thinking is an equivocal and complex concept, in which some definitions are subsumed by others. By attempting to define it and to highlight the relevance of any given definition for teaching and assessing it, we hope to contribute to a better understanding of what we teach, test and expect of our students, as well as what we expect of ourselves, and how we can reasonably conclude that there is evidence of critical thinking in an exam or assignment.

METHODOLOGY

We began our investigation in the summer of 2010 as part of a project on participant research. We asked some exiting EAP students at Nottingham University to sit our integrated reading for writing test in return for feedback on their writing using

---

[1] Students read three texts from different sources (academic, newspaper and advert) dealing with the same topic. They then took selective notes in order to answer an essay question which required them to show evidence of having evaluated the reliability of the sources in order to support their stance.

descriptors that were weighted in favour of critical thinking. We had six volunteer students who were informed that this test was not similar to the pre-sessional tests they were sitting at the time, so that they were not under the impression that we were providing exam practice. The usual research ethical code was abided by in terms of obtaining consent, providing information, safeguarding anonymity and offering gratitude in terms of feedback from ourselves on their writing.

Our investigation was three-fold:

- We sought to 'capture' the meanings of critical thinking by mining the literature for definitions.
- We drew up a taxonomy of critical thinking by searching both published and online materials.
- We solicited student and tutor views on critical thinking using questionnaires which contained both open and closed questions.

Our research on teaching and testing critical thinking in EAP is still in progress as we write.

DEFINITIONS

Several references to critical thinking can be found in Alexander, et al., 2008; Cottrell, 2005; McCarter and Jakes, 2009; Siegel, 2008; Thompson, 2001; Wallace and Wray, 2006; Yamada, 2009, all of whom argue for clarity in communicating what we expect students to be doing when they read and write.

Pally (1997, p. 295) identifies three predominant research areas active in defining critical thinking: EAP, cognitive psychology and transformative pedagogy. She provides an extensive list of sources for each discipline,

which indicates the breadth of interest and debate in this area. Each field appears to approach critical thinking from different perspectives or for different purposes, which may explain why Walker and Finney (1999, p. 531) state that 'there is a significant contention over what is meant by the phrase'.

According to Halpern (2003, p. 6), writing from the perspective of cognitive psychology:

Critical thinking is the use of those cognitive skills or strategies that increase the probability of a desirable outcome. It is used to describe thinking that is purposeful, reasoned, and goal directed – the kind of thinking involved in solving problems, formulating inferences, calculating likelihoods, and making decisions when the thinker is using skills that are thoughtful and effective for the particular context and type of thinking task.

In the field of education, Unrau (2008, p. 14) gives a broad interpretation of the term, defining it as '... a process of reasoned reflection on the meanings of claims about what to believe or what to do,' and, broadening even further, considers it '... a process, a network of dispositions and an outlook – all of which are framed in a social context'.

Some concentrate on attributes, defining '... the essence of CT skills' as 'the willingness to challenge old assumptions and examine alternatives' (Olson, 1992, p. 3) or stating that '[t]he spirit of critical thinking is that we take nothing for granted or as being beyond question ...' (Walker & Finney, 1999, p. 533).

While '[n]o one definition of critical thinking is applicable to every discipline at every level' (Condon & Kelly-Riley, 2004, p. 64–65), Alexander et al. (2008, p. 256) identify three important types of critical thinking: taking a stance, evaluating and making connections, while Vermillion (1997, p. iii) identifies three primary components: understanding the author's intended meaning, synthesising all available information, and analysing.

A TAXONOMY OF DEFINITIONS

We attempted to classify this concept by drawing up a taxonomy of definitions and mapping them onto the 'knowledge telling and knowledge transforming' spectrum outlined in the BALEAP Competency Framework (BALEAP, 2008), which defines critical thinking as the ability to 'transform' (evaluate) knowledge so that it can evolve and not simply 'tell' (or recount) it, which would lead to mere description. The competency framework outlines best practice for EAP teachers, positing that criticality is a defining characteristic of higher education and as such should be part of good EAP teaching.

We have so far drawn up a taxonomy (see an excerpt in Table 1) of approximately 100 definitions from the literature. Most of these are on a cline: they are either consequences of each other (for example, being 'sceptical about claims' can be a consequence of 'questioning claims reasonably') or potential effects (for example, by keeping 'an open mind' we are more likely to 'be open to reasonable persuasion').

Table 1 Definitions of critical thinking grouped according to the 'knowledge telling–knowledge transforming' spectrum (excerpt)

CRITICAL THINKING TAXONOMY		
A critical thinker knows that every text has a purpose and can infer what is not said		
A <u>critical thinker</u> can/has an aptitude, willingness and predisposition to:		
CRITICAL THINKING		
Knowledge Telling ⟵――――――――――⟶		**Knowledge Transforming**
be sceptical about claims		question these reasonably
keep an open mind		be open to reasonable persuasion
	recognise irrelevant and distracting information	
		evaluate statements, sequences of statements, paragraphs and whole texts
		use their curiosity, doubts and prior knowledge to understand and create

The tabular format above seemed to us, however, to be rather reductive and rigid, failing to capture the procedural, cyclical and dynamic nature of thinking. We therefore tried to present the taxonomy in the following diagram (Figure 1), which was animated during our actual presentation of this material to reflect how knowledge is transformed by the questions we ask.

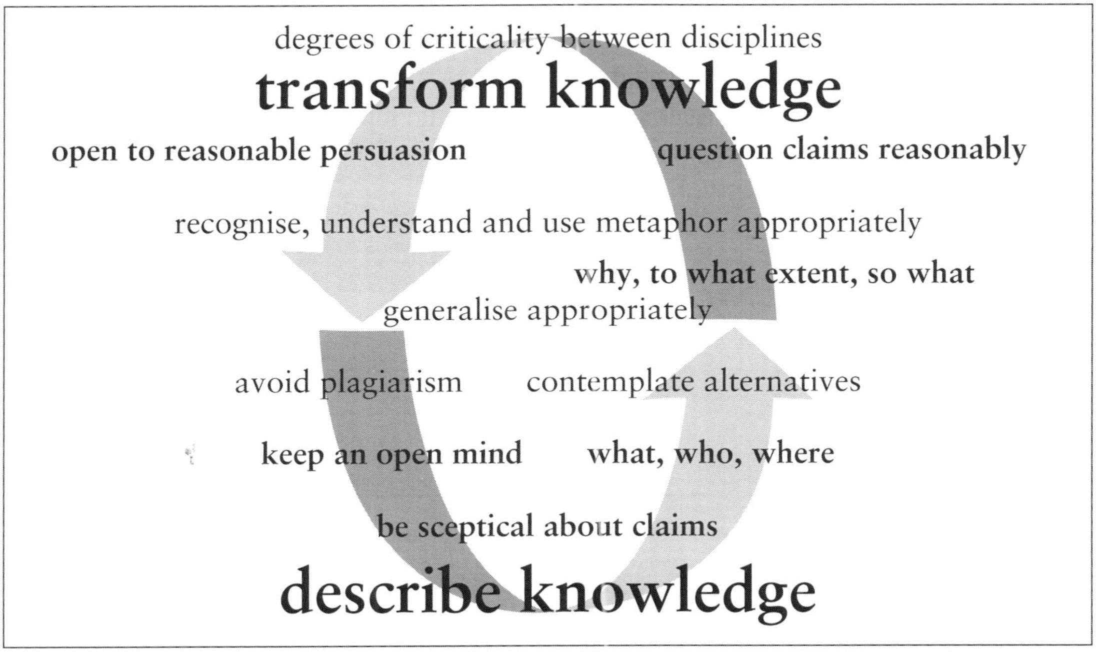

Figure 1 Procedural, cyclical and dynamic nature of critical thinking moving from knowledge telling to knowledge transforming

However, even this classification flagged up other concerns, which were raised in discussions with colleagues, who pointed out that 'what' questions (represented here at the 'describing knowledge' stage of the cycle) can lead both to a description of knowledge (e.g., 'What are the elements of water?' in a subject like chemistry) and to a transformation of knowledge (e.g., 'What are the risks of this investment?' in a subject like business). This further alerted us to the need to be ready to qualify and contextualise our statements, indeed, to think critically about our own utterances when helping students to approach a task critically.

TEXTBOOKS AND WEBSITES

As well as searching the literature for definitions of critical thinking, we also scanned several EAP textbooks for evidence of what definitions of critical thinking were being used and how it was being presented to students. The following summarises what we found.

Table 2 Evidence of critical thinking in published textbooks

Title	Approach	Level	Sample tasks	Critical thinking focus
Study Tasks in English (Waters & Waters, 1995)	Task-based	Intermediate EAP	U2: Thinking it through U3: Critical questions	Who, what, where, why, when, so what? Recognising flawed/invalid arguments
Access EAP (Alexander & Argent, 2010)	Context-based syllabus	Low-level EAP	Unit 1: L1, T2, 2.2 Unit 9: L5, T3, 4	Persuade others by reason Reliability/quality/purpose of sources
EAP Now! (Cox & Hill, 2004)	Eight skills integrated & linked thematically	Int./Upper-Intermediate EAP	U5: Critical reading	Identify stance and purpose; recognise & distinguish fact from opinion
Study Reading (Glendinning & Holmstrom, 2004)	Problem-solving tasks to develop reading strategies	Upper-intermediate	U5: Making links within texts and own knowledge of the world	Infer meanings between and beyond the lines of text

As can be seen, specific tasks in each textbook make explicit reference to the kind of thinking required rather than reductively labelling it as 'critical thinking'. We felt this was encouraging and could help overcome some of the reservations expressed by some of the tutors who responded to our questionnaires (discussed below).

In addition, our scan of materials on the web revealed that there is widespread attention to what critical thinking is and how university students can develop this aptitude. We found many online guides or sequences of tasks on critical thinking, all designed to help students, but also teachers, understand what it is and how to nurture it. These sources fall into two categories: those designed specifically for the EAP context and perhaps targeted directly at international students, such as *Prepare for success* (University of Southampton, 2008) and *UEfAP* (Gillett, 2010); and those that are aimed more generally towards all higher education students, such as individual university webpages and those drawing on collectively produced materials such as *Learn Higher* (2010).

TEST MATERIALS

Having found our definitions of critical thinking in the literature, textbooks and on the web, we then turned our attention to how it is tested to try and gauge whether EAP tests are valid in terms of their content (i.e., whether they test criticality) and construct (i.e., whether the tasks reflect this).

Table 3 Critical thinking in internationally recognised test materials

Test	Key 'academic' features	'Non-academic' features	Evidence of critical thinking
The Official Guide to PTE: Pearson Test of English Academic (2010)	Integrated skills Range of texts from different disciplines (semi-authentic)	20 mins to write a 200–300 word essay All answers in texts Non-selective summaries Instructions: 'do not refer back' to original text	No
IELTS (International English Language Testing System)	Scanning for main ideas Inferred meanings (T/F/NG) It is accepted as a measure of academic proficiency by universities[2]	Relies on personal experience and suggestions, not evidence Discrete items Lacks thematic links Textbooks/general audience texts	No

Here, we found that, although both the Pearson Test and the IELTS purport to test 'academic' English, they do not test the criticality we believe distinguishes EAP from other forms of ELT. In view of this, it is arguable whether they provide a reliable indication of a student's ability to navigate the discourse of the academic community.

In addition to the above summative proficiency tests, we also examined a number of EAP course books to further our understanding of how critical thinking is evaluated in formative assessment and found evidence of good practice in the following sources. In *EAP Now!* (Cox & Hill, 2004, p. 257) students' criticality is assessed according to criteria which match some of the definitions we collated in our taxonomy such as 'clear argument' and 'strong support'. However, one of the criteria is 'critical analysis', which would seem to beg the question, if we accept the starting point of our discussion, i.e., that we need to define what we mean by 'critical' before we can consider assessing it.

---

[2] This is a circular point: the claim is that IELTS is deemed 'academic' simply by virtue of its being widely accepted by most universities worldwide (which in turn begs the question we are asking, i.e., whether IELTS is, in fact, an academic test).

We found *Study Tasks in English* (Waters & Waters, 1995, p. 21) to be particularly helpful in providing a way into assessing critical thinking that avoided being distracted by linguistic accuracy or personal opinions. Indeed, students are informed: 'You are not concerned with whether you agree with him *[the student you are evaluating]* or not, nor are you concerned with his general English ability'. The task involved peer evaluating a student's essay in terms of whether it had:

- a clear purpose
- defined terms
- included relevant information
- excluded bias and unsupported opinion
- considered all viewpoints

To conclude our examination of the different ways critical thinking is assessed in summative and formative assessment in our literature review, we would like to suggest that the Washington State University Guide to rating critical thinking (2004) could help EAP practitioners design useful assessment criteria for critical thinking. This rating scale

has the merit of focusing on seven aspects of critical thinking and considers the relevance of critical thinking within different disciplines. It is a criterion-referenced and competence-based descriptor (i.e., it focuses on what the student can do), which also makes explicit what kind of thinking is being evaluated, so, for example, a student will get a grade on their ability to 'identify and assess the quality of data' or 'consider the influence of context'.

STUDENT FEEDBACK

In order to gauge how aware and receptive students are to critical thinking, we distributed questionnaires to 75 students studying on a foundation programme and at two different levels of a pre-sessional programme, asking both open and closed questions, as indicated in Table 4. Each closed question was followed by an open one (in brackets), which enabled participants who felt they had not heard of critical thinking to participate and provide a response to what they thought it might mean.

Table 4 Student responses

Question / Course type (level)	Pre-sessional (1) (31 responses) Yes/No	Pre-sessional (2) (19 responses) Yes/No	Foundation (15 responses) Yes/No
Have you heard of critical thinking? (What do you think it means?)	27/4	18/1	15/0
Do you think it is necessary to read and write critically? (Why/Why not?)	30/0*	19/0	15/0
Do you think it is possible to learn to think critically? (How/why not?)	24/4*	19/0	12/3

*Discrepancy in total due to no response given to that particular question

We received a total of 65 responses, in which the majority of students seemed to have a grasp of the concept of critical thinking, manifested in such expressions as: 'you have to analyse'; 'understand the writer's stance ... your own stance'; 'include your personal judgement'; 'evaluate'; 'use evidence to support your ideas'. There is also a strong sense of its value for the future with expressions such as, 'useful in future studies' and 'good in our future career life'.

TUTOR FEEDBACK

At the same time, by means of a questionnaire, we asked approximately 40 centre staff questions relating to their understanding of critical thinking, whether they thought it could be taught and why and, if so, at what level of language proficiency. A total of 19 questionnaires were returned. There were wide variations in interpretation and beliefs, with statements on what critical thinking is ranging from 'asking *wh~* questions' to 'synthesising and using evidence from various sources and experience', and respondents described critical thinking as 'culture-bound' and 'discipline-specific'. Conflicting views were evident on whether critical thinking should indeed be a focus of EAP, with some tutors perceiving it as unnecessary on lower-level courses ('irrelevant concept for struggling students'), while others saw it as vital from the very beginning ('should be encouraged from the lowest level we teach') of such courses. There were perceived difficulties in 'teaching' it ('not sure it can be taught', 'can be a difficult concept to get across', 'would like more advice on how to approach it') and in testing it ('how do you measure it?', 'it's hard to test in reading'), and many felt constrained by time ('introducing

more on critical thinking would inevitably mean losing something else' and 'it's hard to get through everything as it is'). Although not a focus here, an area of further interest would be to investigate the relationship between tutors' interpretation of critical thinking and their evaluation of its importance.

IMPLICATIONS AND EMERGING QUESTIONS

Our conclusions draw on the following three assumptions: (i) critical thinking is a distinguishing feature of EAP (as opposed to general ELT) because of its commitment to helping students access the discourse of their academic communities, (ii) critical thinking is a complex term which needs to be qualified depending on context and purpose, and (iii) critical thinking is not something all EAP practitioners feel comfortable engaging with (based on our very small sample).

In order to assuage teachers' discomfort, we would endorse a *systematic* and *informed* approach to critical thinking in teacher training programmes and staff development sessions. *Systematic* attention can be achieved by adopting a critical approach to designing EAP syllabuses, materials and tests, by paying due attention to the language or discourse of critical thinking, and by articulating (both to ourselves and to our students) what exactly we mean by evidence of criticality (see Table 1 and Figure 1). By *informed* attention, we mean that a discussion on what critical thinking is should acknowledge its complexity and 'slipperiness' because the transformation of knowledge is 'complex' and 'slippery': it requires a constant definition of terms and is a process, not a product, of the 'knowledge-telling/knowledge-transforming cycle'.

In keeping with the transformative consequences of adopting a critical approach to knowledge, we feel that our small-scale research has in turn raised other questions such as whether a taxonomy of critical thinking can indeed inform the design of materials and assessment or whether thinking analytically in terms of a taxonomy actually detracts from the nature of critical thinking because it suggests that there are quantifiably set ways of thinking critically. From our perspective, this discussion is worthwhile and ongoing because it contributes to a better understanding of the pivotal role that EAP provision plays in facilitating access to higher education.

REFERENCES

Alexander, O., & Argent, S. (2010). *Access EAP*. Reading: Garnet.

Alexander, O., Argent, S., & Spencer, J. (2008). *EAP essentials: A teacher's guide to principles and practice*. Reading: Garnet.

BALEAP (2008). BALEAP competency framework for teachers of English for Academic Purposes. Retrieved from www.baleap.org.uk

Cardew, S. (2005). Critical thinking about cultural and academic identity. In O. Alexander (Ed.), *New approaches to materials development in language learning*. Oxford: Peter Lang.

Condon, W., & Kelly-Riley, D. (2004). Assessing and teaching what we value: The relationship between college-level writing and critical thinking abilities. *Assessing Writing*, 9(1), 56–75. Retrieved from http://www.sciencedirect.com/science/article/pii/ S1075293504000042

Cottrell, S. (2005). Critical thinking skills: Developing effective analysis and argument. Basingstoke: Palgrave MacMillan.

Cox, K. K., & Hill, D. (2004). *EAP Now!* Frenchs Forest: Pearson Longman.

Glendinning, E. H., & Holmstrom, B. (2004). *Study Reading* (2nd ed.). Cambridge: Cambridge University Press.

Gillett, A. (2010). *UEfAP*. Retrieved from www.uefap.com/reading/readfram.htm

Halpern, D. F. (2003). *Thought and knowledge: An introduction to critical thinking*. Mahwah: Lawrence Erlbaum.

Hammersley, M. (1998). On the teacher as researcher. In M. Hammersley (Ed.), *Educational Research: Current issues* (pp. 211–231). London: The Open University/Paul Chapman Publishing.

IELTS (2011). *Academic reading and writing sample materials*. Retrieved from http://www.ielts.org/test_takers_information/test_sample.aspx

Learn Higher (2010). *Critical thinking and reflection – Resources for students*. Retrieved from http://www.learnhigher.ac.uk/Students/Critical-thinking-and-reflection.html

McCarter, S. & Jakes, P. (2009). *Uncovering EAP: How to teach academic writing and reading*. Oxford: Macmillan.

Olson, C. B. (1992). *Thinking/writing: Fostering critical thinking through writing*. NY: Harper Collins.

Pally, M. (1997). Critical thinking in ESL: An argument for sustained content. *Journal of Second Language Writing, 6*(3), 293–311.

Siegel, H. (2008). Autonomy, critical thinking and the Wittgenstein legacy: Reflections on Christopher Winch, education, autonomy and critical thinking. *Journal of Philosophy of Education, 42*(1), 165–184.

The Official Guide to PTE: Pearson Test of English: Academic. (2010). Hong Kong: Pearson Longman Asia.

Thompson, G. (2001). Interaction in academic writing: Learning to argue with the reader. *Applied Linguistics, 22*(1), 58–78.

University of Southampton (2008). *Prepare for success.* Retrieved from www.prepareforsuccess.org.uk

Unrau, N. (2008). *Thoughtful teachers, thoughtful learners: Helping students think critically.* Pippin Publishing Company. Retrieved from http://site.ebrary.com/lib/uon/

Vermillion, D. M. (1997). *Developing critical thinking skills in EAP students.* Master's Thesis, Biola University. Retrieved from http://www.eric.ed.gov/PDFS/ED424749.pdf

Walker, P., & Finney, N. (1999). Skill development and critical thinking in higher education. *Teaching in Higher Education, 4*(4), 531–547. Retrieved from: http://www.swetswise.com/eAccess/viewAbstract.do?articleID=31052034&titleID=198437

Wallace, M., & Wray, A. (2006). *Critical reading and writing for postgraduates.* London: Sage Publications Ltd.

Washington State University (2004). *Guide to rating critical thinking.* Retrieved from https://my.wsu.edu/pls/portal/docs/PAGE/CTLT/CITRUBRIC/ORIGINAL%20WSU%20CT%20RUBRIC.PDF

Waters, M., & Waters, A. (1995). *Study tasks in English.* Cambridge: Cambridge University Press.

Weigle, S. C. (2002). *Assessing writing.* Cambridge: Cambridge University Press.

Yamada, E. (2009). Discussion on the concept of 'Criticality'. *Literacies WEB Journal, 6*(1), 11–20. Retrieved from http://www.literacies.9640.jp/dat/litera6-1-2.pdf

SECTION V

Promoting best practice in EAP provision

GARRY DYCK

A QUANTITATIVE ASSESSMENT OF THE SUCCESS OF A CANADIAN UNIVERSITY-BASED, ON-SITE EAP PROGRAM: PRELIMINARY RESULTS

The goal of the Intensive Academic English Program (IAEP) of the University of Manitoba English Language Centre is to prepare students for success in degree study. This quantitative analysis seeks to determine how successful graduates of this program are relative to other groups. The four distinct groups include over 1,000 students who successfully completed L5 of IAEP to meet the language requirement of the University of Manitoba, more than 26,000 Canadians (CA), close to 2,400 international students who did not study in L5 to meet the language requirements (IN), and over 500 English-speaking international students (e.g., students from the US or the UK).

BACKGROUND

The primary function of the English Language Centre (ELC) is to teach English for Academic Purposes (EAP) in order to assist students in meeting the language requirement of the University of Manitoba. The ELC's IAEP has five levels with each level consisting of a twenty-four hour per week, fourteen-week course of instruction. The successful completion of the highest level – Level 5 or L5 – meets the language requirements for both graduate and undergraduate study at the University of Manitoba. Students spend an equal amount of time each week in each of the four skill areas: reading, writing, listening and speaking. In addition, they are given opportunities to practice study skills specific to each of these four skill areas and to learn about Canadian university culture and study skills. In order to enter L5, students must have achieved 3.5 in each of the four skill areas in the Canadian Test of English for Scholars and Trainees (CanTEST), 64 on the TOEFL iBT with no individual score lower than 15, 5.5 on IELTS or an equivalent score in a standardized English proficiency test. (In order to meet the language requirement for entry to degree study, they must have a CanTEST score of 4.5 in reading and listening and 4.0 in writing, 6.5 in IELTS, or 80 in iBT with no individual score lower than 19.) In addition, the L5 curriculum is taught at Red River College and the University of Winnipeg. Successful completion of this program at any of the three institutions meets the language requirement for academic study at any of the three institutions. The challenge for the ELC is to determine if the students who pass L5 are indeed ready for academic study relative to those who meet the language requirement by other means. As the program started in 1998, there are now enough students to allow for a quantitative study of the progress of L5 graduates in academic study.

EAP courses generally are based on a needs assessment and include practice of language and skills necessary for success in a degree program. This needs assessment has resulted in the inclusion of a variety of components to help students adapt to the university culture, including improved critical thinking skills necessary for success in a degree program. Terraschke and Wahid (2011) found that students perceived that the 'non-linguistic' components were more valuable in their academic success than the language skills that they achieved. Although it could be argued that students may not be aware of the reasons for their own success, what Terraschke and Wahid called 'non-linguistic' components had a significant impact on student confidence. Furthermore, Evans and Morrison (2011) found that non-native English-speaking (NNES) students with more practice in academic skills prior to entry to university were better prepared than NNES students who only studied English as a subject. Green (2000) also found that students benefited from increased knowledge of academic and social culture and that this was

more valuable than the language skills achieved when they began their degree studies. Lai (2009) found that students using critical thinking skills not only learned language faster but also did better in their degree study.

It is difficult to distinguish the linguistic components from the non-linguistic components in an EAP program. Some of the non-linguistic components could be taught separately in a study skills portion of a larger course, but EAP is more than academic ESL plus study skills. EAP needs to focus on accuracy and precision in all aspects of language and so may be less concerned with communicability (Turner, 2004). Other studies of specific EAP courses have considered EAP as a mixture of all components necessary for success in a degree program, including both linguistic and non-linguistic components (Dooey, 2010; Storch & Tapper, 2009). Indeed, in order for EAP to be successful, this mixture must be more of a fusion of linguistic and non-linguistic components.

The assumption of this paper is that those who have met the general language requirement of the University of Manitoba by language proficiency testing have had limited exposure to EAP. These students will most likely have completed general ESL and/or IELTS or TOEFL preparation courses. Further research would be required to determine the extent of their exposure to EAP. Nevertheless, if the ELC has properly assessed the needs of students and prepared them adequately, graduates of L5 should be successful in their degree study.

To date three studies have examined the success of L5 students at the ELC. The first was a qualitative study that looked at the interview data of six L5 students (Fast, 2003). This study found that the relationship between students within an EAP program contributed to their sense of success in L5.

The second included both qualitative and quantitative aspects (Friesen, 2004). Friesen interviewed eight students about their experience in L5. She also compared the 2002–03 cumulative grade point average (CGPA) of students who had completed L5 with all students including L5 students. In her results, L5 students showed good performance relative to that of other international students; however, her study did not distinguish University of Manitoba L5 students from those who completed L5 at the University of Winnipeg and those at Red River College. Her study, although providing early evidence of the value of L5, was completed too soon after the start of the program in 1998, when the numbers of students who had completed L5 was still relatively low. In addition, she included only CGPAs in her study.

The third study looked at all first-year international students in the academic years 2004–05 and 2005–06 (Blais, n.d.). Blais admits many limitations of the study and refers to the study as a 'report … meant as a guideline for discussion purposes only.'

It is, therefore, timely to examine the role of L5 in the University of Manitoba community. The current study includes a much larger number of students in its database than previous studies and is able to distinguish between the various groups of international students.

This research is interested in how many graduates complete degrees and how quickly they completed those degrees. In addition, how do grade point averages (GPAs) of L5 graduates compare with those of other international students and with those of Canadian students? The answers to these questions should help determine if the L5 graduates are benefiting from L5.

DESCRIPTION OF DATA

The present study is based on data received from the University of Manitoba's Information Services and Technology (IST) office. The data includes information from the archived data system (Information Management System – IMS), as well as from the current data system (SCT Banner known at the University of Manitoba as Aurora Student), where data has been stored since 2006. Data includes entries for 51,564 students admitted for September 1996 to winter 2010; L5 students were identified in the database in 2001 (although the L5 program began in 1998).

In order to examine an adequate number of students who have completed L5, I have limited the database to begin with the academic year starting in September 2001. The year 2001 will be used to refer to the academic year starting in September of 2001 and ending in August of 2002. The last admissions in the data are for January 2010 and so the data for the 2009 academic year are incomplete, as they do not include the May admissions of 2010. I will, therefore, use 2008 as my final year. The academic years 2001 to 2008 will allow for eight years of data as indicated in the table.

The grade point scale used at the University of Manitoba ranges from a low of 0 (Fail) to a high of 4.5 (A+).

STUDENT TYPE

IST was able to distinguish students in the following categories:

- Canadian and permanent resident students (CA)
- international students whose primary language is not English and who did not take L5 to meet the language requirements (IN)
- students who successfully completed L5 (L5)

- international students whose primary language is English (ES)

Students studying in French at the University of Manitoba's Collège universitaire de Saint-Boniface were excluded from the study.

The following table shows the number of students admitted from 2001 to 2008.

Table 1 Number of students admitted from 2001 to 2008 by category

Student type	Number of students	Percentage
L5	1,058	3.5%
IN	2,394	7.8%
ES	547	1.8%
CA	26,642	86.9%
Total	30,641	100.0%

RESULTS

GRADE POINT AVERAGE

Figure 1 illustrates the GPAs for students admitted from the academic years 2001 to 2008. It is interesting to note that L5 have the highest first-year GPA, even higher than CA. They remain higher than IN but lower than CA in second year; however, L5 are the lowest of the three in third year. L5 have a CGPA lower than CA but higher than IN.

ES have the lowest GPA in the first, second, and third years and therefore have the lowest CGPA.

Typical of North American students, CA at the University of Manitoba get higher GPAs as they progress through their programs, while IN have little variation as they progress through three years. Surprisingly, L5 start high and then progressively get lower GPAs. L5 CGPAs are slightly higher than the IN CGPAs.

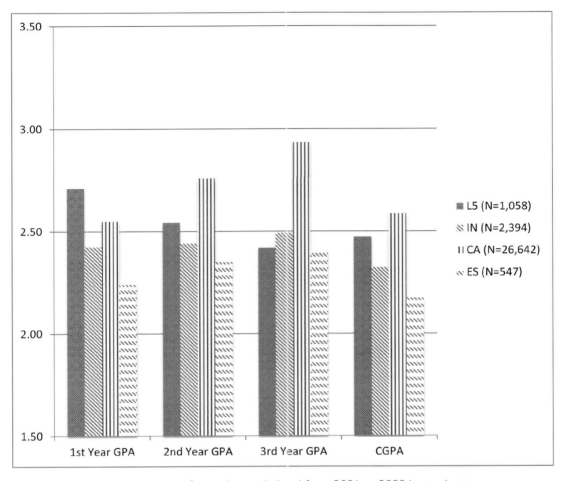

Figure I Grade point averages for students admitted from 2001 to 2008 by student type

The key patterns in this graph are (1) L5 have the highest first-year GPA, (2) L5 GPAs get progressively lower moving from the first to third year, (3) CA GPAs get progressively higher moving from first to third year, (4) L5 CGPAs are higher than IN CGPAs by 0.15, and (5) ES GPA's are lower than those of CA, IN and L5.

The standard deviation was lower for L5 and CA than it was for IN and ES. For first year GPA, L5 had a standard deviation of 1.01, and CA had 1.04. In contrast, IN had 1.13 and ES had 1.09, suggesting a wider range of grades. For CGPA, L5 had a standard deviation of 0.78 and CA had

0.97. This can be contrasted with IN at 1.00 and ES at 1.01.

GRADUATION RATE

In addition to GPA to determine student success, the percentage of students who graduate can also provide valuable information. In order to do this, the data was restricted to students who were admitted prior to 2005 in order to allow these students enough time to complete their degrees. In addition, the students who have transfer credit have been removed so that length of time to complete the degree can also be compared.

As would be expected, Figure 2 shows that L5 and IN graduate sooner than CA, since L5 and IN must be full-time students to keep to the requirements of a study permit. ES take a full six months longer than L5 to graduate.

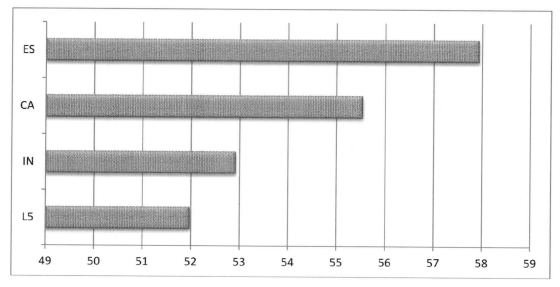

Figure 2 Average number of months to graduate

L5 also have on average completed more credit hours in a five-year period, as indicated in Figure 3. ES have completed the least number of credit hours in a five-year period.

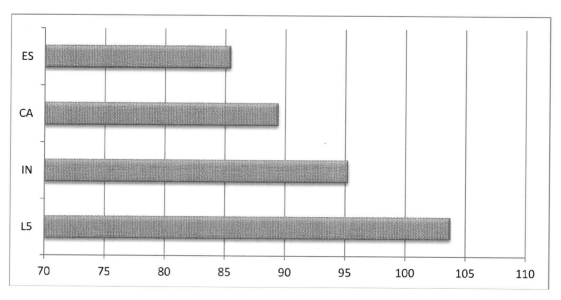

Figure 3 Credit hours completed in 5 years – admitted prior to 2005

Figure 4 indicates that L5 are much more likely to graduate from the University of Manitoba (70.1%) than IN (56.4%). Again, these are students who were admitted before 2005 and therefore had until January 2010 to graduate. CA will be able to continue as part-time students and so may take longer. IN are not permitted part-time status due to the requirements of the study authorization on their passports and so will have transferred to another university, deferred their study while returning to their home country or discontinued their study altogether. Surprisingly, only 48.1% of ES graduate within the five years.

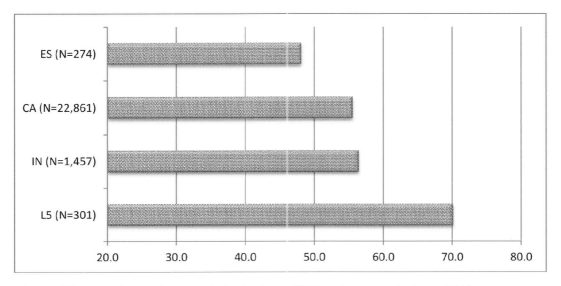

Figure 4 Per cent that graduate – admitted prior to 2005 and graduated prior to 2010

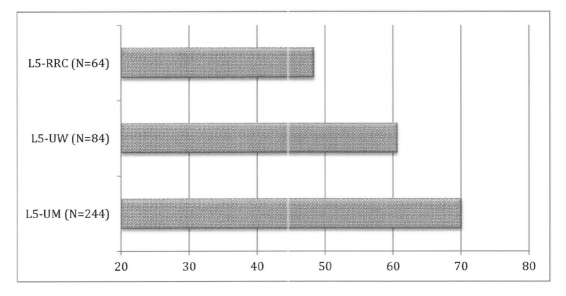

Figure 5 Per cent that graduate at University of Manitoba by institution where L5 was completed – admitted prior to 2005 and graduated prior to 2010

In addition, a comparison of the students who completed L5 at each of the three institutions providing L5: the University of Manitoba, the University of Winnipeg and Red River College provide strong support for English instruction to be taken at the institution in which degree study will be taken. As indicated in Figure 5, students who completed L5 at Red River College were less likely than CAs to graduate, and students completing at the University of Winnipeg were slightly higher than IN but significantly lower than L5 at the University of Manitoba.

DISCUSSION

The data suggests that students who complete L5 at the University of Manitoba are as likely or more likely to succeed than students who meet the language requirements by other means. L5 do better when looking at all programs and do as well or better in the areas where there are adequate numbers for comparison: Arts and Commerce.

Of some concern is the drop in GPA from the first to second year for L5. This pattern also occurs for IN but is more marked for L5, perhaps in part due to high first-year GPAs. L5 appear to have been prepared for the first year but not for the second. There are a few possible reasons for this.

In 2002 I presented research I had completed with Dieter Schönwetter on changes in attitudes of first-year students before and after they had taken the first-year credit course – Introduction to university – at the University of Manitoba (Dyck & Schönwetter, 2002). We found that international students were less likely to take responsibility for their accomplishments or failures. These students were more likely to credit circumstances beyond their control for

their success or failure. Not recognizing their own locus of control could reasonably result in declining GPAs.

The increasing need from first to final year for critical thinking in an academic program requires a change in approach to study and learning. This change would be more difficult to accomplish for students who have less awareness of their own control in achieving high grades. Further research would be required to verify this.

In addition to studying GPAs, this study also examined graduation rates. The graduation rates of L5 (70%) are much higher than IN (56%) or CA (56%) within the specified time frame. L5 may be more likely to stay as they have already spent some time in Winnipeg studying English and are less likely to transfer after beginning an academic program.

It is not surprising that students who completed L5 at the University of Manitoba are most likely to graduate with a degree from that institution. Students taking L5 at the University of Manitoba become familiar with the institution's academic culture, including its library and computer systems. This familiarity can translate to institutional loyalty and confidence within that institution.

The declining GPAs of L5 may be explained by the relatively high percentage of L5 that graduate. It is possible that Canadian students with low GPAs in first and second year choose not to persist to graduation. This could result in higher-average GPAs for the Canadians who remain for third and fourth years. On the other hand, L5 students with lower GPAs in their first and second years may be choosing to complete rather than transfer, delay or discontinue their studies, and, if their GPAs remain low, the overall result would be lower-average GPAs.

Both L5 and IN could benefit from assistance during their degree study. Academic advisors could advise students about degree choices and help them adjust to the critical thinking required for success in the last half of the degree. This could be provided in the form of workshops or tutorials.

Overall, the L5 program at the University of Manitoba has had a positive impact on student success. Graduates of this program have earned higher than average first-year GPAs and have been more likely to graduate by a significant margin. Assuming that students who met the language requirement of the University of Manitoba without L5 focused on language alone, the L5 advantage may be the result of the non-linguistic components of L5. Adding more years to the data in this on-going study will provide a clearer picture for students in particular fields of study.

REFERENCES

Blais, C. (n.d.). *University 1 international profile 2004–2006 and 2005–2006.* Winnipeg, Manitoba: University of Manitoba, University 1.

Dooey, P. (2010). Students' perspectives of an EAP pathway program. *Journal of English for Academic Purposes, 9,* 184–197.

Dyck, G. N., & Schönwetter, D. J. (2002). *Preparing international students for success: A specialized section approach.* Paper presented at International Conference on the First Year Experience, University of Bath, England, UK.

Evans, S., & Morrison, B. (2011). Meeting the challenges of English-medium higher education: The first-year experience in Hong Kong. *English for Specific Purposes, 30,* 198–208.

Fast, R. (2003). Students' perception of effectiveness: The University of Manitoba's Academic English program. *The English Teacher: An International Journal, 6*(1), 71–78.

Friesen, H. (2004). *Report on the success rate of students enrolled in the Academic English Program for University and College Entrance (AEPUCE).* Winnipeg, Manitoba: University of Manitoba, Student Advocacy/Student Resource Services.

Green, R. (2000). Life after the pre-sessional course: How students fare in their departments. In J. M. Blue, J. Milton, & J. Saville (Eds.), *Assessing English for academic purposes* (pp. 131–145). Bern: Peter Lang.

Lai, Y. (2009). Language learning strategy use and English proficiency of university freshmen in Taiwan. *TESOL Quarterly, 43*(2), 255–280.

Storch, N., & Tapper, J. (2009). The impact of an EAP course on postgraduate writing. *Journal of English for Academic Purposes, 8,* 207–223.

Terraschke, A. & Wahid, R. (2011). The impact of EAP study on the academic experiences of international postgraduate students in Australia. *Journal of English for Academic Purposes, 10,* 173–182.

Turner, J. (2004). Language as academic purpose. *Journal of English for Academic Purposes, 3*(2), 95–105.

MICK KAVANAGH AND LISA ROBINSON

EAP TUTOR OBSERVATION AND FEEDBACK: AN EMPIRICAL STUDY

INTRODUCTION

The current EAP scene is characterised by rapid expansion, the development of the profession as distinct from TEFL, and the rarity of EAP-specific teacher qualifications. In common with mainstream teacher education, EAP programmes often include lesson observation and feedback. However, while these areas have long constituted research fields for general educationalists, the EAP experience has been largely overlooked by researchers.

As with many areas of pedagogy/research, the origin of post-observation conferencing can be traced to practices in mainstream education (see, for example, Wragg, 1994). In this context, typical situations include those relating to pre-service teaching practices, and tertiary-level mentoring schemes, which tend to be aimed at researcher–teachers without a teaching background. Within EAP, however, these situations are not encountered in the same way since most university EAP tutors are pre-existent teachers who do not fall under mentoring schemes. Rather, the EAP situation is characterised by intensive courses (as opposed to longer-term teacher development), the distinction between experienced and novice teachers and, in some cases, the importance of BALEAP course accreditation.

This study responds to the lack of attention to EAP post-observation discussion in the literature. Planned to take advantage of the lesson observations typical of summer pre-sessional courses, it examines 11 post-observation digitally-recorded conversations conducted over one EAP pre-sessional term at a British university. The research considers the main themes arising from the data, providing further insight into tutor and observer intentions and understandings, with possible implications for tutor behaviour and development, and observer awareness and training.

CONTEXT

Though the context of summer pre-sessional courses may be familiar to the reader, it is worth summarising in order to set the study aside from more mainstream education research.

The university's English language centre offers a large number of summer courses for international students planning to enter UK Higher Education, most of whom hope to achieve their target IELTS (or equivalent) score within either five or ten weeks.

In summer 2010, of 45 tutors staffing these pre-sessional programmes, 32 required observations, creating a significant observation task. Some of those observed had ten years' EAP experience, while others had less than a year. Observations are required to satisfy both in-house quality assurance expectations and those pertaining to BALEAP Accreditation (BALEAP, 2008; BALEAP, 2011). While observations perform both evaluative and developmental functions, the former element is significant, as the decision to invite tutors to teach on subsequent courses is based largely on the observation and written feedback. Any lesson deemed below standard requires a follow-up observation. In 2010, a trial was coincidentally being carried out of a new observation protocol developed by Julie King and Steve Kirk based on the BALEAP Competency Framework (BALEAP, 2008).

The trial observation protocol included the use of a *reflection box*, which was e-mailed to the tutor after the observation,

completed, and returned to the observer before the post-observation discussion. Delayed feedback took place one to three days after the observed lesson in order to support reflection further (Williams & Watson, 2004).

DATA COLLECTION AND ANALYSIS

Eleven tutors (seven on fixed-term summer contracts and four longer-term tutors) and seven observers agreed to participate in the research interviews after being informed of our aims and procedures. They consented to being audio-recorded, on the understanding that transcripts of the conferences would be available to check, and (for tutors) that neither participation nor withdrawal would affect the evaluative aspects of the observation. Each tutor had a lesson attended by either one or two observers drawn from Course Directors (including ourselves) and senior colleagues, and the resulting data consisted of eleven dialogic post-observation feedback sessions (see Table 1 opposite).

Our analysis followed a system of constant comparison (Boeije, 2002). After individually examining the transcribed data, with attention to both substantive content and conversation structure, and assigning working codes, we compared these in order to identify temporary constructs (Thomas, 2009, p. 199). A second round of individual analysis was conducted to narrow down the number of salient themes, and additional

Table 1 Post-observation conferences

Observee	Observer	Recording length (mins/secs)	Ratio (observee: observer)	Conference structure
A	1	38.25	3:5	2
B	2	54.57	3:5	2
C	3	21.15	1:2	3
D	4	34.42	2:1	4
E	3	20.12	1:3.5	3
F	5	22.36	2:1	1
G	6	25.39	1:4	3
H	2	39.43	2:3	2
I	7	42.17	1:1.5	2
J	5	17.41	1:1	1
K	1	27.50	1:4	2
			Average 2:3	

sub-categories emerged as we again compared the themes; further collaboration enabled selected extracts to form the basis of our narrative enquiry.

THEMES

Our analysis identified four main themes, divided into a number of sub-themes (see Table 2). The first two themes were *classroom skills* and the *nature of observation*, where the participants exhibited similarities with more general EFL teachers.

Table 2 Themes

Classroom skills	Nature of observation	Challenge	Projection
timing and instructions	planning and behaving differently	short-term	general
atmosphere	perceived pressure on students	targets	specific contexts and disciplines
'higher order'	empathy/solidarity	long-term	
	effect on the observer		

For example, while we might assume that issues like *timing* and *instructions* have been finessed by the typical EAP tutor, it appears that they remain a concern. Two other sub-themes were *atmosphere* and '*higher order*', while comments on the *nature of observation* referred to *planning and behaving differently*, *perceived pressure on students*, *empathy/solidarity* (between observer and observee), and *effect on the observer*.

Where our data revealed distinct EAP features, however, was in the remaining themes of *challenge* and *projection*. While these themes are EAP-specific, the actuality of the conferences appears less so; the tendency of the observer to initiate topics with in-service EAP tutors is reminiscent of the situation regarding pre-service teachers (see Hyland & Lo, 2006, p. 169). It can be seen from the extracts which follow that very little dialogue was evident; in other words, not only were the two categories largely dependent on observer topic-initiation, but also tutors tended not to respond.

CHALLENGE

Originally termed 'pushing students' (i.e., challenge for students) the *challenge* category comprised three sub-categories: *short-term* (within the lesson), *targets* (expressed as IELTS equivalents, and necessary for university admission), and *long-term* (within the course).

SHORT-TERM

Short-term challenges were mentioned in relation to the classroom situation and the course being taught. Using the observed lesson as a starting point, then, one observer focused on the use of materials, drawing a comparison with a more typical EFL

situation, where teachers' decisions need to be based on the students as they find them:

> **Observer 3:** *My question here is … it's just like you walk into a language school and they say you have to use this book but you know that the book is not challenging enough for the students, so how do you make the task? How do you use that material, same materials, same task, just slightly more challenging?*
>
> **Tutor D:** *That's fair enough, completely fair enough, I understand [reads]. Quiet students, they're never normally, they were terrified that you that you were there, to be honest.*

Observer 3 found it helpful to characterise students as 'robust' in order to encourage the tutor to push them harder in pursuit of the end goal. The students, as willing collaborators, were ready to undertake the challenge and the tutor needed to see this:

> **Observer 3:** *Some of the students … we always get this with writing … they feel they want to write straightaway and there's a lot of input, but the fact that they're raring to go – I think … they're ready for a challenge. They're quite robust.*

Observer 3's other respondent became a conversational collaborator by examining the term 'oomph', first proposed by the observer. Though a rather vague concept, this was seen by the observer as something different from speed or pace, and as lacking in the class by the tutor. Whatever it might be, the speakers seemed to agree on it; more seriously, it was seen to be necessary to student success:

> **Observer 3:** *… the good thing … is you've done it before … so you know the type of student and … the pressures they're going to be under, you can deal with it … I think …*

probably speed and the pace is the wrong thing, they need a bit more oomph as a class. [They're not a very oomph class.] I think you could get them there because they have to be bloody oomph when it comes to the timed writing and stuff like that … I wonder if their lack of oomph is going to hold them back.

Tutor C: *I can compare with the course two years ago, where the business students really had to work. Even on the ten-week course they had three essays in the five weeks.*

Clearly, one of Observer 3's conferencing strategies is to refer to the tutor's previous experience in order to build tutor confidence. Tutor C's response contrasts sharply with the defensiveness of Tutor D (above), a difference which may be due to a disparity in experience.

Thus far, challenge has encompassed using materials to challenge students, students' readiness to be pushed and their motivation.

TARGETS

Reminding tutors of the students' targets was a way of encouraging them to reassess the level of challenge they were presenting. Sometimes this was done in a general way:

Observer 3: *Bear in mind that students on this particular course have a high level to reach in a short time.*

Tutor E: *Yeah, I see that … I hadn't really thought … the thing … you just mentioned like them, after doing the task – analysing, discussing.*

and on other occasions a specific (IELTS) target was mentioned:

Observer 3: *I suppose the bottom line is they've still got to get into that 7 and how we get there is something always to be kept in mind. You said you're aware of that and*

you've had the experience before … they can be put under a bit of pressure to get it. It all sounds a bit like being on the students' case. We're not doing them any favours unless we get them into shape ready for that …

Tutor C: *Which I don't think they ever really appreciate until they get there.*

In each case, Observer 3 was keen to ensure that the tutors received a clear message about the job expected of them, and for whose benefit. Once more, there is a reference to the tutor's previous experience, though the observer is seemingly not quite so convinced that the tutor is judging the students' ability correctly.

Observer 1, reacting to a slightly different situation, was able to be more positive, encouraging the tutor and affirming the challenge being offered to students:

Observer 1: *You're encouraging them and pushing them up to a level that they need to be because … some of these students are even needing an IELTS 7. So … you're doing what we want or what any academic environment needs – you're pushing them up … and certainly I didn't notice students lost … They're … capable of … meeting that … level.*

Quality assurance requires that tutors challenge students to reach a standard, including a particular IELTS equivalent, and this was clearly important to observers.

LONG TERM

With longer-term *challenge* comments, the observer found it possible, and usually necessary, to remind the tutor of what students would be facing further ahead. There is still the sense that they need to be pushed, indeed in our initial stages of analysis, *challenge* was temporarily termed 'pushing students', as the verb was frequently encountered. Observer 7 explicitly described what students were faced with in terms of the course they were studying. Indeed, the term 'duty' was invoked in order to allay any fears that the tutor might have had about pushing students too hard:

> **Observer 7:** *I think you have to push them … they haven't got a lot of time, they've only got eight weeks now … it's a very limited period of time and … because of the nature of the course – it's short, it's intensive, it's very high stakes, there's an exam at the end of it … we have to be pushing them … which might well mean that … occasionally the weaker ones are not going to be exactly with you all the time … We've got a duty to get as many as possible through and up to the best level that they're capable of.*

The short, intensive, high-stakes, exam-dependent nature of the course meant that tutors should be pushing students, even sometimes at the expense of weaker ones. Observer 3 also advised pushing students and applying pressure:

> **Observer 3:** *I think it's a bit too comfortable for where they've got to get cos they've got a hell of a test at the end of the course and up to IELTS 7 and they should be sweating a bit really … so I think they need more pressure … across the board … but especially … where they've got to come out with a 7 … we're not doing them any favours by coasting.*

Again there is reference to target scores and 'not doing them any favours,' adding to the sense that EAP must challenge students and move them out of their comfort zone.

There is a lack of tutor response to these suggestions, exacerbated in the *projection* category.

PROJECTION

GENERAL

Projection differed from *challenge* in the sense that it invoked a longer-term perspective, succinctly summed-up in the following extract:

> **Observer 7:** *You didn't talk about that explicitly to the students. The end goal is not the … timed essay … There's another goal beyond that … It's also very helpful for the much longer term, what you'll be doing in your departments in nine months' time and you didn't mention that once … you could by adding that kind of extra layer, just making those pointers to the future.*

By referring to the 'goal beyond' and 'pointers to the future', Observer 7 highlights the reason for teaching, and for students undertaking, pre-sessional EAP courses. This 'extra layer' of referring to future context represents a core difference between EAP and EFL, which often lacks an explicit end goal.

SPECIFIC CONTEXTS AND DISCIPLINES

Continuing where *challenge* left off, *projection* comments often referred to departments:

> **Observer 3:** *We're kind of giving a university class in that sense … the whole kind of … experience they're gonna get … in any department.*

> **Observer 2:** *That's what's going to be expected when they go to their departments.*

Taking this theme further, Observer 1 advised that constant classroom reference to departments was expected:

> **Observer 1:** *The other … big thing … [we're] looking for … is to constantly be referring to that future department, this is what you'll be doing … this is how this helps you now with what you will be doing, and you … have that knowledge … you've got an MA …. you know about university departments … Give them that information …*

In some cases, observers found it useful to refer to specific contexts and disciplines:

> **Observer 3:** *The MBA, as you know – you've taught on it – it's an assault course, it's a test of stamina, like a PhD is really. If people flop out it's not because they're not bright, it's because they can't handle it and I suppose it's preparing you for that ruthless world of business.*
>
> **Tutor C:** *I think it's interesting that I picked up on some of the points that you …*

In another case, the observer emphasised elements of the *challenge* category (the target score) alongside references to the department and a specific course:

> **Observer 6:** *… to go further forward … you perhaps need to look at matching your level or at least the target level, with the activities you're expecting them to do and to try and consider more what will they be expected to do in their department. How high can I ramp this up so that they're not going to have too big a jump to make between finishing [here] and going to do their MBA course? … when you think of it like that … you think of what they're going into and that really we can best serve the students by taking them to as high a level and as challenging a work as we possibly can.*

Without doubt, observers felt it important to attempt to lift tutors' – and by extension, students' – gaze to the further academic horizon.

The lack of tutor response is notable here. In the data, references to *projection*, in particular, are generally embedded in lengthy observer monologues, often leaving the tutors' response to such information unclear. While deliberate observer efforts to mention these areas indicates the partial training function of feedback, purposive solicitation of responses after key points during the post-observation conference would confirm tutor understanding.

STRUCTURING THE POST-OBSERVATION CONFERENCE

Observer-dominated feedback is well-documented (Vásquez, 2004; Hyland & Lo, 2006; Copland, 2010), and in our data the observer spoke more than the observee; in some cases, observer talk was as much as four times that of the tutor, though in two others (both the same observer) the situation was reversed and the tutors spoke more than they were spoken to. Table 1 shows that the post-lesson conferences ranged in length from 17+ minutes to almost 55. The range may be attributable to, for example, the timing of the discussion relative to other ongoing work, or whether the discussion touched on more than the observed lesson itself, but the quantitative data indicates a strong tendency for the observer to take charge of the conference.

Williams and Watson (2004, p. 88) hypothesise that reflection before the conference may lead to more observee-initiated topics. Apart from the benefits to the observee, we certainly found the inclusion of a *reflection box* helpful for the observer, providing a useful starting point on which to base the conversation. Five observers used this strategy and in these cases, observed tutors did initiate topics.

While it is difficult in such a small-scale study to claim that 'models' have been established, several general approaches to the feedback can be noted. By summarising each post-lesson conference several patterns emerge (see Table 3). The four observers for whom we have two sets of data each tended to adhere to one of these patterns. In other words, neither the relative success of the lesson nor the atmosphere of the conference seemed to affect the choice of approach, which, we would contend, is most likely to be linked to the observer's own preferences.

CONCLUSION

Implications can be suggested in two main areas: tutor behaviour and development, and observer awareness and training. We see the greatest potential value, however, in the latter.

The findings may help to indicate desirable elements of both tutor behaviour and development. Both pre-arrival material and induction content need to reiterate the necessity to challenge students and relate their present context to the future academic environment, a relationship which should be monitored throughout the course. Tutor behaviour – that is, what happens in the classroom – might be modified through attention to the issues that have been discussed in the conversations represented here. Such modification constitutes development, though more formal developmental activities, such as sessions based on the issues highlighted in post-lesson conferences, would certainly also be possible.

It is our belief that the greatest scope lies in the area of observer awareness and training. Barrera, Braley & Slate (2010, p. 72) have identified a need, among mentors, for guidelines, training and well-

Table 3 Conference structures

1	2	3	4
general questions to begin	feedback session outlined	immediate and sustained observer talk (based on pre-prepared written feedback)	apparent prepared set of questions
dialogue based on observer's written feedback	moves from general to specific questions		ample tutor response opportunities
	discussion generally shared		
	observer control of conference		

defined goals. Following Borg (1998), we would like to see raw data such as our interview transcripts used for increasing observer awareness and contributing to training. In the absence of video footage of real EAP lessons, such data provides a valuable means of looking into the classroom. Indeed, real possibilities exist to exploit the material with both existing and prospective observers and to provide an insight into both the teacher's and the observer's minds.

While it has been suggested that a range of conferencing frameworks be set so that tutors experience different forms of feedback according to their learning styles (Copland, 2010, p. 467), we feel that a more balanced dialogue and clearer expectations could be possible by discussing with observers the conference structures outlined above. Furthermore, Hyland and Lo (2006, p. 182) suggest that teacher educators record their post-observation conferences as a form of critical self-reflection. This may be effective in boosting observer confidence and encouraging a willingness to experiment with alternative conference structures.

REFERENCES

BALEAP. (2008). *Competency framework for teachers of English for Academic Purposes.* Retrieved from www.baleap.org.uk/teap/teap-competency-framework.pdf

BALEAP. (2011). *BALEAP accreditation scheme handbook.* Retrieved from http://www.baleap.org.uk/media/uploads/pdfs/baleap-accreditation-scheme-handbook.pdf

Barrera, A., Braley, R.T., & Slate, J. R. (2010). Beginning teacher success: An investigation into the feedback from mentors of formal mentoring programs. *Mentoring & Tutoring, 18*(1), 61–74.

Boeije, H. (2002). A purposeful approach to the constant comparative method in the analysis of qualitative interviews. *Quality & Quantity, 36,* 391–409.

Borg, S. (1998). Data-based teacher development. *ELT Journal, 52*(4), 273–281.

Copland, F. (2010). Causes of tension in post-observation feedback in pre-service teacher training: An alternative view. *Teaching and Teacher Education, 26,* 466–472.

Hyland, F., & Lo, M. (2006). Examining interaction in the teaching practicum: Issues of language, power and control. *Mentoring and Tutoring, 14*(2), 163–186.

Thomas, G. (2009). *How to do your research project.* London: Sage.

Vásquez, C. (2004). 'Very carefully managed': Advice and suggestions in post-observation meetings. *Linguistics and Education, 15,* 33–58.

Williams, M., & Watson, A. (2004). Post-lesson debriefing: delayed or immediate? An investigation of student teacher talk. *Journal of Education for Teaching: International Research and Pedagogy, 30*(2), 85–96.

Wragg, E. C. (1994*). An introduction to classroom observation.* London: Routledge.

Tijen Akşit

Teacher action research: a means of reflection to improve EAP teaching practice

Introduction

This paper describes a group of English for Academic Purposes (EAP) instructors' experience of conducting action research (AR) for professional development purposes as part of an in-house teacher development course.

Part of effective teaching is 'a teacher's reflective practice, or careful review of and thoughtfulness about one's own teaching processes.' These teachers 'seek and try out new approaches in the classroom to better meet the needs of their learners' (Stronge, 2007, p. 30), acting in a cycle of identifying issues in their teaching, exploring the possible reasons, finding viable solutions, trying these solutions, and starting the whole cycle again with the same, similar or totally new issues (Dymoke & Harrison, 2008; Gay, Mills & Airasian, 2009; Jordan, 1997; Stringer, 1996; West, 2011). When teachers go through these cycles in an intentional, systematic and critical way, they become engaged in teacher research or classroom based AR. Altrichter, Feldman,

Posch and Somekh (2008, p. 8) visualize AR (Figure 1) 'as an iterative process that integrates theory with practice, through reflection and action planning'.

Having reviewed the relevant literature, Burns (1999, p. 30) outlines the main features of action research as follows:

- *Action research is contextual, small-scale and localized – it identifies and investigates problems within a specific situation.*
- *It is evaluative and reflective as it aims at bring about change and improvement in practice.*
- *It is participatory as it provides for collaborative investigation by teams of colleagues, practitioners and researchers.*
- *Changes in practice are based on the collection of information or data which provides the impetus for change.*

AR is classroom-based and makes teachers systematically reflect on the teaching/learning issues, so it is a perfect tool for systematic reflective teacher practice. Academic research, with its emphasis on theory, has been

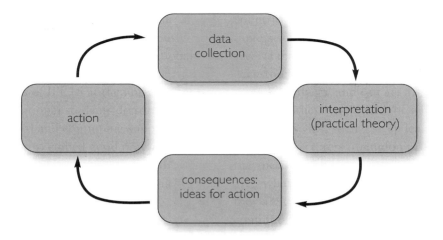

Figure 1 The circle of action and reflection (Altrichter et al., 2008, p. 8)

criticized for being distant from actual practice (Hopkins, 1993). According to Gay, Mills & Airasian (2009), unlike academic research, AR is more accessible to practitioner teachers, as it is conducted by practitioners for themselves, it tries to find solutions to everyday problems of teachers, and, unlike many academic research reports, its reports are more accessible to practitioners, as they are written by and for teachers.

In education, AR 'is frequently used to assist pre-service and master's-level candidates to research their own practice as a way to strengthen reflection, professional learning, and changes in practice' (Young, Crow, Murphy & Ogawa, 2009, p. 352). Apart from assisting pre-service and master's level candidates, AR is also a very effective tool that 'can be used to enhance the craft of teaching by assisting teachers to organize and facilitate effective programs of student learning' (Stringer, Christensen, & Baldwin, 2010, p. 1). The '[t]eaching and learning centers [also] provide an array of programs and services to assist the instructor who is struggling or the excellent teacher looking for something new' (Mettetal, 2002, p. 1) on university campuses, supporting the AR

efforts in tertiary education.

Jordan (1997) highlights the main purpose of AR in English language teaching context as 'find[ing] solutions to problems and … enabl[ing] teachers to improve aspects of teaching and learning.' He describes the aim of 'pure or basic research' as 'to add to knowledge in a certain area … finding evidence to support a theory'. Creswell (2008, p. 596–605) also highlights the relevance of AR to practitioners, stating that it is 'a practical design and is a way of self-development'. Allwright and Bailey (1991, p. 35) emphasize that AR 'basically involves taking an action and systematically observing what follows'; however, unlike academic research, 'a carefully controlled experimental design is not needed to answer this question in a local context'. Jordan (1997) lists common methodologies used in AR into EAP as observations, case studies, diaries, questionnaires and interviews, and student test results. AR in EAP settings is also highly encouraged by BALEAP, recognizing AR as a possible indicator of the importance that an EAP teacher gives 'to continuing professional development' and to 'the critical reflection on own practice' (2008, p. 5).

Despite all the benefits in all educational contexts, some concerns have been raised by practitioner teachers who conducted AR. Burns (1999) reports that lack of time is placed as number one in teachers' list of concerns. The list also contains, but is not limited to, the following: additional work, limited local support for continuing or recognizing the research, anxiety about research skills and timetable pressures. For similar reasons, Allwright (2005, p. 353) criticizes AR and claims that '... common emphases on practical problem-solving and making measureable improvements in student achievement [is] not only unhelpfully short-sighted but also potentially counterproductive', especially when the pressure and the burden it places on teachers and their daily teaching practice (Allwright & Bailey, 1991) are concerned.

Allwright (2005, p. 355) asserts that the only context where AR fits would be 'an in-service teacher development course, where good support was available, and [it would] be used as the framework for a final project'. He believes that the participants of such a course would carry out their AR 'with such great enthusiasm and at a level of energy expenditure that it would not be possible to repeat after the course was over and the teacher was back in the classroom full-time.' Burns (1999, p. 53), on the other hand, acknowledging the criticisms raised on AR, proposes that AR is better to be a collaborative activity since, 'when it is collaborative and framed by supporting structures, such as a school or teacher center decision to integrate action research within a professional development programme, or research' carried out as part of a degree program, it works better.

THE CONTEXT

The AR experience described in this paper is part of an in-service professional development course offered in-house. Participating instructors teach in the Faculty Academic English Program (FAEP) of Bilkent University (BU) in Ankara, Turkey. The university, where the medium of instruction is English, ranks top in Turkey, and 112th in the Top 400 World Universities list (*Times Higher Education*, 2011). FAEP offers credit-bearing in-sessional EAP courses to around 3,000 degree program students from more than ten disciplines. There are 70 instructors (one-third native speakers of English) in FAEP, (11 PhDs., 53 Master's and 6 Bachelor degrees), with an average of over 12 years' professional experience.

THE EAP CERTIFICATE PROGRAM

FAEP runs an in-house EAP teacher-development certificate program on designing, teaching and evaluating credit-bearing in-sessional EAP courses. Lasting one calendar year, the program has three modules:

- theory and practice in EAP course design
- course implementation and evaluation
- action research in teaching EAP

In the first two modules participants explore their context, design a 14-week course, teach and evaluate this course and compare the planned and the implemented curricula. In the third module, they conduct and report on a piece of action research.

To date, 20 experienced and qualified EAP instructors finished the program. Table 1 shows participant profile to date.

Table 1 EAP certificate program participant profile (n=20)

Teaching experience	Bachelor relevant field/Total	Masters relevant field/Total	PhD. relevant field/Total	Cambridge Teaching Certification	Cambridge Teaching Diploma
~18yrs	16/20	15/20	1/2	9	6

ACTION RESEARCH MODULE

In the AR module, participants study key principles and stages of AR, write an AR proposal, conduct AR, reflect on and evaluate practice and finally draw up an action plan to improve their EAP practice.

In the 2010–2011 Academic Year, seven participating instructors (pseudonyms will be used to ensure anonymity), two of whom were native speakers of English, explored some research problems/questions emerging from their classroom teaching practice (Figure 2).

Participant	Research problems/questions
Serkan	Does the use of reading worksheets improve student participation in classroom discussions that are based on assigned readings?
Selma	Why are my ENG 102 students reluctant to use library sources? How can I change this?
Can	What are my ENG 101 students' outside class reading habits and attitudes to reading?
Steve	Do the use of graphic organizers and SQ3R technique enhance my ENG 101 students' reading comprehension?
Ozden	Can my ENG 101 students' classroom discussion skills be improved by two teaching strategies: advance preparation and role taking?
Sevil	Does the use of class-led moodle glossary activity enhance my ENG 101 students' content and academic vocabulary
Julie	Why do my ENG 102 students feel reluctant to speak English? How can I change this?

Figure 2 Action research problems/questions of module participants

A closer look at one of the studies can illustrate the nature and the stages of the processes that the participants followed. Julie's case was chosen randomly to be presented in more detail. Any of the seven studies would be equally representative to exemplify the kind of AR studies conducted.

JULIE'S STUDY

Julie wanted to explore why her in-sessional (ENG 102) students feel reluctant to speak English in class and used four different sources of data collection to triangulate her results:

- student questionnaire
- weekly overview
- classroom observation
- mid-term evaluation of teaching and learning

More detailed information about these data sources is presented in the appendix.

Having finished collecting data, Julie analyzed them using content-analysis techniques, looking for patterns, and comparing and contrasting the findings from each data source. The following is an excerpt from Julie's AR report regarding the conclusions of her study:

Students want to speak in English, however there are certain conditions which may encourage, and motivate them to speak. It is important to capture the interest of students through careful choice of topic and class activity. When students interact with each other by doing an activity they enjoy or see as meaningful, they will use the target language.

In her AR report Julie reflects on her experience of conducting AR on an area that she has always found problematic as an EAP instructor. The following is taken from her report.

From this action research I have become more aware of classroom dynamics and student motivation. I realize how careful I have to be in planning lessons to ensure that activities aim to involve all the class in meaningful tasks that foster greater student interaction and participation that could lead to more use of English in class. Students will feel motivated to speak in English if they are allowed to work in groups or with peers, and when they have background knowledge of the topic. The importance of choosing topics for discussion that are provocative enough to engage students, and lead to communication is evident. I need to see my role as facilitator not only as teacher, and to provide a safe classroom environment, and opportunities where active communication can take place.

Julie's answer to a survey question about her feelings for the AR module is as follows:

The course made me more critical about my teaching practice. It encouraged me to do background reading related to the problem I

was interested in. I became aware of the variety of methods of collecting information, and how to do data analysis.

In the follow-up interview Julie talked about how her classroom teaching changed after AR:

... an effort to give more responsibility to the students, more work in pairs and groups. I also made changes in giving them more opportunities for speaking after they do exploit the text in pairs. They do mind-mapping, and come to the board, they share their experiences with their friends. I think this gives them more confidence.

I feel I become more student centered. I try to take a backward role from the main person. I try to set up the task, give the students the responsibility, and get them to explain the text or whatever the things being discussed

When asked why she was not doing these before as a very experienced EAP instructor, she responded:

Lack of awareness! Maybe I always thought students couldn't do it. Maybe lack of confidence in student ability. Because if they don't speak very much you just assume that they can't. Whereas, there may be other reasons why they don't speak.

OTHER PARTICIPANT REFLECTIONS

All seven participants had a section in their AR final report to share their reflections on the experience of conducting AR. They also answered two open-ended survey questions. Their answers were collected anonymously. Three of the instructors volunteered to participate in follow-up interviews, which were audio-recorded and transcribed. Data coming from all three sources (AR reports, survey questions and the interviews) were analyzed using content analysis techniques to identify themes and to check evolving concepts as to how the participants reflect on their AR experience. The descriptive information collected allowed the categories to emerge (Fraenkel & Wallen, 2008).

The results show that, like Julie, all participating instructors found the experience of carrying out an AR over a period of one semester (15 weeks) extremely rewarding, since it provided the researchers with a lot of benefits, such as the following:

AR

- *makes one critical about one's teaching*
- *motivates the teacher to reflect on own practice*

AR is

- *the best way to test one's own teaching*
- *something I'll continue to do even after this certificate program is over*
- *not overwhelming*
- *not frightening like research*

In their AR report and while answering survey and interview questions, the participating instructors provided answers to two main questions:

1) Was conducting AR beneficial? Why/why not?
2) What were the problems you faced and what are your suggestions to further improve the AR module of the certificate program?

The participants unanimously agreed that conducting AR was beneficial. Table 2 lists the variety of reasons why they think so, as categorized under *Benefits of AR*. The participants had little to say, however, about

problems faced and possible solutions. Table 2 presents these views under *Problems with AR*. Conducting AR in pairs and/or small groups and reduction of teaching load to carry out *AR* were presented as possible solutions. Italics are used to show emphasis in the responses.

The participants did not expound on the problems of carrying out an AR study in detail. To illustrate, no one raised concerns about being observed as part of the AR. This could be due to the fact that classroom observations are already an integral part of the academic life in the FAEP for all instructors, including the non-EAP course participants. Therefore, the notion of observations for developmental purposes was not alien for them.

Although the problems and suggested solutions did not cover a wide range of areas, the ones expressed have implications for institutional structures. In order to further encourage AR, FAEP should consider reducing the teaching load of those instructors involved in AR and/or creating opportunities for them to be involved in collaborative AR.

FINAL REMARKS

The AR experience of the group of instructors presented in this paper suggests that promotion of AR among EAP practitioners via various means, like the in-house teacher development program as presented in this paper, would encourage systematic EAP-teacher reflective inquiry, which as a matter of fact would further enrich and enhance the instruction in EAP classrooms.

Table 2 Common areas

Area	Participant answers
Benefits of AR	AR made me *better realize* …
	• Now I *can understand why* my students were …
	• I have *become more aware* of …
	• I *used to think* it was my students' fault …
	• My intuition now became *systematic*.
	• Now, I have *concrete tools* to help my students with …
	• I *realized* teachers can do a lot to change students …
	• I *realized* how careful I have to be …
	AR helped me to see …
	• Provided the *opportunity* to try to do a serious AR
	• *Confidence* building (can conduct AR alone now time permitting)
	• Guidance from the tutor helped me to *do it right* (better than trying to learn AR on my own)
	• Experimenting and receiving feedback from the tutor/getting confirmation from literature during the process was very *beneficial*
	• Hands on experience
	• Encouraged me to do background reading
	• Became aware of what makes quality materials
Problems with AR	• Too *time demanding*
	• *Stressful* due to *time limitations*
	Possible solutions:
	• Could be done in *pairs or small groups*
	• Need reduced teaching load to conduct AR

However, it would be interesting to observe if the instructors, whose positive AR experiences are shared in this paper, will continue conducting AR as they plan when they go back to their normal teaching routine and when it is not a required part of a teacher development course, as asserted by Allwright (2005). Acknowledging the demanding nature of conducting AR, though, EAP programs can reconsider the current teaching load of the teachers and/or consider collaborative AR to encourage the continuity of such efforts as part of teacher development, independent of formal training and development programs, as proposed by Burns (1999).

REFERENCES

Allright, D., & Bailey, K. M. (1991). *Focus on the language classroom: An introduction to classroom research for language teachers.* Cambridge: CUP.

Allright, D. (2005). Developing principles for practitioner research: The case of exploratory practice. *The Modern Language Journal, 89*(3), 353–366.

Altrichter, H., Feldman, A., Posch, P., & Somekh, B. (2008). *Teachers investigate their work: An introduction to action research across the professions* (2nd ed.). New York: Routledge.

BALEAP. (2008, August). *The competence framework for teachers of English for Academic Purposes.* Retrieved from www.baleap.org.uk/teap/teap-competency-framework.pdf

Burns, A. (1999). *Collaborative action research for English language teachers.* Cambridge: CUP.

Creswell, J. W. (2008). *Educational research: Planning, conducting, and evaluating quantitative and qualitative research* (3rd ed.). New Jersey: Pearson.

Dymoke, S., & Harrison, J. (Eds.). (2008). *Reflective teaching and learning.* London: Sage Publications Ltd.

Fraenkel, J. R., & Wallen, N. E. (2008). *How to design and evaluate research in education* (6th ed.). NY: McGraw-Hill.

Gay, L. R, Mills, G. E., & Airasian, P. (2009). *Educational research: Competencies for analysis and applications* (9th ed.). New Jersey: Pearson.

Hopkins, D. (1993). *A teacher's guide to classroom research* (2nd ed.). Buckingham: Open University Press.

Jordan, R. R. (1997*). English for academic purposes: A guide and resource book for teachers.* Cambridge: CUP.

Mettetal, G. (2002). Improving teaching through classroom action research. *Essays on Teaching Excellence: Towards the Best in the Academy, 14*(7). Retrieved from http://podnetwork.org/

Stringer, E. T. (1996). *Action research: A handbook for practitioners.* Thousand Oaks, California: Sage Publications, Inc.

Stringer, E. T., Christensen, L. M. F., & Baldwin, S. C. (2010). *Integrating teaching, learning, and action research.* Thousand Oaks, California: Sage Publications, Inc.

Stronge, J. H. (2007). *Qualities of effective teachers* (2nd ed.). Virginia: Association for Supervision and Curriculum Development.

Times Higher Education (2011). *World university rankings 2010–2011 of top 400 world universities list.* Retrieved from www.timeshighereducation.co.uk/world-university-rankings/

West, C. (2011). Action research as a professional development activity. *Arts Education Policy Review, 112*, 89–94.

Young, M. D., Crow, G. M., Murphy, J., & Ogawa, R. T. (Eds.) (2009). *Handbook of research on the education of school leaders*. New York, NY: Routledge.

APPENDIX: JULIE'S DATA COLLECTION TOOLS

STUDENT QUESTIONNAIRE

Nineteen questions aimed at finding out students' attitude towards and perspective about speaking in English in Julie's classes. Below are some sample questions:

*How important is it for you to speak English in every ENG 102 class?
A) Very important   ☐
B) Quite important   ☐
C) Important   ☐
D) Unimportant   ☐

*When do you usually speak English in ENG 102 class?
A) Only when the teacher asks me a question   ☐
B) When I do group work   ☐
C) When I want to ask a question   ☐
D) When I have an opinion about the topic   ☐
E) Other please specify: _____

*How do you feel most often when the teacher asks you a question in ENG 102 class?
A) Confident (I speak English well)   ☐
B) Happy (I get the chance to speak)   ☐
C) Worried (I might not know the answer)   ☐
D) Afraid (I might make a mistake)   ☐
E) Panic (I never know what to say)   ☐
F) Disinterested (I am not interested in the topic)   ☐
G) Other please specify

_____

_____

_____

* Which of the following give you the best opportunity to speak English in ENG 102?
A) Small groups (5 students)   ☐
B) Pair work   ☐
C) Whole class discussions   ☐
D) Debates   ☐
E) Tutorials (individual)   ☐
F) Tutorials (group)   ☐
G) Individual oral presentation   ☐

WEEKLY OVERVIEW

Each week students anonymously answered three questions for Julie:

- When did you feel most comfortable speaking English in ENG 102 class this week?
- What motivated you to speak in ENG 102 class this week?
- Which situation would have motivated you to speak in ENG 102 class this week?

CLASSROOM OBSERVATIONS

Julie was observed twice (participant observation by Julie herself and non-participant observation by course tutor). Both observers used a tally sheet to record types of communication happening in class. The following prompts were ticked if observed in class:

Student:
- asks peer a question
- asks peer to clarify a point
- disagrees with a peer
- asks teacher to clarify
- answers teacher's question
- comments on teacher's response
- comments on peer's response
- talks off-task in English
- talks off-task in Turkish (L1)

Peer:
- answers a student's question
- clarifies

MID-TERM EVALUATION OF TEACHING AND LEARNING

Julie added the following question to FAEP's mid-semester evaluation of teaching and learning questionnaire and asked for anonymous answers.

- How have you benefited from the ENG 102 class regarding speaking for the last seven weeks?

NOTES ON CONTRIBUTORS

TIJEN AKŞIT is the Director of the Faculty Academic English Program at Bilkent University, and she has more than 20 years of EAP teaching experience. She also teaches in the MA in Management in Education programme, and Bilkent University Postgraduate Certificate Program in Teaching EAP.

HELEN ARMSTRONG has been a lecturer in English for Academic Purposes at Teesside University since 2006. She coordinates the in-sessional courses and teaches on the summer pre-sessional course. Her teaching and research interests lie in student motivation and social integration of international and home students in higher education.

HILARY ARNOLD has over 30 years' experience in the field of English language teaching and examining both abroad and in the UK. Since 2001 she has been a tutor in EAP at the University of Surrey. She currently specialises in designing materials and running writing workshops for PhD students.

SARAH BEAUMONT is a Senior Lecturer in Accounting at the University of Hertfordshire. She has taught for the past three years on the innovative pre-masters programme, working in partnership with English language specialists to prepare mainly overseas students for Master's courses in the Business School.

IAN BRUCE is a Senior Lecturer in Applied Linguistics at the University of Waikato, Hamilton, New Zealand. His research relates to the application of genre theory to EAP writing instruction. His most recent book is *Theory and Concepts of English for Academic Purposes* (Palgrave Macmillan).

FIONA DALZIEL is Assistant Professor at Padua University in northern Italy, where she teaches EAP on the undergraduate programme in Modern Languages. She is also deputy director of the University Language Centre and coordinates the EFL theatre workshop. Her research interests include academic writing, learner autonomy and drama in language teaching.

JACKIE DANNAT has taught academic skills on year-round pre-sessional and in-sessional courses, and effective writing for native and non-native students on undergraduate programmes in the disciplines. She coordinates an Academic Writing For Engineering course, and has delivered writing input on the University of Bath MA (TESOL) programme. She now teaches at the University of Bristol, where she is continuing to postgraduate level.

MARY DAVIS is Senior Lecturer of EAP at Oxford Brookes University, where she leads the Pre-Master's programme. She is undertaking PhD research in plagiarism education at the Institute of Education, University of London. Her research interests also include the formative use of Turnitin and the role of academic phrases.

JIANYING DU works as an Associate Professor at the School of Foreign Languages, Huazhong University of Science and Technology in China. She teaches on MA applied linguistics and English academic writing courses. Her research interests are in the area of second language acquisition and the interface between language learning and critical thinking.

GARRY DYCK, B.Ed. (Manitoba), M.Ed. International (Lesley), started at the University of Manitoba English Language Centre as an instructor in 1990 and has served as the Centre's Director since 2005. Since 2008, he has also served as the President of the Manitoba Council for International Education.

SUZANNE EVANS has worked in EAP for over nine years. Suzanne is the Coordinator of English Language Support at Teesside University and is a member of the Internationalization working group. Her teaching and research interests are in academic writing, student engagement and course design.

MAUREEN FINN is an EAP tutor at the University Language Centre of the University of Manchester. She has extensive experience in Spain and South America as a TESOL/EAP teacher, teacher trainer, examiner and materials developer. Her current interest is the study of genres and communicative conventions in medical English.

GLENN FULCHER is Professor of Education and Language Assessment at the University of Leicester, UK. His main interests lie in the field of language testing and educational assessment. He is a former president of the *International Language Testing Association* (ILTA) and is currently co-editor of the journal *Language Testing*. He has published widely, his latest monograph being *Practical Language Testing* (Hodder 2010). Glenn's website http://languagetesting.info/ is widely used by practitioners, students and researchers.

ANDY GILLETT is Director of Andy Gillett Consulting Ltd. He is involved in a range of projects connected with electronic and paper-based EAP materials writing, editing and proofreading as well as course planning, materials design and evaluation, and teaching for a number of clients around the world.

JULIAN INGLE works for Thinking Writing at Queen Mary, University of London. Much of his recent work has been in medicine and engineering on disciplinary-focused scientific writing, and developing e-learning resources. Recent research is informed by Academic Literacies and explores how ideas of power and identity can help students think about their writing in their discipline. Prior to his present post, Julian taught philosophy, English and Spanish language.

ANNE KAVANAGH teaches EAP at the University of Nottingham, UK. She has several years' teaching experience in China with pre-service English language teachers and is interested in influences of L1 on second language acquisition. She holds a BEd (Hons), DTEFLA, PG certificate in TEAP, and is currently studying for an MA in TESOL.

MICK KAVANAGH is an EAP tutor at the University of Nottingham. He is interested in teacher education and support, and in particular the lesson observation and feedback cycle.

JENNY KEMP is a Tutor in English for Academic Purposes (EAP) at the University of Leicester, UK. She is involved in the development, teaching and assessment of pre-sessional programmes and also coordinates credit-bearing modules for incoming Erasmus and Study Abroad students. Her research interests are mainly related to discourse analysis, vocabulary and listening.

JULIA MOLINARI teaches EAP at the University of Nottingham, UK. Her interests are mainly in the socio-linguistic aspects of second language acquisition. She has an MA (Hons) in Philosophy and an MEd (Applied Linguistics). She also holds a postgraduate teaching certificate in EAP and is bilingual in English and Italian.

JOHN MORLEY is Director of the University-wide Language Programmes at the University of Manchester. Part of this work involves organising and running classes and workshops in academic writing for students and staff. He has a special interest in pedagogical role of academic phraseology. He holds a PhD in Applied Linguistics.

GAMZE ONCUL has a BA and MA in English Language and Literature and a PhD in ELT. She has been teaching self-designed content-based EAP courses at Bilkent University in Ankara, Turkey, since 2004. Her research areas of interest include contrastive rhetoric, writing assessment, and EAP course and material design.

LISA ROBINSON is an EAP tutor at the University of Nottingham, UK, with an interest in teacher education, in particular research into the observation process. She is currently studying for an MA in TESOL.

FRANCINE ROUSSEL is a Senior Lecturer in Applied Linguistics and a member of the I.D.E.A. research team at the Université de Lorraine (France). Her interest in multilingualism and in Tim Johns' Data-Driven Language Learning approach have led her to initiate and coordinate the development of a multilingual concordancer for 12 European languages, MultiConcord, with EU funding at first, and then funds from her university.

JANETTE RYAN is Director of the Teaching International Students Project hosted by the Higher Education Academy and a Research Associate at the China Centre at the University of Oxford. Her publications include *International education and the Chinese learner* (2010) and *Cross cultural teaching and learning for home and international students: Internationalisation of pedagogy and curriculum in higher education* (2012).

CAROLE SEDGWICK is Senior Lecturer at the University of Roehampton where she has delivered undergraduate modules in sociolinguistics, semantics and pragmatics and individual differences in language learning, and contributed to the MRes in Sociolinguistics. Her PhD research was a study of academic literacy practices in two different national locations in Europe.

JOHN SLAGHT is Director of Assessment and Test Development at the University of Reading. He has worked in EAP in various locations worldwide and is also an author of EAP textbooks. He is particularly interested in the testing and teaching of academic reading.

JOAN TURNER is a Senior Lecturer and Director of the Centre for English Language and Academic Writing at Goldsmiths, University of London. Her research focuses on language in higher education, including EAP, academic literacies and intercultural communication. She is the author of *Language in the Academy: Cultural Reflexivity and Intercultural Dynamics* (2011), Multilingual Matters.

CHITRA VARAPRASAD has been teaching EAP and ESP courses for more than 20 years. She obtained her PhD in Applied Linguistics in 2005. Chitra is a reflective teacher and has undertaken classroom-based research and published several papers on teaching methodologies and learning processes. She currently teaches thesis writing to postgraduate students at the Centre for English Language Communication, National University of Singapore.

SIMON WILLIAMS is a Teaching Fellow at the University of Sussex, where he convenes the Pre-Masters in EAP programme and teaches on the MA ELT. He is also involved with supervising doctoral research students in the area of ELT. His particular interests are EAP writing, MALL and discourse analysis.

NADYA YAKOVCHUK works as a Student Learning Adviser at the University of Surrey and as an associate lecturer at the Open University. Her previous post in Thinking Writing at Queen Mary, University of London has inspired her interest in writing and knowledge construction in the disciplines. Nadya's doctoral research focused on student source use and plagiarism prevention, and she has taught at several UK universities over the last decade.